THE LONDON
HIPPODROME

An entertainment of unexampled brilliance

INTRODUCTION BY DAME SHIRLEY BASSEY – FOREWORD BY SIR MICHAEL GRADE

LUCINDA GOSLING

This book is dedicated to my fellow Hippodrome custodians. Those who, for the last 120 years, have worked, lived and breathed life into this most extraordinary building. I salute you.
Simon Thomas

First published by Memory Lane Media Ltd
Third Floor, Scottish Mutual House,
27–29 North Street, Hornchurch, Essex, RM11 1RS.
www.memory-lane.co.uk

Text © Lucinda Gosling, 2021

© The London Hippodrome, 2021. All rights reserved.

Without limiting the rights under copyright reserved above, no part of this publication may be reproduced, stored in or introduced into a retrieval system, or transmitted, in any form or by any means (electronic, mechanical, photocopying, recording or otherwise), without the written permission of the publisher and the copyright holders.

ISBN: 978-1-9196381-3-3

Author: Lucinda Gosling
Design & Artwork: Louise Sword
Contributor: Rosalyn Wilder
Picture research: Lucinda Gosling
Proofreader: Alison Griffiths
Publishers: Ian Haworth, Andrew Humphries
Executive Producer: Simon Thomas

Printed and bound in England by Pure Print Ltd

Contents

Introduction		6
Foreword		7
Welcome		**8**
The circus of variety	1900–1909	**10**
Ragtime and revue	1909–1919	**42**
The comedy musical	1920–1939	**64**
From blackouts to rock 'n' roll	1939–1958	**96**
The Talk of the Town	1958–1982	**126**
The greatest disco in the world	1983–2009	**152**
The Hippodrome Casino	2009–present	**168**
Acknowledgements		**182**

Introduction

I will always remember my first appearance at the Hippodrome in 1957, and then later, in 1962, when it had transformed into the Talk of the Town, stepping into the shoes of Diana Ross, Judy Garland, Sammy Davis Jr., Lena Horne, Engelbert Humperdinck and Liza Minnelli.

It was a home for all of us and will always hold a special place in my heart and in the world of show business - it is part of our lives!

All my love,

Shirley Bassey

Dame Shirley Bassey

Foreword

For tourists, the major London landmarks are Big Ben, the Tower of London and Buckingham Palace. For this Londoner, the key landmarks are our West End theatres. From the age of five, a trip to the Palladium and the others was an almost weekly occurrence for me. My whole family were in live show business, as producers, agents and performers. The London Hippodrome, that iconic theatre bang in the middle of the golden square mile that is the West End, holds my earliest memory. I could only have been five years old when I was taken to see my Aunt Carole (then Carole Lynne, later Lady Delfont) starring in *Babes in the Wood*, the big Christmas pantomime. I can still remember the thrills, the laughter and the excitement at that matinee performance.

Little could I realise then how big a part the Hippodrome would play in my career in the 1960s and 70s. My uncle Bernard (Lord) Delfont realised that with the demise of variety theatre, a regular staple at the Hippodrome, the future was big musicals or straight plays. The beautiful Hippodrome theatre was unlikely to survive as it was too small for big musicals and too big for straight plays.

Delfont and his partner Sir Charles Forte hit on the idea of creating a mass entertainment, cabaret venue where, for an all-in package price, audiences could eat, drink and dance, and see a spectacular floor show and a big star. So, the Hippodrome became the iconic Talk of the Town, the best value in show business.

I was a booking agent by this time, and with my partner Billy Marsh, our job was to book the star attractions. What a list: Diana Ross and the Supremes, Stevie Wonder, Judy Garland, Ethel Merman, Victor Borge, Sammy Davis Jr., plus all the greatest home-grown talent like Tom Jones, Bruce Forsyth, Frankie Vaughan, Shirley Bassey. You name a star of the period and they played at The Talk of the Town.

The rows of red velvet seats were replaced by tables and chairs, the stage transformed from its original, classic proscenium to a state-of-the-art system of rising and falling sections, plus a dance floor... all at an affordable price for families celebrating, couples courting and fans of the big stars. I was lucky enough to see them all.

When that fashion changed, the ever-adaptable Hippodrome became a disco and then, finally, a very classy casino. It retains its place in the entertainment life of London, a premium venue with a rich history. The ability of the original Hippodrome to adapt and reinvent itself over the decades, again and again, has ensured its survival.

This publication ensures that its place in London's popular cultural history is secure. A magical building.

Michael Grade, Lord Grade of Yarmouth

An entertainment of unexampled brilliance

15th January 1900

It is 7:30pm on a damp, Monday evening in January and London's newest theatre has opened for business. In the gleaming marble foyer, the front-of-house staff welcome their first customers. Top hats and fur-lined wraps are deposited in the cloakroom, chocolates and bon-bons are purchased and the hems of silk evening gowns swish across the mosaic floor. Outside, people who have been unable to purchase a ticket loiter and wait anyway, caught up in the air of excitement and craning their necks for a view as cabs draw up on Charing Cross Road to disgorge VIPs and members of the press. As the auditorium begins to fill, the powdery scents of Violette de Parme and Florida Water mingle with a whisper of cigar smoke and the odour of new paint and plaster. The low buzz of conversation begins to amplify and rise towards the proscenium and domed ceiling, from where plasterwork nymphs and cherubs gaze sightlessly across at the grand and upper circles. In one of the boxes encircling the stalls, Edward Moss, chairman of Moss Empires, takes his seat. With ten minutes until curtain up, he takes the opportunity to survey and admire this, the latest, and most significant, property in his expanding empire.

The scene before him is, even by his standards, impressive. Mr. Matcham's opulent interior is a feast for the eyes; an iced confection in cream and gold, sparkling under the electric lights and set off by seating upholstered in ruby red velvet. In each box, a bouquet of white flowers tied with coloured streamers is left as a gift for the ladies and a special programme has been printed on silk to mark the occasion.

At the back of the auditorium, Mr. Moss sees his front-of-house manager, known to everyone as 'Mac', guiding the last few arrivals to their seats. His business partner, Mr. Thornton, is in a box across the auditorium, deep in conversation with Mr. Rothschild, who gave them the honour of laying the foundation stone of the building just over a year ago. And Mr. Allen, his general manager, dependable as always, has disappeared backstage, anxious to check that all is in order. Moss catches Mr. Thornton's eye and the two men nod to each other. Everything is in place.

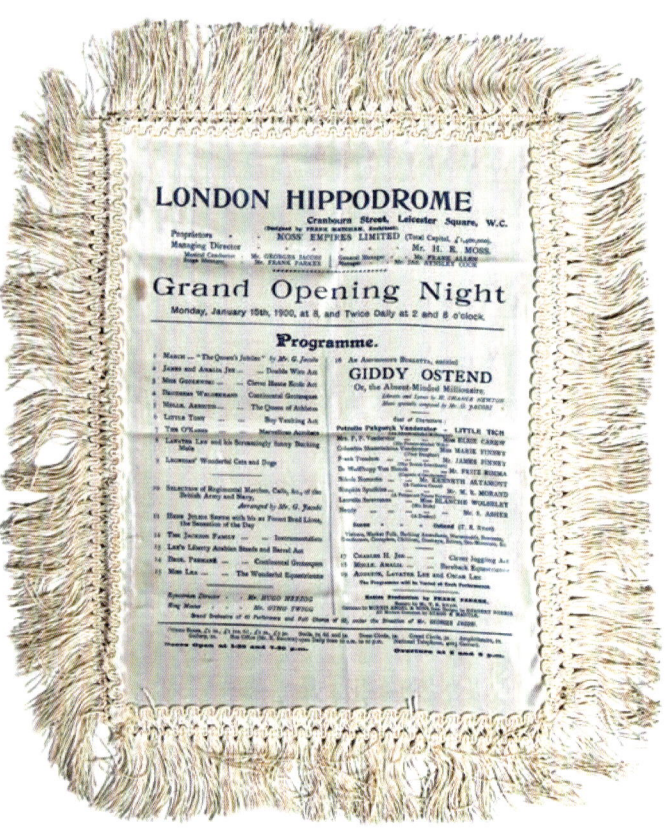

Special silk programmes were popular during the nineteenth century as a way to ceremoniously mark an opening night or special theatrical performance. This fringed example commemorates the Hippodrome's Grand Opening Night on 15th January 1900.

The best programme of speciality turns ever presented

For several weeks now, Moss has placed advertisements for his new theatre in the press with what appears to be an audacious promise to theatre-goers. That the brand-new London Hippodrome will stage "the best programme of speciality turns ever presented". Moss has spent twenty years opening or taking over theatres, giving his audiences what they want, looking for gaps in the market, ensuring he moves with the times. The London Hippodrome is built on a prime spot between Charing Cross Road and Leicester Square, but it is also a stone's throw from established variety theatres, the Alhambra, the Empire and the Pavilion. What can his new venue offer that others theatres cannot? Moss believes he has the answer.

The lights lower, a hush descends across the auditorium.
The show is about to begin. Welcome to what Edward Moss declared:
"an entertainment of unexampled brilliance".

Welcome to the London Hippodrome.

Taken in August 1902 by the photographers Bedford Lemere & Company – an exterior view of the Hippodrome showing the shop fronts lining both the Charing Cross Road and Cranbourn Street aspects. Above this, rooms in Cranbourn Mansions provided office space for Moss Empires Ltd.

Illustrations from a children's picture book of the London Hippodrome, 1901.

The circus of variety 1900-1909

An impression of country visitors in 'the Gods', contrasting with the elegance and disdainful expressions of the more well-heeled town visitors in the expensive seats. Cartoon by Thomas Downey in *The Illustrated Sporting and Dramatic News*, reflecting the popularity of the London Hippodrome and its diverse entertainment programme, catering to a broad range of tastes.

> **The usual dreariness associated with a circus is entirely missing here, the visitor experiencing a sense of cheery comfort equal to any London theatre**
>
> The Illustrated Sporting and Dramatic News, 20th January 1900

An original pair of opera glasses punched with 'London Hippodrome', early 1900s.

Poster, printed by the leading theatrical advertisers David Allen & Sons, announcing the Hippodrome's eclectic array of acts in January 1900.

Reading the morning papers over breakfast on the 16th January 1900 must have been a particular pleasure for Edward Moss, managing director of the London Hippodrome and chairman of Moss Empires Limited.

"Stupendous, even in these days of magnificence – putting its immediate rivals in the shade" was the conclusion of *The Telegraph*'s theatre critic after attending the grand opening night at London's latest entertainment venue. "There are few more brilliant things to be seen in London than the auditorium of this Hippodrome when lighted by electricity, and thronged, as it was last night, by well-dressed pleasure-seekers," wrote *The Globe*. *The Evening Standard* echoed this admiration, noting how, "both in comfort, and the quality of the entertainment, everything that money can command would be provided", adding that the show, "ran with the precision of a machine". Moss could not have wished for better reviews.

The final preparations had not been without difficulties. Having given a preview tour of the building to members of the press in September, the Hippodrome was initially due to open over the Christmas period in 1899. When the schedule of preparations appeared to be delayed, the management took the decision to postpone until the 6th January, and then were forced to delay further, setting the opening night for the 15th. For the newly appointed press manager, Henry Garrick, fresh from Earls Court, it was a baptism of fire. Press releases were hastily despatched, explaining the reason for the postponement. "The magnificent new Hippodrome was to open on Saturday evening, but the management, anxious to feel entire confidence as to the elaborate mechanical effects, have postponed the opening until Monday 15th January." It was a minor hiccup, rather than a disaster. It may have even been advantageous. The intriguing mention of "elaborate mechanical effects" served only to pique the curiosity of those who had watched the magnificent terracotta building rise up on the corner of Cranbourn Street and Charing Cross Road over the past twelve months. This was surely something worth waiting for.

Moss and his team must have been relieved that their decision to delay was rewarded with such plaudits. There was, after all, a lot to get right, and much that could go wrong. Edward Moss had engaged the renowned theatre architect Frank Matcham to design most of his theatres, but for the London Hippodrome, his first venue in London and the flagship of Moss Empires Ltd., his plans were particularly ambitious. Moss's vision for his new theatre was to combine circus entertainment with variety acts, all enjoyed by audience members in a setting of well-appointed opulence. "The usual dreariness associated with a circus is entirely missing here, the visitor experiencing a sense of cheery comfort equal to any London theatre," remarked *The Illustrated Sporting and Dramatic News* with satisfaction in its report on the first night. Equally important to Moss, the amusements on offer would be free of the bawdy innuendo associated with music hall. Even the Empire and Alhambra theatres, just a short walk away in Leicester Square, while not exactly disreputable, were renowned for a certain type of clientele. In the previous decade there had been a moral crusade against the Empire's promenade (the bar area behind the stalls), where it was argued that prostitutes prowled among the cosmopolitan crowd, and the Empire's gentleman patrons were only too willing to give them custom.

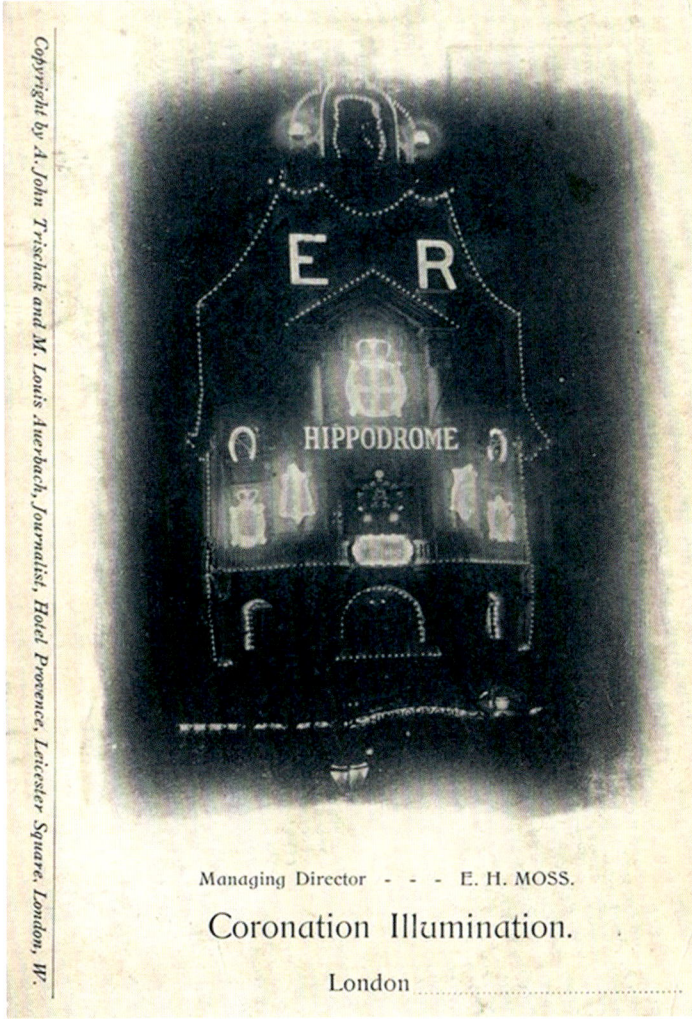

The Hippodrome illuminated for the coronation of King Edward VII in August 1902.

"There is no finer interior in the kingdom, and an absolute wealth of architectural and ornamental beauty has been lavished upon every detail." *The Illustrated Sporting and Dramatic News*, 10th February 1900. This illustration of the Hippodrome's auditorium appeared in its first programme and was reproduced in *The Sketch* magazine. The configuration of the ornate auditorium, with the circular water tank surrounded by the stalls, and the gallery with its balustrade high above the upper circle, gives an accurate impression of the theatre's scale.

The circus of variety 1900-1909

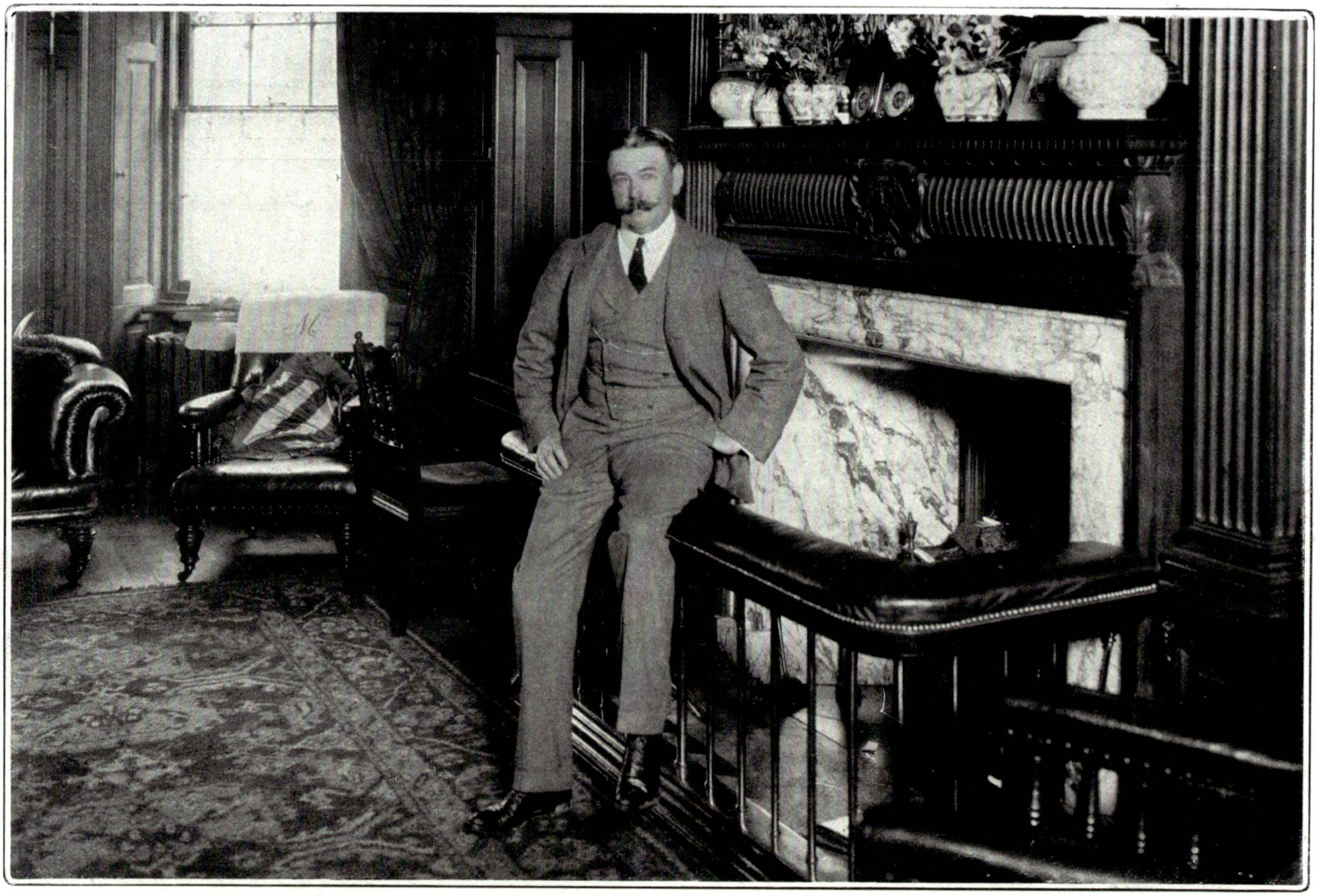

MR. H. E. MOSS, MANAGING-DIRECTOR OF THE LONDON HIPPODROME, AT MIDDLETON HALL, MIDDLETON, N.B.

LONDON HIPPODROME,

CRANBOURN STREET, LEICESTER SQUARE, W.C.

(Designed by FRANK MATCHAM, Architect.)

Proprietors - - MOSS' EMPIRES LIMITED (Total Capital, £1,400,000).
Managing Director - - - - Mr. H. E. MOSS.
Musical Conductor, Mr. GEORGES JACOBI : General Manager - Mr. FRANK ALLEN.
Manager - Mr. JAS. AYNSLEY COOK.

TWICE DAILY at 2 and 8 O'CLOCK.

PROGRAMME.

1—OVERTURE - - - - - - Orchestra

2—MIRA AMORAS in her Clever and Graceful Trapeze Act.

3—AGNES KREMBSER, the Female Champion Juggler on Horseback.

4—MAISANOS - - Continental Musical Grotesques

5—TONY WILSON and CLOWN in the Cleverest Horizontal Bar Act ever seen.

6—MARCELINE - - - - - Continental Auguste

7—SELECTION - - - - - - Orchestra

8—MONS. EMILE GAUTIER, with his Marvellous Equestrian Act, entitled, "La Table Arienne."

9—THE ATHOS TROUPE of Marvellous Acrobats.

10—TSCHERNOFF'S DOGS in a Marvellous Instance of Animal Training.

11—LAFAYETTE, the Marvellous Magician and Mimic.

12—THE LATEST WAR PICTURES, depicted by "GIBBONS' BIO-TABLEAUX."

3—GHEZZI, the Famous Clown.

—THE CONTINENTAL MUSICAL STARS.

—NEWHOUSE and WARD - American Trick Cyclists

1 FATMA & SMAUN - - - Dwarf Acrobats

17 ISS DARLING - - - - - Equestrienne

18— NEW HIPPODROME SENSATION, entitled—

"SIBERIA!"

Ac y W. H. RISQUE. Music composed and arranged by GEORGES JACOBI. Produced by FRANK PARKER.

Introducing Mr. HENCLER'S Magnificent Stud of Horses.

General Ivanoff (Military Governor of a District in Siberia) Mr. CECIL M. YORK
Major Karoutsky ... Mr. GASTON MERVALE
Captain Orloff ... Officers of a Regiment in the Garrison Town ... Mr. DRELINCOURT ODLUM
Captain Rentsef ... Mr. WINDHAM GUISE
Lieut. Hermanof ... Mr. T. ELLIS-BUXTON
Lieut. Maletsky ... Mr. ROLAND BOTTOMLEY
Nikolai ... (a Soldier) ... Mr. HUGH SETON
Dimitri ... (a Sleigh Driver) ... Mr. F. STRICKLAND
Vera Ivanoff ... (the General's Sister) Miss MARY ALLESTREE
Officers, Soldiers, Citizens, Siberian Exiles, &c., &c., &c.

Scene I.—Cafe in Siberian Military Town ... T. E. Ryan
Scene II.—The Road to the Mines ... T. E. Ryan
Scene III.—The Frozen River ... T. E. Ryan

N.B.—Owing to the elaborate nature of the Programme, which has to be constantly varied, it is impossible for the numbers to run consecutively.

Equestrian and Stage Director - - - - FRANK PARKER
Grand Orchestra of 40 Performers, under the Direction of Mr. GEORGES JACOBI
Ring Master, Mr. OTHO TWIGG.

Private Boxes, £1 1s., £1 11s. 6d., £2 2s., £3 3s. Stalls, 7/6 and 5/-. Dress Circle, 5/-. Grand Circle, 3/-. Amphitheatre Stalls, 2/-. Amphitheatre, 1/-. Box Office open Daily from 10 a.m. to 10 p.m. National Telephone 4035, Gerrard.

DOORS OPEN at 1-30 and 7-30 p.m. OVERTURE at 2 and 8-0 p.m.

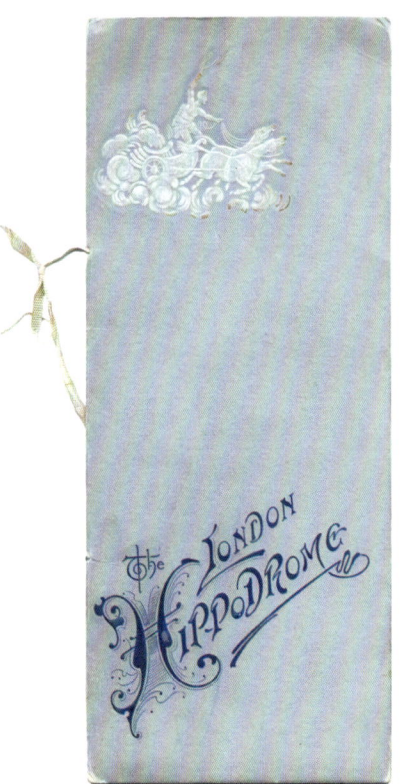

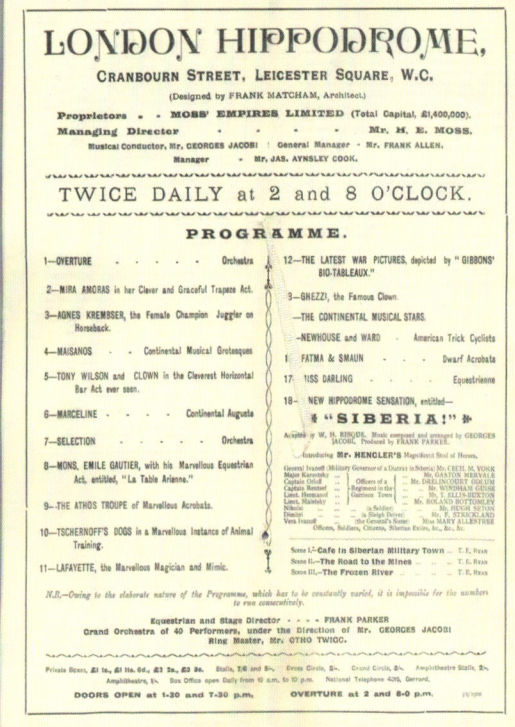

Sir Horace Edward Moss (1852–1912), the man behind the London Hippodrome. The son of a theatre manager, Moss learnt his craft at his father's music hall in Greenock and while still a teenager became manager of a travelling company exhibiting a diorama of the Franco-Prussian War.

He leased his first premises, Edinburgh's Gaiety Music Hall, in 1877 and in 1880 bought a theatre in Leith. He engaged performers to work across both venues, establishing a system that would underpin and ensure the success of later ventures. In the 1890s, he joined forces with Richard Thornton, and built the Empire Theatre in Newcastle, adding more premises in Edinburgh, Sheffield, Glasgow, Leeds and Nottingham throughout the 1890s. By this time, he was also in partnership with Oswald Stoll and in December 1899, just before the London Hippodrome was due to open, they merged their individual businesses into Moss Empires Ltd. with a capital of £1.4 million, 80% of which was financed by ordinary share capital, such was Moss and his partners' reputation by this point.

Although he did not court publicity, he was admired as a trustworthy businessman, whose perception of public taste gave him something of a Midas touch in the theatre world. Following an operation in April 1912, he did not appear in public again and died at his home, Middleton Hall at Gorebridge, Midlothian on 25th November that year.

Hippodrome programme from 1900 listing Hippodrome favourite, Marceline as well as performing animal, acrobatic and equestrian acts. 'Siberia', staged in June of that year, was the first in a series of dramatic water spectacles. M. Willson Disher, writing in his 1938 memoir of the entertainment industry, recalled the thrill of watching, 'Siberia': "The moment we lived for in 'Siberia' occurred when fugitives drove their sleigh by night through the snowstorm down stage, across the bridge (over the place where the orchestra had been earlier in the evening), and slap into the paper-flecked waters of the tank, with Cossacks in pursuit."

From a child's point of view, the London Hippodrome offered the best of both worlds. Thomas Downey caricatures Edward Moss in *The Illustrated Sporting and Dramatic News* as a kindly father figure, who gives his juvenile audiences what they want. The Hippodrome's family-friendly policy included half-price tickets for children during matinee performances.

Illustration from a popular children's book of the period, *The Visit to London* by Frances D. Bedford, published in 1902. Already, just two years after opening, the theatre had managed to establish itself as an essential highlight of London's array of amusements, alongside London Zoo and the Tower of London. Note the act drop behind the clowns in the arena, painted with a Hippodrome race from the classical world.

No such unsavoury scandals would cast a shadow over the London Hippodrome. Twenty years later, at his testimonial, Frank Allen, a fellow director of Moss Empires and manager of the Hippodrome, recalled Moss's objective verbatim: "Let us present a programme to the public which a man can safely bring his wife and family to witness." The London Hippodrome would serve up thrills, spills, fantasy and fun; but it would be good, clean fun. In agreement with Moss was his business partner in Moss Empires, Oswald Stoll, another great Edwardian theatre entrepreneur. Stoll was a teetotaller and non-smoker, but also a canny businessman, who understood that a guarantee of respectability in his theatres would naturally attract a more affluent, middle-class audience. Advertisements in programmes from this period reflect the tastes and aspirations of the Hippodrome's audience; Warings furniture specialists, Rudge-Whitworth bicycles, Klauss's chocolates, The Rendezvous "drawing room tea rooms", Kettner's restaurant, Peter Robinson's of Oxford Street, as well as several small ads for plots of land in London's outer suburbs. The Hippodrome's family-friendly policy included half-price tickets for children during matinee performances, and a popular children's book of the period, *The Visit to London* by Frances D. Bedford, published in 1902, featured an illustration and description of the Hippodrome. Already, just two years after opening, the theatre had managed to establish itself as an essential highlight of London's array of amusements, muscling in alongside London Zoo and the Tower of London.

Central to the Hippodrome's quest to present its audience with the most novel, innovative and spectacular programme of variety was a water tank situated underneath the arena, capable of holding 100,000 gallons of water drawn from the River Bourne, which ran directly underneath the building. A table, operated by hydraulic rams, could be raised in line with the stage or lowered to create a pool eight feet deep, illuminated by electric lights, equipped with fountains, and capacious enough to accommodate dives even from as high as the Hippodrome's roof. 'Water spectacles' would be the lead feature in the theatre's programme for the next nine years. Underneath the stalls and arena, mechanical apparatus was operated by a large team of stagehands, who, crucially, ensured a smooth and seamless changeover between acts. With a matinee and evening performance six days a week, and with around twelve to fifteen acts a show, it was essential the venue ran like a well-oiled machine.

For its opening night, the Hippodrome was to stage an 'aquatic burletta' entitled 'Giddy Ostend – or the Absent-Minded Millionaire'. Written by the theatre critic and librettist Henry Chance Newton, it starred one of variety's most popular and well-loved turns, Little Tich (real name, Harry Relph), whose diminutive height was accentuated for comic effect by his famous elongated clown shoes, in which he often performed a 'big boot dance'. 'Giddy Ostend' was scheduled towards the end of a programme into which no fewer than eighteen separate acts were packed; it was often reported in the press that Edward Moss believed in giving his audiences value for money.

Launching the evening's proceedings was the Hippodrome's 40-strong orchestra, led by its conductor, Georges Jacobi, poached from the Alhambra nearby where he had been musical director for over twenty-five years, during which time he had composed over one hundred ballets. Unlike the majority of theatres, the Hippodrome's orchestra did not have a pit at the front of the stage, as the space had been given over to the arena. Instead, the musicians were situated to one side of the grand circle (the 'OP' or 'off prompt' side) with a

Frank Parker, stage manager of the London Hippodrome during its first decade. Parker began his career in 1878 at the Adelphi Theatre under his uncle, John Parker, where he was involved in all aspects of production "from gas to stagework". He also worked at Drury Lane as a prompter and at the Gaiety. By the time he arrived at the Hippodrome in 1900 he had 25 years of stage management experience under his belt and was well-placed to devise and oversee the complicated ambitions of the Hippodrome's water spectacles and circus entertainment. From constructing a ramp strong enough to hold the weight of fourteen elephants to replicating an earthquake, Frank Parker's ingenuity knew no bounds.

Although much of his work took place behind the scenes, Parker was in demand for interviews, and in 1906 was featured in *The Tatler* in an article entitled 'Earthquakes I Have Made'. The interview was witty but evasive, Parker perhaps preferring to keep some of his stagecraft secrets to himself.

Scene beneath the arena of the London Hippodrome with stage hands and ponies readying themselves to convey large wooden 'properties' above for the next act. Frank Parker, the stage manager, can be seen at the front right of the picture, in bowler hat.

BENEATH THE ARENA (HIPPODROME).

CINDERELLA LEAVES A DELIGHTFUL IMPRESSION OF LAVISH PROFUSION.

Frank Parker deservedly takes a bow in this charming illustration by Thomas Downey for *The Illustrated Sporting and Dramatic News*, celebrating the Hippodrome's first pantomime, *Cinderella*. Moss, who was never coy about the cost of his productions, let it be known that over £10,000 had been lavished on this show, an enormous amount especially considering the pantomime itself had a run-time of just forty minutes. Among the expenses reported in the press was a glass coach studded with electric bulbs, costing £800–1000 (reports vary), and Cinderella's £100 shoes, made with over a thousand Abyssinian brilliants, displayed in the vestibule of the Hippodrome as a glittering symbol of the theatre's no-expense-spared policy.

Songs on topical subjects were popular during the late 19th and early 20th century. So it is perhaps unsurprising that the London Hippodrome inspired the 'Hippodrome March' composed by Theo Bonheur and published in London by W. Paxton. The cover design shows both the exterior and interior of the celebrated building.

> **Let us present a programme to the public which a man can safely bring his wife and family to witness**
>
> Edward Moss

A bewildering collection of switches and levers behind the scenes at the London Hippodrome. Mr. Hawkins, the electrical engineer in the switch-room, which was situated behind the stage and exclusively used for lighting that part of the building. Photograph from *The Illustrated Sporting and Dramatic News*, 1904.

shell-like cover ensuring an acoustically perfect projection of sound. On stage walked the American contralto, Madame Belle Cole, along with a chorus of ninety to lead the audience in a rousing rendition of the National Anthem. Cole, despite being American, was a crowd-pleaser with the necessary gravitas to handle a prestigious occasion; a few years earlier she had earned star status in London after being commanded by Queen Victoria to perform at the Royal Albert Hall during the visit of the German Emperor. To ensure a full measure of patriotism had been served, Jacobi's orchestra followed 'God Save the Queen' with 'God Bless the Prince of Wales' and the 'Queen's Jubilee March'. It was a suitably auspicious beginning.

The first half consisted of acts that alternately took place on the stage and in the arena. The Jees performed a double wire act with a skill that prompted *The Telegraph* to compare them to the great tightrope walkers Blondin and Maria Speltarini. They were followed by equestrienne Miss Godlewski who gave an elegant exhibition of 'haute ecole' (dressage). More acrobatics were performed by The O'Kabes, a Japanese troupe specialising in contortion, and Little Tony, 'the boy vaulting act' who leapt nimbly on and off a piebald pony. Mademoiselle Arnotis, a female strong woman, lifted five men seated on a table, drawing much admiration and applause, and Lavater Lee provoked laughter as he attempted to coax and cajole his "screamingly funny bucking mule" around the arena. Leonidas' Wonderful Cats and Dogs provided some audience interaction when one dog from the troupe headed a football back and forth between people in the stalls. The highlight of the performance was Nellie the cat, who ran up a rope to the roof, climbed deftly into a parachute, fell to the floor and, according to one newspaper report, "trotted away apparently well-satisfied with herself".

'Giddy Ostend' the programme's piece de resistance, was an opportunity for the Hippodrome to show off its state-of-the-art water tank. The rather flimsy plot featured an 'absent-minded millionaire' who wished to rid himself of his wife, while his daughter, desperate to avoid marrying a Count in pursuit of her, flings herself into the sea in order to end it all. Constructed more as a vehicle for the stars of the show – Little Tich as Petrolio Vanderstor the millionaire, the exhibition swimmers, James and Marie Finney and of course, the tank itself – *The Stage* newspaper sympathised with H. Chance Newton, who, "must have been hampered in his work. With no straw he could turn out very few tricks". It was Little Tich, the paper concluded, who sustained the piece with his, "nimble dancing, eccentric tricks and mannerisms" causing endless amusement. Providing the aquatic entertainment was Marie Finney, playing the suicidal daughter who is rescued only to miraculously display exceptional swimming skills. With other cast members singing and dancing in swimming costumes, and even the background scenery, painted by T. E. Ryan, offering an authentic view of Ostend's famous Kursaal, the novelty and spectacle alone made it a pleasant diversion for the audience.

But in fact, the highlight of the evening, and the act to receive the most column inches in the press, was Herr Julius Seeth and his Twenty-One Forest-Bred Lions. Their arrival in Britain had already caused ripples of interest as far as Essex, where the local papers reported on a curious consignment of twenty-one lions landing at Harwich on 5th January. Their debut at the Hippodrome ten days later was heralded by the smooth raising of a silver grille around the arena, providing a protective barrier approximately twenty feet high between audience and performers. The 'cage' as it was known, was formed by circular lengths of railings fixed upon the tops of the eight

Frank Matcham, caricatured in *Vanity Fair*, 1911

The London Hippodrome featured in postcard publisher Raphael Tuck's 'Famous Playhouses' series from around 1902 with sketches not only of the exterior and auditorium, but also the nautically inspired cabin saloon, the vestibule and the royal box, all giving an impression of the lavish ornamentation and rich red colour scheme.

Matcham's Magnificence

Frank Matcham was born in Newton Abbot, Devon in 1854 and at the age of fourteen began his career at the office of a Torquay architect, George Bridgeman. His grounding in theatre architecture began when he joined the practice of Jethro Thomas Robinson, who, as well as being responsible for the interiors of the Old Vic in London and Theatre Royal in Margate, was theatre architectural advisor to the Lord Chamberlain. Matcham married Robinson's daughter Hannah and, when his father-in-law died in 1878, took over his architectural practice. Matcham's productivity was astounding. Between 1879 and 1912, he built or re-modelled over 150 theatres around the United Kingdom, working on commissions that covered a spectrum ranging from smaller, provincial theatres to landmark buildings such as Oswald Stoll's Coliseum, opened in 1904 and of course, the London Hippodrome in 1900. Considering his firm's prolific output, relatively few of Matcham's buildings have survived; if not victims of wartime bombing raids, they instead succumbed to the developer's wrecking ball in the mid-twentieth century when appreciation of Matcham's ornate flamboyance was at its lowest ebb. Frank Matcham's interiors were an exuberant and unapologetic pick-and-mix of florid architectural styles. There was extravagant use of fibrous plaster mouldings, statuary and painted murals, creating an effect that provided his clients (and subsequently their audiences) with a place of escapism and fantasy. But his talents were technical as well as artistic, and his pioneering use of cantilevers in his theatre's galleries, abolished columns and vastly improved sight lines. Equally, the demands of theatre impresarios such as Edward Moss and Oswald Stoll saw Matcham devise and install state-of-the-art mechanical features such as the Hippodrome's tank and the Coliseum's revolving stages. After falling out of favour with architectural purists for a number of years, Frank Matcham's incomparable contribution to theatre was recognised when over seven thousand of his drawings were acquired by the Theatre Museum in 1995 (now part of the Theatre & Performing Arts Collection at the V&A), and the establishment of the Frank Matcham Society in 1994 has ensured his legacy is not forgotten. Among his best-known surviving buildings are the Grand Opera House in Belfast, Grand Theatre, Blackpool, Richmond Theatre in Surrey, Hackney Empire and the London Palladium. In 1958, when the London Hippodrome was transformed into The Talk of the Town, another exquisite Matcham interior was lost to modernisation. More than half a century later, when the Hippodrome was acquired by Jimmy and Simon Thomas, £700,000 was invested in restoring and reinstating much of the original mouldings, going some way to restoring the Hippodrome to its former glory.

Why the 'Hippodrome'?

In ancient Greece, a hippodrome was a stadium used for chariot racing, and by the nineteenth century had become associated with a new form of entertainment – circus. The London Hippodrome was just one of many theatres to borrow the name from antiquity; in the capital alone there were several Hippodrome theatres including in Lewisham, Ilford and Golders Green. Previous to that, there had been a horse racing course in Notting Hill also called the Hippodrome. But Matcham's new Hippodrome in London's West End was to wholeheartedly embrace the classical theme, with Imperial guards standing sentry on the roof top over the entrance, and the magnificent bronze horse-drawn Roman chariot, frozen in motion atop the corner tower's dome. Built at a time when London was the centre of the British Empire, the London Hippodrome's exterior details reinforces the strong sense of patriotism and imperialism prevalent in Britain at the turn of the twentieth century.

> "There is no finer interior in the kingdom, and an absolute wealth of architectural and ornamental beauty has been lavished upon every details"
>
> The Illustrated Sporting and Dramatic News, 10th February 1900

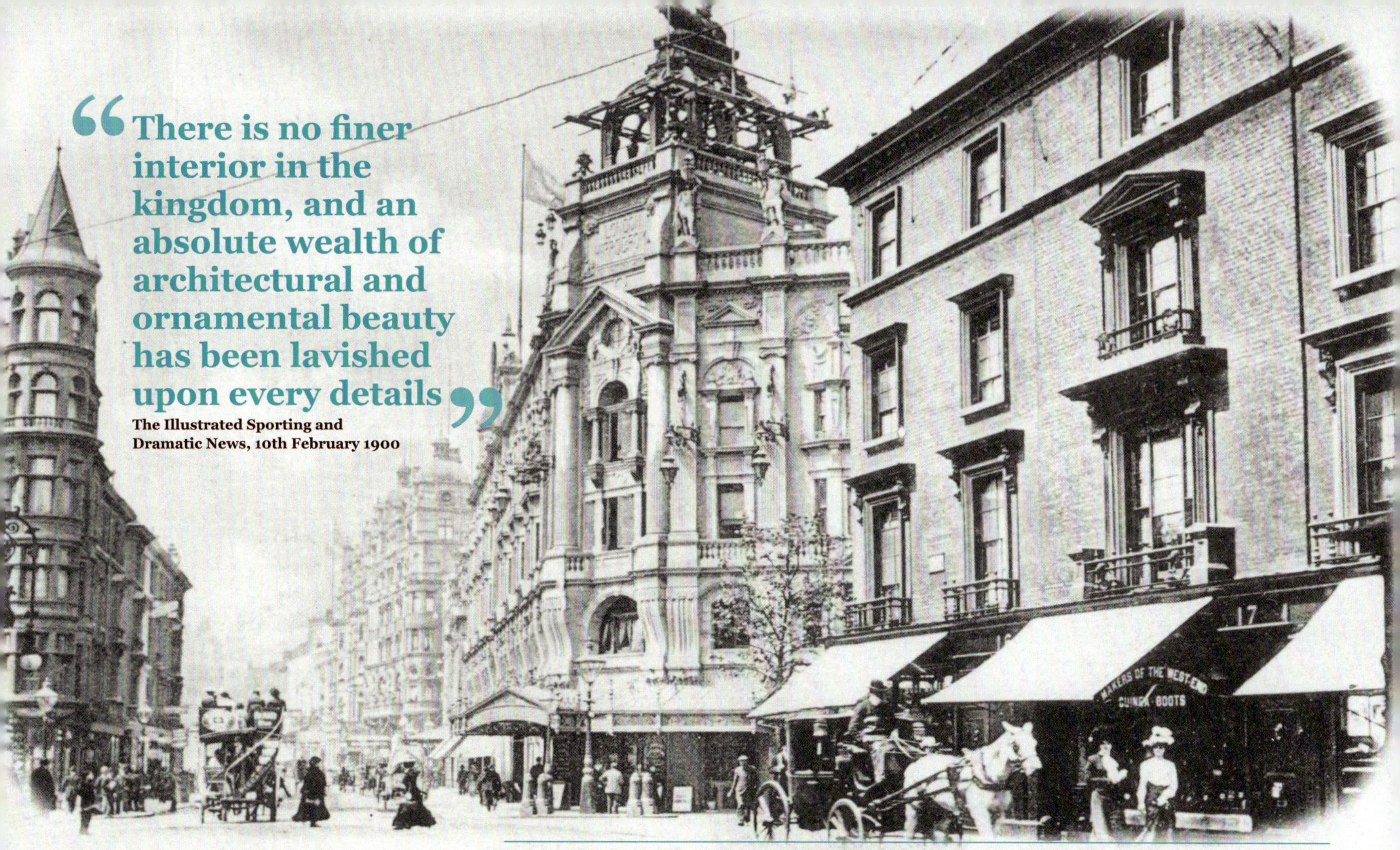

The Hippodrome, probably 1899 – construction almost complete but scaffolding still visible around the metal cupola.

Inside the Hippodrome

When interviewed about his new theatre, Edward Moss told reporters that he and Frank Matcham had travelled around all the big European cities, "to see if there were any wrinkles to be picked up, and there is nothing that skill and more skill can do to make the place a success that has not been done". Detailed descriptions in the press as well as in early programmes build up a picture of the Hippodrome's spectacular 'Flemish Renaissance' interior when it first opened in 1900. Entering from the main entrance on the corner of Charing Cross Road and Cranbourn Street, the vestibule, with its mosaic floor, mahogany doors and Italian marble walls, led through to the foyer. Here, the surroundings were "sumptuously furnished with velvet pile carpet and luxuriously upholstered settees, etc.", alongside the white marble stairs, marble columns, "artistic paintings" and oval ornamental plaster ceiling. Leading right off the foyer was the grand saloon, fitted out like a ship's saloon (and named the 'Cabin Saloon'), complete with portholes, brass fittings and attendants in "semi-naval costume". Through the crush room into the 'Flemish Renaissance' auditorium, the tip-up seats were upholstered in red velvet, all with a fine view of the stage and arena. The proscenium, measuring forty feet by thirty-six feet and sixty feet at its apex, was embellished with a statue of Britannia at its centre and side groups of sea monsters and nymphs, continuing the aquatic theme in décor.

Behind the opulent décor were some impressive technical and engineering innovations. To further cater to its patrons' comfort, a state-of-the-art ventilation system had been installed, drawing air through a perforated opening in the roof, which was then filtered through a saturated screen of matting which revolved in water. In the winter, the air was then driven over hot water coils into the ventilating chamber and through the perforated ceiling and in warm weather, it was drawn through iced water to create a cooling effect in the auditorium. Between the smog of London outside, and the smoky clouds from cigars inside, it is no surprise that this innovative air conditioning system was frequently remarked upon. Above the auditorium, a large square opening in the ceiling was surrounded by an open colonnade, creating a gallery from which high dives could be taken into the tank below, and snowstorms and limelight could be worked. The tank itself was made from steel boiler plates and measured 230 feet in circumference and eight feet in depth. When filled with water it weighed approximately four hundred tons, the weight supported by a strong steel platform with eight radiating lattice steel girders and circular bearers.

In the Hippodrome, Matcham had created state-of-the-art facilities, wrapped them in a cloak of magnificence and delivered to Edward Moss the means with which to conquer London.

The Grand Saloon of the Hippodrome, to the left of the foyer, was fitted out in a nautical style with portholes even showing a view of the (fake) sea through them. Staff were kitted out in semi-nautical uniforms. Note the themed life buoys with 'Hippodrome' printed upon them.

The circus of variety 1900-1909

In 1902, Eddie Gifford, the one-legged cyclist, performed his death-defying dive on his bicycle from the roof of the Hippodrome, a distance of seventy feet, into the tank below. Chicot, the theatre critic of the *Illustrated Sporting and Dramatic News*, had this to say about Gifford's act:

"The great thrill of the evening, however, is kindly provided by Mr. Eddie Gifford, described upon the programme as 'the world's most daring cyclist.' I should imagine the description to be perfectly accurate. Mr Gifford, I must tell you, has one leg instead of two, the usual number… The last thing that Eddie accomplishes is to climb up to the roof of the Hippodrome and ride along a little platform near the ceiling. Before he does it, they fill the arena with several feet of water. This is just as well, because, when Mr. Gifford gets to the end of the platform near the roof, there is no rail to protect him from falling, and so he just rides off. If there were no water there, he might get a nasty jar. I saw several people go out before this 'turn'. I didn't go out myself, but at the most exciting moment, I gave the man sitting next to me rather a sharp clutch on the fleshy part of the thigh. Unfortunately, he was sitting with his mouth open at the time, and I believe the sudden shock caused him to bite his tongue."

Gifford returned to the Hippodrome in 1903 with a new act he had devised and constructed. This time he did not take part himself but instead, Miss Mina Alix, so-called 'Heroine of the Hoop' thundered down a 'rake' in a small car, whizzing three times round an enormous hoop at lightning speed before making a rapid and effective exit via a trap.

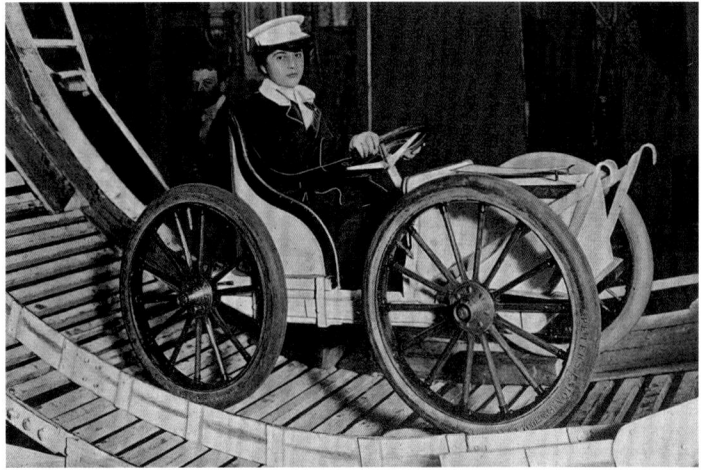

In order to book the very best acts; the Hippodrome's management cast their net wide and, in 1905, flung it as far as the Congo in central Africa. Colonel James Harrison, of Brandesburton Hall in East Yorkshire, a traveller and big game hunter, met a group of Pygmies while on a hunting trip, who, according to him, volunteered to travel with him back to the UK. The Mbuti Pygmies of the Ituri Forest remain one of the most ancient groups of hunter-gatherers in the world. It is therefore unsettling to read about these four men and two women who were taken from their home to be exhibited in front of audiences as a form of exotic entertainment. *The Era* magazine described the scene at the Hippodrome:

"The curtain rose upon a scene which represented a tropical forest, in the midst of which is an opening, containing four wigwams of small dimensions. Outside were the group of little people who will for some time be objects of curiosity to amusement-seeking Londoners."

The intention was to replicate the Pygmies' own homes in the Ituri forest. Whether this was a genuine attempt to educate the public about cultural difference, or an exploitative venture designed to sate voyeuristic appetites, we can only wonder. But the visitors do seem to have been treated well and took their celebrity status in their stride. Appearing at the Hippodrome for fourteen weeks, they then toured the provinces and in between times, lived at Brandesburton Hall with Colonel Harrison, where they hunted rabbits and birds in the grounds. The locals found them sociable, if rather unconventional, neighbours. They returned home in December 1907, two years since they had arrived in England, apparently none the worse for their extended sabbatical.

DRAWN BY CHARLES A. BUCHEL

Another hero of the looping the loop genre, albeit on a smaller scale, was Diavolino, a small monkey who appeared at the Hippodrome in 1902. Overseen by his trainer, Herr Grais, Diavolino peddled furiously round a hoop on a miniature tricycle. "I do not know whether he really likes it, but he seems extraordinarily keen to start," observed *The Tatler* after witnessing Diavolino's act.

A mock New Year card drawn by A. A. F. Kennett and published in *The Sketch* magazine, addressed to Edward Moss, "presiding genius" of the London Hippodrome, congratulating him on the pantomime production of *Cinderella*. Note the sparkling slipper on his right foot as he steps from 1900 into 1901!

hydraulic rams, simultaneously raising to enclose the arena. Despite these safety precautions, as Seeth entered the ring, several audience members were heard to nervously ask how high lions could jump. An imposing figure at six feet two inches and eighteen stone, Seeth appeared fearless as he strode on with two lions, two ponies and two dogs; the lions leaping over the latter as they circled the arena. As the act progressed, all twenty-one lions gathered in the arena, obliging Seeth by riding on a merry-go-round and see-saw; allowing him to lie across them, and to ride on the back of one of the largest. As his grand finale, Seeth walked around the arena carrying one lion over his shoulders. It was a triumph. "A large troupe of forest kings go through a startling performance so sensational as to be uncanny," raved *The Telegraph*.

Lion taming acts were nothing new in London, but Seeth's performance took the genre to a new level with its sheer ambition. Nobody had ever seen twenty-one lions kept under control, and guided through a performance, by just one man, and such was the applause from the audience (who were no doubt impressed but also relieved not to have witnessed a massacre), Seeth took no fewer than six curtain calls.

The evening concluded with more curtain calls, this time for Georges Jacobi, Edward Moss and Frank Parker who all appeared on stage together to take a bow. Parker, as producer and stage manager, was the mastermind behind the staging, scene changes, and smooth operation of the Hippodrome's complicated backstage mechanics. One can only imagine the sleepless nights he may have endured in the months leading up to this night. His moment in the spotlight was undoubtedly well deserved.

For the next nine years, the London Hippodrome's speciality was this flamboyant mix of circus, variety and spectacle. Having set the bar high, the theatre continued to work hard to attract the world's finest performers and maintain the Hippodrome as a leading provider of event entertainment in the capital. Henry Garrick, as publicity manager, was kept busy notifying the press of forthcoming acts, supplying photographs and arranging tours and tickets for reporters and press artists. While undoubtedly a pressurised job, the Hippodrome was providing just the sort of entertainment the papers, and especially the quality illustrated weeklies, liked to cover – original, occasionally bizarre, often ground-breaking and consistently spectacular.

In the first year of operation, acts on the bill included the equestrienne Milly Capell, the Meister Glee Singers Quartette, the Sisters O'Meers 'clever wire artists', Eugene Sandow, the world-famous strong man and the regular appearance of the Finney family of swimmers. In May of that year, the climax of the Finneys' act was a thrilling dive by Marie from sixty feet above the arena into the tank below. 'Mr Goodnight', the horse who undresses and puts himself to bed, was another popular attraction in March. Following the comparatively lukewarm reception to the light-hearted 'Giddy Ostend' sketch, Frank Parker decided to take a more dramatic direction with the centrepiece shows. In June 1900, the Hippodrome presented a new water spectacle entitled 'Siberia'. Featuring snow and a climactic scene where horses thundered across the stage and plunged into the water, it was such a sensation the Hippodrome simply printed snippets of its glowing reviews in the theatre listings of the daily papers. "It is not likely to be surpassed. A triumph of realistic spectacle. No other place of amusement could attempt so huge and audacious a spectacle,

The circus of variety 1900-1909

Marceline, a 'clown Auguste' reliant on mime, whistling and physicality to make audiences laugh, was a Hippodrome favourite during its first four years, delighting all with his meddlesome antics and acting as a mischievous foil to some of the more serious acts. Hailed a "true genius" by the *Cornhill* magazine in 1901, and just over a year later, declared by *The Sketch* as "funnier than ever" in the pantomime *Dick Whittington*, Marceline was one of London's most popular stars during his residency at the Hippodrome.

> **I was a cat and Marceline would back away from a dog and fall over my back while I drank milk. He always complained that I did not arch my back enough to break his fall.**
>
> Charlie Chaplin recalling his time performing with Marceline at the London Hippodrome

Caricature of Marceline with Otto Twigg, the Hippodrome's ringmaster, by Thomas Downey in *The Illustrated Sporting and Dramatic News*, from June 1901.

Promotional postcard for Marceline. In 1902 'The Playgoer' said, "Since the opening of the Hippodrome, Marceline has scarcely been 'out of the bill'. He is the unqualified delight of the grown-ups as well as that of the children."

Marceline performing with a 'moving statue' at the London Hippodrome in December 1902.

Performing with Marceline the Droll at the London Hippodrome was a formative experience for the young Charlie Chaplin. From the crumpled, baggy suit to the physical poses, Marceline's influence on the on-screen persona Chaplin created is plain to see.

and not even the Hippodrome itself, despite its excellent record in the past, is likely to surpass the frozen river of 'Siberia'" wrote *The Daily Telegraph*. *The Morning Advertiser*'s praise was similarly effusive: "It is an intensely dramatic moment and its successful achievement is another triumph for stagecraft and perfect organisation at the Hippodrome." M. Willson Disher, in '*Winkles and Champagne*,' his 1938 memoir of the entertainment industry, recalled the thrill of watching 'Siberia':

"The moment we lived for in 'Siberia' occurred when fugitives drove their sleigh by night through the snowstorm down stage, across the bridge (over the place where the orchestra had been earlier in the evening), and slap into the paper-flecked waters of the tank, with Cossacks in pursuit."

'Siberia' was a sensation and thereafter, the water spectacles at the Hippodrome frequently followed a melodramatic narrative, sometimes written around a fictional natural disaster, which brought a watery death and destruction in its wake. 'The Flood' (1906), 'The Typhoon' (1907), 'The Earthquake' (1907) and 'The Volcano' (1908), were all ambitious but superbly realised according to contemporary accounts and might be considered the forebears of the disaster movie of more recent times. The writers behind these 'disaster' spectacles, the husband-and-wife team Alicia Ramsey and Rudolph de Cordova, did in fact go on to script a number of silent films. It was unfortunate that rehearsals for 'The Earthquake' were already in progress when a devastating real-life earthquake, at Valparaiso in Chile, demolished most of the city and killed over 20,000 people. "The management desires to explain (the show) was in rehearsal weeks before the great disaster at Valparaiso and hopes that the production will be regarded as an inventable coincidence and not be ascribed to want of taste," reported *The Illustrated Sporting and Dramatic News*.

'Tally-ho', staged in the summer of 1901, recreated a hunting scene, complete with horses and hounds splashing into the water and on 21 August 1902, such was the renown of the new theatre's water spectacles, the Shah of Persia came to see 'The Bandits'. The Shah arrived at the Hippodrome which had been specially lit for the occasion and hung with the Persian flag over the main entrance. Inside, the auditorium was festooned with silver and white floral arrangements. It was later recalled the entire cost of decorations for this gala performance amounted to £6000. The Shah and his party watched the show from the comfort of a private box where, just metres away, he witnessed the moment when an explosion blew up a mill-house setting free thousands of gallons of pent-up water and sweeping away a stagecoach and horses in the torrent. Having missed the Edisonograph presentation, which apparently included pictures of his own arrival in London, he requested the Hippodrome set up a private viewing for him at Marlborough House where he was staying, a request which they duly obliged.

In 1908's 'Sands of Dee', the heroine of the play was submerged in water and tied to a post while five-ton waves crashed down one after another, an effect created by a suspended tank of water above the stage releasing a deluge onto a concave board. As with many water spectacles, the helpless heroine was rescued at the last minute, and the villain was dealt with correctly in that he invariably drowned. 'The Redskins' in 1903, which was inspired by the tales of frontier life and Native Americans in the stories of Fenimore Cooper, included a scene with a waterfall over which the Redskins paddled in their canoes.

> "There are few more brilliant things to be seen in London than the auditorium of this Hippodrome when lighted by electricity, and thronged, as it was last night, by well-dressed pleasure-seekers"
>
> The Globe, 16th January 1900

The Aberdeen Press and Journal in its 'Our London Letter' summed up the kind of impact it had on spectators:

"Horses as well as men come plunging and swimming through the water. The final scene of all – the Indian canoes shooting down a cataract – is the most exciting and marvellous scene of all. It was rapturously applauded. With such attractions as this, the Hippodrome has won a distinctive place amongst houses of entertainment in London, and a visit to it now comes within the category of all juvenile aspirations."

Incredible water spectacles and the finest animal performers were the Hippodrome's speciality, but a combination of the two could provide the ultimate in theatrical experiences. Horses and dogs had already been trained to jump into the water tank with great effect, but pantomimes were an excuse to indulge in fantasy and perhaps some ambitious amphibious experimentation. Frank Parker appears to have been a man undaunted by a challenge and for the Hippodrome's 1903-4 pantomime, hired fifteen elephants from Herr Busch's circus in Berlin to be the highlight of the show, sliding in succession down a tropical water chute into the water-filled arena below. An incredible feat of theatrical engineering, as well as one of the most novel animal acts London had seen, the plunging elephants at the Hippodrome received rave reviews. The news that on one particular day a recalcitrant elephant called Charlie had decided to rampage through the backstage area seems to have done little harm to the Hippodrome's reputation, perhaps even encouraging more people to buy a ticket to satisfy their curiosity and dabble with some dramatic danger.

A few weeks after Charlie's very destructive protest, the *Music Hall and Theatre Review* reported that the Home Secretary had asked if any action would be taken, "in connection with the performance at the London Hippodrome in which elephants were forced on to a steep incline and precipitated into the water?" A Mr. Buxton replied, "I have no special power in the matter, but, having made inquiry, I am informed that no force is used in the performance. The elephants, under the direction of a keeper, proceed to the head of the chute, and thence slide into the water. There is no cruelty, and the animals are said to be well-kept and cared for."

Nothing more seems to have been said about the matter, but it demonstrates that even over a century ago, animal welfare was a growing concern, and considered worth debating in parliament. We cannot know fully the methods used by trainers, or the conditions animals were kept in. However, the Hippodrome's bespoke construction took into account the requirements of animal acts. There were extensive stables and stalls underneath the theatre, for animals to stay in prior and immediately after a performance, and a number of rooms reserved for trainers and keepers. For a high-profile venue such as the Hippodrome, it would not do for the facilities to be anything less than first class, or for animals to appear unhappy or out of condition. We can only assume the animals that performed at the Hippodrome were, as Mr. Buxton confirmed, well looked after.

The Hippodrome, London by Everett Shinn (1876–1953)
The American painter Everett Shinn would become renowned for his theatrical subjects, but this unusual view of the audience at the Hippodrome, dappled by limelight as a trapeze artist swoops to their level, was his first attempt at the genre. The painting, which now hangs in the Art Institute of Chicago, was inspired by Shinn's visit to the Hippodrome during his only trip to Europe in 1900.

Annette Kellermann

As a child, Annette Kellermann wore steel supports to support her weak legs and was encouraged to swim in order to build her strength. A natural water baby, swimming soon became second nature to her, and the more competitions she won and aquatic feats she performed, the more famous she became.

Female swimmers in the late nineteenth and early twentieth centuries were encumbered by bulky bathing costumes, designed for modesty rather than performance, but Annette Kellermann pioneered a new, sleeveless, figure-hugging swimsuit that would allow ease of movement in the water. "I cannot swim wearing more stuff than a clothesline," she declared, quite reasonably.

The costume also sealed her celebrity when she was arrested on a Massachusetts beach for indecency in 1907, earning her a very useful notoriety that Kellermann cannily turned to her advantage. When a Harvard academic, Professor Dudley A. Sargent, announced that he had scientifically and statistically deduced Kellermann had the world's most perfect figure, there cannot have been an announcement more likely to entice the public to want to see this modern-day mermaid in the flesh. And if water spectacles were the highlight of the London Hippodrome, then surely the world's most famous female swimmer should be its centrepiece?

In 1906, she appeared in *The Treasure Ship and the Fairy Seas* alongside the Finney sisters. These were opportunities for the electric lighting scheme surrounding the Hippodrome's water tank to be used for full effect and as Kellerman dived into the illuminated water members of the audience had a good view of the submerged scenery, complete with octopus, no matter where they sat.

Annette Kellermann, chief mermaid, never had a better setting for her lovely, casual dives

M. Willson Disher, recalling Kellermann's aquatic performances at the Hippodrome in his theatrical memoirs

MISS ANNETTE KELLERMANN, WHO IS GIVING EXHIBITIONS OF DIVING AT THE HIPPODROME.

Miss Kellermann, the Australian lady swimmer, came to this country in order to make an attempt to swim the Channel, and will renew her efforts next year, when she hopes to meet with success. It will be remembered that she failed last summer owing to an unfortunate attack of mal-de-mer. At the London Hippodrome, Miss Kellermann is giving an exhibition of fancy diving, and is showing how Holbein, Burgess, and herself endeavoured to emulate Captain Webb's great feat. Our illustration shows her making what is, perhaps, her most perfect dive.

Based on a photograph by Sears.

The Treasure Ship and The Fairy Seas. The 1906 Christmas production at the London Hippodrome used its famous water tank to enact an underwater scene about treasure seekers beneath the sea. Attacked by an octopus, but rescued by fairies, Annette Kellermann and the Finney sisters starred in the aquatic drama.

James Finney and his sister Marie, champion exhibition swimmers, were among the first acts to appear at the London Hippodrome and continued to perform regularly during its early years. Marie appeared as the heroine in 'Giddy Ostend' and in May 1900, the climax of the Finneys' act was a thrilling dive by Marie from sixty feet above the arena into the tank below. She also starred alongside Annette Kellermann in *The Treasure Ship and the Fairy Seas* as illustrated above.

Herr Seeth returned to the Hippodrome in 1903, having increased his pride of lions from twenty-one to thirty-one, though it would be one of his final performances and he retired soon afterwards. To keep up with the public's appetite, new wild animal acts had been introduced. Herr Richard Sawade was born in Frankfurt but gained his training at Hagenbek's zoological emporium in Hamburg, where Seeth had also learnt his craft. As well as two lions, Sawade's troupe in 1901 consisted of four Bengal tigers, three Himalayan black bears, two polar bears and two German boar hounds, which harmoniously combined to form pyramids, balance on a see-saw, jump through hoops and walk on cylinders. One of the black bears was the comedian of the troupe, walking on its hind legs, "with all the pompous decorum of a Turveydrop" according to *The Sketch*.

Even those members of the press who confessed to feeling uncomfortable about performing animals could not help being won over by the turns at the Hippodrome. *The Sketch* magazine, although admitting it was not, "as a rule 'gone on' animal acts", was enchanted by Captain Woodward's seals and sea-lions in January 1901. The magazine observed how their obedience was won by Woodward feeding them "herrings and whiting galore" through the whole performance, as half of his seals swam in the tank which had been specially anointed with rock-salt from Turk's Island in the Pacific. The "truly marvellous" Lion was able to dribble a football and balance an air ball perfectly on his snout. Frisco, a skilful trumpet player, and Mr. Toby, who performed on the guitar, were "scarcely less astonishing".

Woodward's seals formed part of the Hippodrome's Christmas programme, the main attraction of which was its first pantomime, *Cinderella*. Moss, who was never coy about the cost of his productions, let it be known that over £10,000 had been lavished on this show, an enormous amount especially considering the pantomime itself had a run-time of just forty minutes. Among the expenses reported in the press was a glass coach studded with electric bulbs, costing £800, and *Cinderella*'s £100 shoes, made with over a thousand Abyssinian brilliants, displayed in the Hippodrome's vestibule. With *Cinderella*, the Hippodrome had set the bar high and the following year, *The Illustrated Sporting and Dramatic News* reported that *Aladdin* would be, "the most expensive version of the fairy story ever put on stage". For the 1902–3 production, this time *Dick Whittington*, Frank Parker promised a city guild scene costing £5000. Extravagant financial outlay together with a carefully choreographed publicity campaign proved to be a winning formula. Theatregoers were keen to see the best that money could buy and were rarely disappointed by what they saw at the Hippodrome.

The cast of *Cinderella* in the first Christmas season of 1900–1 included Marceline 'The Droll' playing Buttons opposite Amy Farrell as Cinders, and Hetty Chattell in the role of Prince Charming. Marceline, born Marcelino Orbes in Saragossa, Spain, despite his Gallic-sounding name, was a 'clown Auguste' in that he was mute and performed purely through mime, action and whistles. A regular fixture at the Hippodrome in its first four years, his speciality was meddling and generally getting in the way. *The Stage*, in a 1903 review of the Hippodrome's latest programme, listed Robert Cottrell and Miss Louise, the famous Continental equestrians who gave, "an exhibition of daring and skilful horsemanship which it would be hard to equal". Meanwhile, during their performance, "Marceline, the Hippodrome clown, who, beside possessing a natural fund of humour, is a most agile acrobat" ran amok, much to the delight of the audience.

AN EARTHQUAKE NEAR LEICESTER SQUARE
The Latest Sensation at the Hippodrome.

DRAWN BY F. MATANIA

'The Earthquake' from 1906, and 'The Typhoon', 1907, both by Fortunino Matania for *The Sphere* magazine. Matania was an artist committed to producing the most authentic pictures of what he saw for *The Sphere*'s readers, and these two images give a good impression of how dramatic the Hippodrome's spectacles were, with audience members in smart evening dress just feet away from the aquatic mayhem.

> **To be appreciated 'The Earthquake' has to be seen. Put briefly it is a wonderful piece of stage production... it is a very clever illusion**
>
> The Sphere, 15th September 1906

The Shah of Persia's visit to the London Hippodrome during which he witnessed the catastrophic scene in 'The Bandits'. A prettily arranged box draped with white, had been constructed facing the stage, bearing the arms of Persia and the triple plumes of the Prince of Wales. The Shah and his suite seemed to be particularly pleased with the riding of M. Salamonsky and the finale in which the coach was overwhelmed with water. Illustration by F. C. Dickinson in *The Graphic*, 1902.

For those lucky enough to secure a front row seat at the Hippodrome, twenty-foot high 'splash panes' were raised around the perimeter of the arena to protect fine silks and velvet evening cloaks from being drenched! Illustration by Thomas Downey in *The Illustrated Sporting and Dramatic News*, 1901.

As a mischievous foil to some of the Hippodrome's more serious acts, Marceline was particularly effective. He quickly became a star.

Also in the cast of *Cinderella*, as a member of the chorus, was an eleven-year old boy just embarking on his comic career. A year earlier, Charles Chaplin had left school and begun his ascent out of a childhood existence that had seen him constantly teetering on the brink of destitution. He had joined 'The Lancashire Lads', an eight-strong clog-dancing troupe, and travelled round halls and theatres nationwide performing. Now on an agent's books, they found a job at the Hippodrome, playing cats and dogs in the Baron's Kitchen scene. It was an opportunity that would at least keep them in regular employment for the best part of four months; during this era, pantomimes traditionally opened after Christmas and often ran until April the following year. Working alongside Marceline was to be a formative experience for Chaplin, and it is easy to see how he picked up the characteristics and quirks of Marceline and made them his own when he embarked on his film career a decade and a half later. In *Cinderella*, Marceline appeared in an ill-fitting dinner suit tied with string and battered opera hat, using a fishing rod to fish for the chorus girls that had disappeared into the water tank. For bait, he threw jewels into the water with a casual yet innocent nonchalance that seems, in retrospect, along with his eccentrically shabby appearance, peculiarly Chaplinesque. While soaking up these comic influences, it was clear Chaplin also had ideas of his own, as exemplified by one matinee performance, which he recounted in *My Autobiography*.

"I was given a little comedy bit to do with Marceline. I was a cat and Marceline would back away from a dog and fall over my back while I drank milk. He always complained that I did not arch my back enough to break his fall. I wore a cat mask which had a look of surprise and during the first matinee for children, I went up to the rear end of a dog and began to sniff. When the audience laughed I turned and looked surprised at them, pulling a string which winked a staring eye. After several sniffs and winks the house-manager came bounding back stage, waving frantically in the wings, but I carried on. After smelling the dog, I smelt the proscenium, then I lifted my leg. The audience roared – possibly because the gesture was so uncatlike. Eventually the manager caught my eye and I capered off to great applause. 'Never do that again!' he said breathlessly, 'You'll have the Lord Chamberlain close down the theatre.'"

No doubt hundreds of Edwardian children went home that evening with the lavatorial exploits of the cat in *Cinderella* etched on their memory forever. But while Chaplin's maverick performance is an early indication of the comedy genius he would become, the story is doubly interesting for the reaction of the Hippodrome's management to his antics. We can only deduce it was J. Aynsley Cook, the Hippodrome's manager, who lectured him afterwards, understandably anxious that a juvenile chorus member had jeopardised the Hippodrome's squeaky-clean reputation.

Chaplin recalled that *Cinderella* was, "a great success, and although Marceline had little to do with plot or story, he was the star attraction." One newspaper reported how Marceline was the recipient of numerous gifts from an admiring female audience member, who insisted on sending him expensive pieces of jewellery, night after night. In those first few years, Marceline was such a regular in the programme, he was known simply as the "Hippodrome's clown". But in 1905, he was lured across the Atlantic by Frederic Thompson and

The circus of variety 1900-1909

Diagram showing a cross-section of the London Hippodrome, and specifically how Busch's elephants slid down a slide into the water-filled arena. Illustration by Percy Home in *The Sphere*, 1904.

Chorus girls and messenger boys screamed and dashed about… Charlie had developed an obstreperous mood

The Daily Mail, January 1903

For the grand finale of the Hippodrome's 1903–4 pantomime, *The Golden Princess and the Elephant Hunters*, something quite unique was planned. As the arena floor was lowered, and the tank filled to create a shimmering lake, the stage curtains opened to reveal a steep chute of about forty-five degrees, bordered by rocks and tropical plants. Appearing at the top of the slope was a real, live elephant, trumpeting to signal its presence (in case anybody had failed to notice) before sliding down the slope and plunging into the water below. As if one elephant was not enough, another fourteen elephants, all weighing around two tonnes each, appeared at the top of the slope before making their descent into the water.

The plunging elephants at the Hippodrome were, unsurprisingly, the talk of London. There are no reports that suggest any of the performances, as seen from the front of house, went anything but smoothly, but on the 23rd January, an incident took place that proved just how unpredictable and dangerous elephants in captivity could be.

The Daily Mail reported, "There was an unrehearsed scene at the London Hippodrome on the 23rd inst. Chorus girls and messenger boys screamed and dashed about wildly; the cracking of doors and the breaking of furniture filled the air; and above all could be heard exultant trumpetings. Charlie, an elephant, had developed an obstreperous mood…"

Apparently Charlie, due to begin his performance, had assumed a "sudden air of independence", flatly refused to slide down the chute and began his escape as swiftly as his bulk allowed him, climbing the stairs up to Frank Parker's office. He butted open the door and on entering, proceeded to wreck everything in sight. In the dressing room next door, chorus girls, some in flimsy costumes, tried to escape out of windows and by running along the low glass roof that sheltered waiting queues on the street below, much to the bemusement of passers-by.

One chorus girl, interviewed afterwards, remembered some girls gripping onto the door of their dressing room, as if that would prevent the forceful entry of an irritable elephant. She eventually persuaded them to let her and some others out. They ran to the top storey and climbed to the roof via a ladder where they sat shivering until news eventually came that Charlie had been lassoed, presumably by his trainer, Mr. Busch, and returned safely to his stable. On the way back down, passing Parker's office she noticed there was no door, just some splintered timber hanging by a hinge. The desk and sofa were ground to pieces, chairs were smashed and fragments from a shattered mirror were scattered across the floor.

The moment of impact as one of the elephants plunges into the water tank. A photograph proving the necessity of the arena's protective splash panes.

Elmer S. Dunday, the proprietors of the newly built New York Hippodrome, an enterprise inspired by the Hippodrome in London, but even more vast in scale and ambition. For about a decade, Marceline enjoyed fame and fortune in New York, and, unlike many variety performers, he was in the fortunate position of being able to take holidays due to drawing a regular salary all year round. But around the time of the First World War, the appetite for circus entertainment rapidly declined. The New York Hippodrome found it increasingly difficult to fill its vast auditorium, and as its fortunes changed, so did Marceline's. In 1918, Chaplin encountered his hero once again at a point when his own career had far eclipsed Marceline's. He was shocked to discover him performing at Ringling Brothers' three-ring circus in Los Angeles, not as the star, but as one of a number of clowns running around the arena – "a great artist lost in the vulgar extravagance of a three-ring circus". On visiting his dressing room afterwards to introduce himself, Chaplin found Marceline "apathetic and sullen under his make up", apparently uninterested in reminiscing about his time as a star in London.

By the 1920s, any fortune Marceline had amassed from his glory days had been sunk into disastrous restaurant schemes, and he was penniless. A report in the *Western Daily Press*, abrupt in its brevity, disclosed a tragic end to a once-great star:

"Famous Clown's Death
New York – Sunday – The famous clown, Marceline, who delighted children at Christmas pantomimes in London 25 years ago, was found dead in bed yesterday afternoon with a bullet in his head. His name was Martinez Orbes and he was born at Saragossa in 1873 – Reuter."

Marceline had shot himself, and was found in his room in a shabby hotel surrounded by photographs of happier, more successful times. He had pawned a diamond stickpin just two days earlier, in order to pay alimony to his wife.

If anything can be taken from the tragedy of Marceline, it is that tastes change, and theatres and entertainers must keep pace. For the London Hippodrome, Marceline's departure does not seem to have had any negative effects. New clowns replaced him: first there was Anderson, known as 'Andy' whose father Bob Anderson had been a famous clown in the 1870s; another clown went by the rather sinister name of 'Sliver'. The programme continued to serve up a tantalisingly eclectic – if lengthy - variety of novel performers. Edward Moss, once responding to one reviewer who complained the programme was too long, agreed but gestured towards the completely full auditorium with a shrug, wordlessly indicating that this was clearly what the public wanted.

These early years saw the Hippodrome enjoy tremendous success. Moss and his business partners had clearly settled on a winning formula, and it is difficult not to be seduced by the colourful descriptions in the contemporary press. If granted the power of time travel for just one evening, choosing which Hippodrome show to see would present a dilemma. Perhaps one could go back to April 1901 to witness Herbert's Wonderful Dogs whose star turn, a mongrel called Dink, could jump through hoops, perform a cakewalk and dive, while a maternal dachshund from the same troupe pushed a pram of furry colleagues around the arena. Or maybe to 1904 to see strongman Herr George Lettl preventing two 8 ½ h.p. cars from moving off at top speed in opposite directions by the sheer strength in his arms.

Houdini and the handcuff challenge

Born Ehrich Weisz in Hungary in 1874, Harry Houdini's family had emigrated to America in 1878 where they settled in Milwaukee. As a boy, he experimented with various circus and entertainment disciplines from trapeze to card tricks, until he eventually found his metier with a handcuffs act, with which he toured the United States, performing at top vaudeville venues. In 1900, his manager booked him on a tour of Europe where he impressed Charles Dundas Slater, then the manager of the Alhambra Theatre. Gaining fame through a series of widely publicised 'jail breaks' that baffled police, his show at the Alhambra ran for six months and established him as a global phenomenon.

Repeatedly plagued by imitators and detractors keen to expose his methods, Houdini was perpetually under pressure to keep ahead of competition and when he was booked to appear at the London Hippodrome in March 1904, he was thrown a challenge that would surpass any previous achievements. On his first appearance, he asked the audience, as he usually did, if anyone cared to offer him a challenge, managing to slip out of several ordinary cuffs given to him with ease. Then a man walked on stage announcing himself as a representative of *The Daily Mirror*. He proffered a heavy, steel handcuff which, he told the audience, was the result of five years' work by a Birmingham blacksmith called Nathaniel Hart, who had been determined to engineer something that would defeat any escapologist or handcuff king. Houdini examined the cuff, which was fastened with two main Bramah locks, and twelve smaller locks concealed within, designed to hold both wrists within a single clasp. Shaking his head, he refused the challenge, claiming the cuff was "not regulation", at which point the journalist, who was later found to be a man called Will A. Bennett, questioned Houdini's claim to be the world's "handcuff king" if he would not attempt to do battle with the handcuffs. After three refusals, Houdini eventually relented, saying he could not carry out the challenge there and then, as the time remaining would not be sufficient to escape from such a complicated device. In consultation with the stage director Frank Parker, a date was set for five days later, on Thursday 17th March, just enough time for the newspapers, and particularly the circulation-hungry *Mirror,* to stir up a frenzy of public interest. It was a masterful piece of manufactured publicity.

On the day, Houdini was joined on stage by a large group of 'officials' and audience members, keen to examine the cuff being secured. Houdini stood centre stage and made a brief speech: "Ladies and Gentlemen, I am now locked up in a handcuff that has taken a British mechanic five years to make. I do not know whether I am going to get out of it or not, but I can assure you I am going to do my best." Houdini retreated to what he called his "ghost house", a cabinet around three feet high that screened his movements from the audience, to begin his extrication as the orchestra played a succession of popular tunes. Several times he emerged from the cabinet and the audience prematurely cheered thinking he had escaped. But the handcuffs were proving fiendishly difficult. He appeared increasingly distressed and dishevelled as he emerged at intervals; to see the mechanism in better light; to ask for a glass of water; at one point he requested to be temporarily released so he could remove his jacket. When this request was refused, he flipped his jacket upside down, and used a penknife to cut it to shreds, much to the delight of the crowd. Unrestricted by his jacket and given a cushion by Frank Parker to make kneeling more comfortable, Houdini's escape had now taken over an hour and the tension in the auditorium was palpable. "Those who were present are not likely to forget the tense excitement of that hour," reported *The Illustrated Sporting and Dramatic News*. "And probably

Houdini, on stage at the Hippodrome, having the specially made cuffs locked to his wrists in the presence of representatives of some London newspapers.

Publicity photographs published in *The Illustrated Sporting and Dramatic News* to coincide with Houdini's appearance.

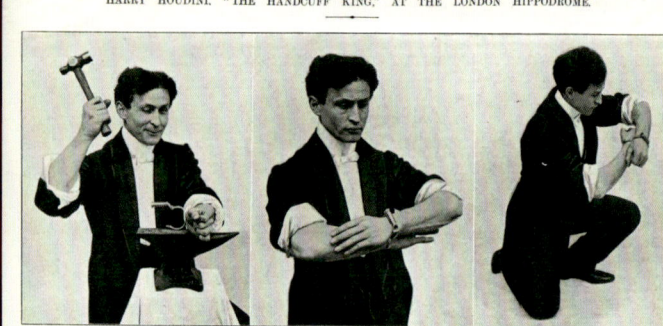

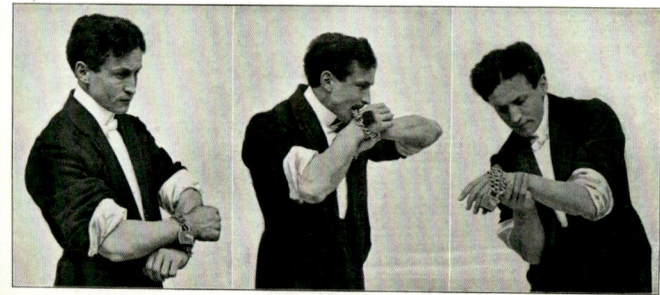

> "The Hippodrome maintains its prestige by a constant change of bill. The latest addition is the well-known Houdini, the handcuff king"
>
> The Sphere, 12th March 1904

only those who were present can realise all that it did mean, and the sincerity and significance of the roar of delight and applause that broke from the huge audience when, with a triumphant cry that was half a sob of physical and emotional relief, Houdini ultimately held aloft the shining handcuffs from which he had freed himself." It sounds like one of entertainment history's greatest moments, perfected by reports that Houdini was afterwards carried on shoulders around the arena in a celebratory lap of honour to receive the adoration of the audience.

Conspiracy theories abound about how Houdini escaped from these apparently inescapable handcuffs. Many assume that the key was smuggled to Houdini via the glass of water, or a tiny cut-off version was concealed on him somewhere. Others suggest Houdini worked with Hart, whose very existence remains unproven, to manufacture the bespoke cuff. In their biography of Houdini, magician William Kalush and writer Larry Sloman unpick the challenge and conclude that it was indeed a carefully choreographed stunt in which Houdini and *The Daily Mirror* both colluded. Houdini was a friend of Alfred Harmsworth, proprietor of the fledgling *Daily Illustrated Mirror* so it seems logical that the two might contrive the challenge as mutually beneficial. Kalush and Sloman also ask why a locksmith would begin work on handcuffs to beat an escapologist in 1899, a time when Houdini was only just embarking on his career and escapology acts such as his were unfamiliar in Britain. They also suggest the specially commissioned silver replica of the cuff, given to Houdini by the *Mirror* as a memento of his feat, bears a hallmark from 1903, the year before the challenge. Yet hallmarks run from May to May meaning it is feasible the cuffs were made after the challenge at the Hippodrome. Like so many aspects of Houdini's life, the incident remains shrouded in mystery, which is no doubt exactly what Houdini intended. "The secret of showmanship consists not of what you really do, but what the mystery-loving public thinks you do," he once said. Maintaining his own mythology, Houdini always declared that escape at the Hippodrome, "one of the hardest, but at the same time one of the fairest, tests I ever had". A plaque commemorating the feat was unveiled at the Hippodrome in 2013.

Illustration by Thomas Downey in *The Illustrated Sporting and Dramatic News*, 1904

Herr Julius Seeth and his twenty-one forest-bred lions, in a publicity shot practising their swing-boat ride for the Hippodrome in 1903.

In a 1900 interview with Seeth, *The Sketch* marvelled, "probably never before had a more remarkable exhibition been given of the domination of the human will over brute intelligence". It added, "The peril run by the performer gave, undoubtedly, an alluring zest to the entertainment; and Herr Seeth ran no fanciful risk." Seeth knew the risks. He had been a lion-tamer since the age of fifteen, and told *The Sketch* about the time he was performing in a show called *Nero* in Paris in 1891, where a recreation of Christians versus lions in the Coliseum had gone badly wrong. Seeth had been so mauled about the legs by one lion, he spent two and a half months in hospital.

The lions in his current troupe came with a particularly exotic back-story. They had been a gift of King Menelik of Abyssinia who had heard of Seeth's skills and summoned him to his court to demonstrate his training methods on some raw, and extremely wild, recruits. Working day and night, Seeth trained three lions in eleven days and as reward, Menelik gifted him with over twenty lions – "as a keepsake, I suppose" remarked Seeth dryly to *The Sketch* reporter.

> **The peril run by the performer gave, undoubtedly, an alluring zest to the entertainment; and Herr Seeth ran no fanciful risk**
> The Sketch, 1900

Mr. A. Ford appearing in the arena of the London Hippodrome where he finally came to a stop after completing a record-breaking non-stop drive of 2,390 miles between Liverpool, Brighton, Perth and London in 1904. Here, the engine that had been running continuously for 204 hours came to a stop and Fred Trussell, manager of the Hippodrome, gave the audience, many of whom were well-known motorists, a brief account of the run. Finally, Mr. H. Rawlinson, a director of the Darracq Company, presented Mr. Ford with a brand-new car as recognition of his achievements. The photograph gives a good view of the Hippodrome's vast auditorium.

In 1906, the star attraction was the Three Olympiers who posed to recreate some startlingly authentic classical bronzes. It's also tempting to choose 1902 when you could hear Mendel the blind pianist and marvel at Herr Paul Conchas with his balancing act using shells and bombs. On the same bill was Eddie Gifford the one-legged cyclist (described in the programme as "the world's most daring cyclist") who performed his death-defying dive on his bicycle from the roof, a distance of seventy feet, into the tank below.

Jumping or diving from the roof into the tank below remained one of the Hippodrome's crowd-pleasers and in 1907, one performer took the dive quite literally to a whole new level. K. P. Speedy's reputation preceded him. He had become notorious through a jump he had made from the Big Four Bridge in Memphis. Although local police had tried to prevent him, Speedy had managed to carry out his attempt by pretending to cancel the event and go on a fishing trip instead. But, unknown to the authorities, he caught a train that delivered him to the bridge just in time for him to dramatically jump off it, injuring himself on a log in the river below, but nevertheless accomplishing his feat. At the Hippodrome, Speedy decided to make a feature of the hole in the Hippodrome's roof. On top of the roof, a platform had been constructed forty feet in height. Speedy was hoisted onto this platform via a ladder held in place by a system of pulleys and then made his dive off the platform, through the hole in the roof and into the tank below, a total distance of 135 feet. *The Sketch* magazine, reeling off Speedy's accomplishments (134 medals for diving, 63 of them for life saving), claimed he never went deeper into the water than eighteen inches, and never wet the whole of his back while performing a feat.

There were non-human performers too with seriously impressive acrobatic or balancing acts, such as Diavolino, a small monkey who pedalled a trike continually round in a loop the loop in 1902, overseen by his trainer, Herr Grais. On the same bill, Grais also performed with an acrobatic baboon that expertly traversed a tight rope. One of the most celebrated monkey performers at the Hippodrome was Consul the Chimp, who by the time he made an appearance in December 1903, was already the toast of Paris where he had charmed audiences. He was the second famous chimpanzee to be named Consul, the first having died of dysentery in 1902. Consul II was engaged by Moss to appear for three weeks at the Hippodrome, and commanded the enormous fee of £200 per week. He seems to have been worth the investment. Consul's publicity photographs showed him looking quite the dandy in gentleman's evening attire and silk hat. He could play the piano, ride a bicycle, dress and undress, and when eating and drinking, displayed most impressive table manners. *The Illustrated London News* published several drawings of Consul by Melton Prior, showing the chimpanzee raising his glass in a toast and engrossed in a copy of *The Sketch*. *The Bystander* magazine, for its very first issue, sent its artist, Charles Sykes, to meet Consul in his dressing room. Sykes found himself won over by Consul's "prescribed formality with a most sagacious expression in his dark, sparkling eyes". The chimp sat obediently for the artist and enthusiastically shook hands when Sykes took his leave. Sadly, Consul died the following year, the cold, damp weather of northern Europe and his habit of chain smoking American cigarettes probably the reason behind the five-year-old chimpanzee's demise from bronchitis. Following in Consul's footsteps was Mr. Link, who appeared at the Hippodrome in 1906, and in 1912, Max and Moritz, "the most extraordinary chimps ever seen behind footlights". Among their skills were the ability to play whist and bagatelle, operate a modern typewriter and understand modern languages. Perhaps they

In 1905, when the animal trainer Richard Sawade was appearing again at the Hippodrome, Queen Alexandra paid a visit to the theatre with her brother, King George of Greece. After the show, the Queen was introduced to a young tiger cub called Babs, the first male Sawade had managed to successfully breed in captivity. A keen animal lover, the Queen insisted on holding the cub and patting it for a time, although much to the discomfort of the management and Sawade, Babs soon became excitable and got his claws entangled in the Queen's lace dress. He was carefully extricated from the royal lap as efficiently as decorum would allow. Despite disgracing himself, Babs's brush with royalty led to a number of society ladies offering extravagant sums of money to buy him. Illustration by A. Forestier in *The Illustrated London News*.

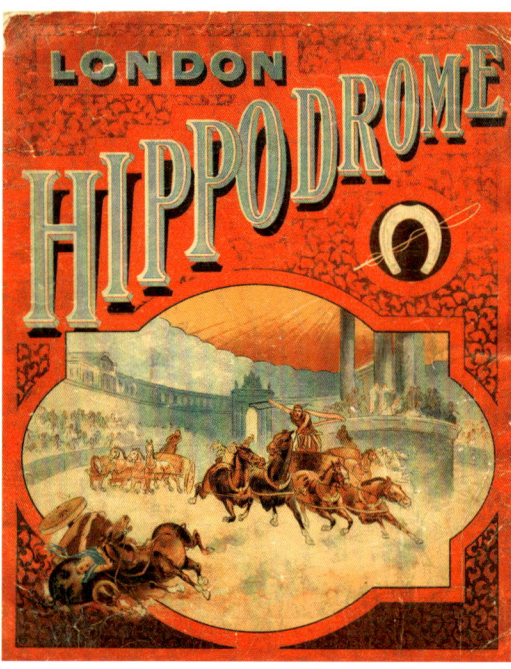

Children's picture book of the London Hippodrome. The illustrations inside, from Herr Seeth and his lions to a glorious double page spread of a scene from *Cinderella*, date the book to 1901. The front cover features the theatre's stage drop, which depicted a dramatic scene of a hippodrome in ancient times.

The circus of variety 1900-1909

Madame Claire Heliot feeding raw beef to her lions at the Hippodrome, by Percy F. S. Spence in *The Sphere*, 1901.

Madame Claire Heliot, a young Anglo-German lion tamer, revealed her methods in an interview with T. Hanson Lewis in *The Illustrated Sporting and Dramatic News*. When Lewis asked, "You train entirely by kindness I believe?" Madame Heliot responded, "It's the only safe way. Treat your charges as you would your dogs and cats about you. Look at my whip which makes such a noise. I merely use it to measure the distance between my lions and myself more than for any purpose. I don't want my skirts torn by their claws." She also elaborated on the upkeep of her charges, explaining that medicine was never required, but she might feed them beef extract from time to time, while their daily diet consisted of 80lbs of best beef when in England, or 100lbs of horseflesh when in Germany. Heliot, in contrast to Julius Seeth, had only been performing for four years, stressing that she did not feel she could embark on her preferred career, which was kindled during many hours spent at Leipzig Zoo, while her parents were alive. "The feeling against women taming and training animals in Germany is very strong," she explained. Petite and fair in appearance, her style was in contrast to the more bombastic Seeth, and the image of Heliot with her lions captured the public's imagination. Claire Heliot's legendary appearances at the Hippodrome have not been forgotten. The steak restaurant at the Hippodrome Casino today is named the Heliot in her honour.

I merely use my whip to measure the distance between my lions and myself more than for any purpose. I don't want my skirts torn by their claws
Madame Claire Heliot

may have been able to converse with Coocoo the parakeet who performed in May 1908, speaking three languages at the command of Mr. Victor Niblo?

Unusually talented animals were a mainstay of the Hippodrome's repertoire, but so too were unusual humans. In 1905, the arrival of Feodor Machnow, the Russian giant, caused ripples of excitement through the press which, through a number of reports, fed the public with eye-popping statistics and details about Machnow's size and diet. Born in Charkow, Russia to parents of ordinary height, the twenty-three-year-old Machnow reportedly measured nine feet, three inches, weighed just under twenty-six stone and had hands which, from wrist to the tip of his middle finger, measured two feet. In fact, his measurements have never been verified, and the tall fur Russian hat he wore as part of his act gave the impression he was taller than his true height, which was likely to have been a still impressive seven feet ten inches. To emphasise his immense size, at each performance Machnow was introduced to the audience by the tiny figure of Madame Chiquita, who was just eighteen inches tall.

From great heights to small stature, Madame Chiquita was just one of several 'midget' acts to appear at the Hippodrome, which, like many purveyors of entertainment, exploited the public curiosity for extremes of height. The nine-strong Colibris Midgets, veterans of the variety circuit since the early 1890s, were regularly on the bill at the Hippodrome, enchanting audiences as they walked in formation wearing tiny ballgowns and dinner jackets. Rossow's midgets took part in a three-way boxing match in their act, "with a quaintness which is very taking, and a zest which shows that they like it." In 1912, Anita, The Doll Lady, standing just twenty-five inches tall, appeared at the Hippodrome, having visited London a year or so earlier to stay at the Savoy Hotel while she purchased her trousseau.

What and who appeared on the stage and in the arena at the London Hippodrome constituted only one part of the reason behind the theatre's meteoric success. From what we can glean from contemporary descriptions and accounts, the Hippodrome was also exceptionally well run. Members of the management, men like Edward Moss (who was knighted in 1905) and Oswald Stoll, were celebrities in their own right, as well known, wealthy and influential as leading film directors or theatre moguls of today. In December 1901, Alfred de Rothschild formally unveiled a marble bust of Edward Moss by the sculptor William Birnie Rhind in the vestibule of the theatre, where it was to remain (though its whereabouts today are unknown). Rothschild, the second son of Baron Lionel de Rothschild, was a well-known public figure, a sociable bachelor, patron of the arts and a director of the Bank of England, National Gallery and the Wallace Collection. He took a special interest in the Hippodrome, partly due to its specialisation in animal acts. Before its opening, he had been a regular visitor to the Empire Theatre where he took the corner box nearest to the stage so he could get the best view of the performing animals. It was Alfred who not only unveiled the bust of Moss, but who laid the foundation stone of the Hippodrome and who, a fortnight after its grand opening, gave a banquet to Georges Jacobi, his orchestra and other members of the Hippodrome management at the Trocadero restaurant. The Hippodrome also enjoyed royal patronage. As well as the famous visits of Queen Alexandra and the Shah of Persia, in 1907, at Princess Victoria's birthday party, the entertainment was organised by the Hippodrome's manager, Fred Trussell, who devised a miniature circus worked by monkeys. Such lofty social connections suggest the Hippodrome as a theatre to

The Russian giant, Feodor Machnow, pictured dining with his manager and members of the Hippodrome staff in 1905. His phenomenal appetite was satisfied by a daily diet that consisted of sixteen hard-boiled eggs and six to eight loaves of bread for breakfast alone. During his London stay, he resided in a capacious room at the top of the Hippodrome, and took his daily exercise in the empty auditorium, "when no curious eyes are upon him".

Growing bored with this routine, he one day, asked for a car and, in an Oldsmobile, motored down to Brighton with his wife, manager and interpreter. On the way, he stopped at several spots to meet and shake hands with villagers who must have been truly amazed to see such a gargantuan human in their midst. For the Oldsmobile Company, they were gifted with some welcome free publicity when it was reported the car, "carried him splendidly despite the fact he weighs about 26st".

Even the back cover of the Hippodrome's programme featured an advertisement for Oxo using a photograph of Machnow with the slogan, "Oxo for Strength". Not only was Machnow drawing crowds at the Hippodrome, he was a walking, talking, readymade endorsement opportunity.

Sadly, he was never able to retire and enjoy the fruits of his labour. With a heavy smoking habit to match his insatiable appetite, Machnow's health finally broke down after touring Europe and America and he began to suffer bronchial problems. He returned to Russia where he died of pneumonia in 1913.

> **The marvellous dexterity, accuracy, and physical strength displayed by these men have aroused an enthusiasm which has exceeded any other exhibition we have ever placed before the public**
>
> Fred Trussell, recalling the Australian tree-fellers act, in The Tatler

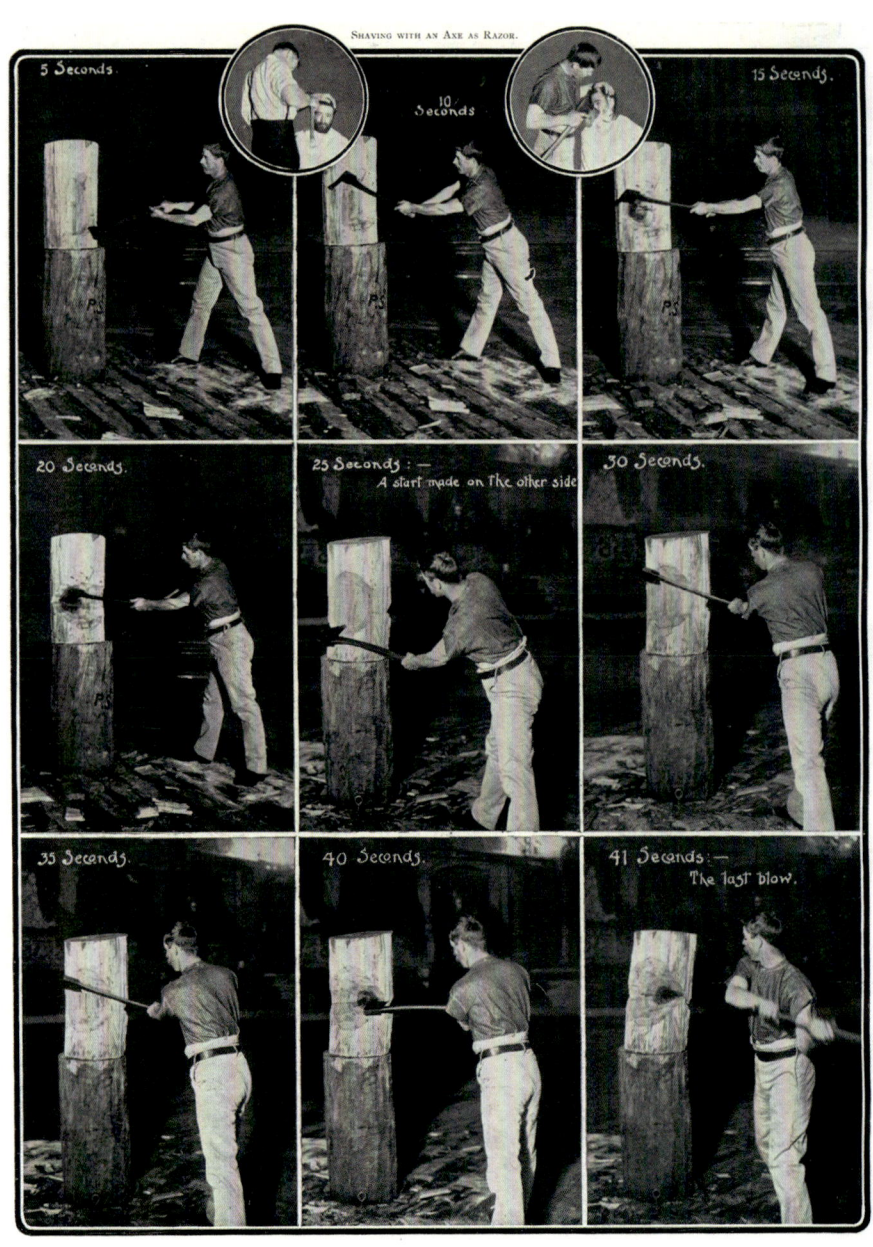

In 1907, Fred Trussell, the Hippodrome's general manager, went to great lengths to secure a new act from the other side of the world, which he was sure would make a thoroughly original piece of entertainment. Harry H. Jackson and Peter MacLaren were champion tree-fellers in their home country and were discovered by Trussell after he had met Mr. T. W. Dougall of Dallesford, Victoria, who discussed the idea with him. "The difficulties were enormous," he explained in an interview with *The Tatler*, "not only had we to induce the men, who to be any good to us must be the two champions of the colony, to leave their homes for a considerable period and to give up their entire business surroundings, but it was absolutely essential that the actual trees should be imported."

Jackson, who was champion of the world in tree-felling, and MacLaren, who was a close second, agreed to travel to London, and Trussell arranged for 100 tons of blue gum trees to be shipped direct from the Australian bush. Photographs were taken of the site at which the trees had been cut down so that the scenery painters could recreate an authentic scene on stage.

The venture was considered such a useful PR opportunity for colonial relationships that it received the support of Thomas Bent, the Prime Minister of Victoria, and Winston Churchill, who at the time was President of the Board of Trade. The public found Jackson and MacLaren's act riveting. "The marvellous dexterity, accuracy, and physical strength displayed by these men have aroused an enthusiasm which has exceeded any other exhibition we have ever placed before the public," confirmed Trussell.

Besides tree cutting, the men also gave an amusing demonstration of shaving, using just the blade of an axe. No mention is made however, of where 100 tons of blue gum trees were stored in the vicinity of Leicester Square.

One of the most celebrated monkey performers at the Hippodrome was **Consul the Chimp,** who appeared for three weeks at the Hippodrome in 1903, commanding a superstar salary of £200 per week. In a succession of dapper outfits, Consul played the piano, rode a bicycle, and went through several costume changes. He sadly died the following year from bronchitis, no doubt caused in part by his chain smoking habit. In an interview with the comic paper, *Judy*, the journalist described how Consul was, "no abstainer from either wine or tobacco, and therefore makes a very sociable companion".

reckon with, the flagship at the centre of a powerful entertainment cartel. And yet there was also the familiarity of an old friend about the Hippodrome. Within a matter of a few years, it had become part of London's fabric. R. B. Elliott, writing in *The Stage* in 1958, recalled:

"People not only went to the Hippodrome for some of their enjoyable light entertainment. They met 'on the Hippodrome Corner', they spoke of the Hippodrome as a landmark almost as fixed as Eros in Piccadilly Circus; there was a personal, friendly air associated with the Hippodrome as well as with the particular spot it occupied in the streets of London, and which perhaps was associated with no other theatre in quite the same way."

Staff members seem to have been treated very well and recognised for their contribution. With an intensive schedule of twelve shows a week, it was recognised that staff needed holiday allowance, which was usually taken during a lull and before the next busy season. In common with most theatres, an annual special day out was arranged each summer for different departments (the entire staff being too numerous to take a day trip together). The first outing was to Kingston and to Old Windsor via a boat trip. In 1903 and again in 1904, some staff went to Clacton-on-Sea, while the front-of-house team enjoyed a day trip to the Isle of Wight, where sightseeing was punctuated with a generous lunch and dinner featuring such delights as salmon mayonnaise, cooked meats and salads accompanied by claret and Bass's Ale. The following year, acting-manager Fred Trussell met his staff at Victoria station from where they departed in specially allocated saloon carriages for a day trip to Horley where "half-a-hundred hungry lads and lasses sat down to a capitally-prepared repast" at the Chequers Hotel. They enjoyed a drive around the leafy Surrey lanes in charabancs and after lunch, walked to the local cricket ground for a match and a comic costume race before returning to the hotel for tea. It is difficult to imagine a more idyllic Edwardian summer outing. Reports of the speeches made that day suggest a sense of familial pride in being a part of such a successful enterprise. Mr. McGrath (the front of house manager known as 'Mac'), raising a toast to the ladies present declared, "Every one was a real gem, and the zealous manner in which they performed their duties proved they were a valuable asset to the Hippodrome." Fred Trussell proposed a toast to "The Hippodrome" and said that particular toast was "nearest and dearest to everyone present. There was not a single person there who did not love the show... It was a most extraordinary thing, that in spite of the new places which had sprung up of late, the takings at the Hippodrome were day by day better than they were last year, and they were proud of the position which they occupied with regard to the show itself. It was not always that they found in theatres that concreteness of feeling between the front and the back that brought a house into the harmonised whole."

But the very root of the Hippodrome's success was its ability to read and forecast public taste, to take its pulse and deliver an entertainment that felt fresh and exciting. By the end of the decade, the popularity of circus and water shows was beginning to fade, and perceiving this, the Hippodrome embarked on what would be the first of several transformations during its lifetime. On 31 March 1909, the Hippodrome closed its doors for four months. Frank Matcham was drafted in to remodel the auditorium, increasing the stage size and adding removable seats to the area formerly occupied by the arena and water tank. A new era was about to begin.

William 'Billy' Ellsworth Robinson, the real man behind the mysterious persona of Chung Ling Soo. His true identity was only revealed after his death.

Willow-pattern plate promotional flyer for Chung Ling Soo.

Chung Ling Soo vs. Ching Ling Foo

Chung Ling Soo was the most successful conjuror and illusionist of his day, and first appeared at the Hippodrome in 1903. Dressed in ceremonial robes and wearing his hair in a traditional cue (plait), Chung Ling Soo, with the aid of his assistant and wife, Suee Seen, performed his illusions in enigmatic silence, a quirk that only added to his air of mystique. But Chung Ling Soo was not all he seemed. He was in fact William 'Billy' Ellsworth Robinson, an American vaudeville performer with Scottish parents, who had worked with celebrated magicians Alexander Herrmann and Harry Kellar in the United States.

A talented mechanical magician, he had ambitions to be more than a support act, though a weak stage presence meant headline status eluded him. So instead he contrived a stage persona that would mask his inadequacies. Having seen a Chinese conjuror called Ching Ling Foo perform in New York, Robinson audaciously copied him, transforming himself into Chung Ling Soo, "the Celestial Magician" or "the marvellous Chinese conjuror", only ever speaking in snippets of broken English and using an interpreter to communicate with journalists. He kept up the pretence and soon began to garner praise and celebrity with a series of mystifying tricks, one of which involved him throwing dead rabbits and pigeons into a boiling cauldron only for them to emerge from it alive, followed finally

This was all too much for the understandably irritated Ching Ling Foo, and in 1905, their rivalry came to a head when Chung Ling Soo was performing at the Hippodrome and Ching Ling Foo at the Empire nearby, both with posters claiming to be the 'original Chinese conjuror'. Ching Ling Foo challenged Chung Ling Soo to a competition, where the latter would be asked to perform ten of the former's tricks to prove his skill. The fact that Ching Ling Foo did not turn up on the day of the challenge led some papers to joke and speculate that Chung Ling Soo had conjured his rival's disappearance. Less was made of the fact Chung Ling Soo had refused to take part in a challenge a few months earlier reasoning that, "his dignity was too sublime". There seems to have been a bias towards Chung Ling Soo in the press, which may well be attributed to the Hippodrome's sophisticated use of spin. One critic complained of Ching Ling Foo that, "he performs his tricks slowly, with a tedious amount of movement" whereas *The Tatler* appreciated how Chung Ling Soo "performs conjuring tricks with a quiet neatness that is delightful".

Ultimately, Ching Ling Foo's run at the Empire ended after four weeks whereas Chung Ling Soo's turn at the Hippodrome was extended to three months. If that is a measure of success, then the imposter can be said to have prevailed.

most frequently appearing at the Hippodrome. Sometimes, his friend Houdini, one of the few people to know his true identity and who himself caused a sensation at the Hippodrome in 1904, would come to watch one of his performances.

In 1918, Chung Ling Soo was appearing at the Wood Green Empire in north London and one night decided to perform the bullet trick, recreating a scene from the Boxer Rebellion where he was meant to catch a bullet in his teeth. This time there was no illusion, and instead the bullet penetrated his chest causing him to crumple to the floor. "My God, I've been shot. Lower the curtain," he was heard to moan in perfect English before losing consciousness. He died a few hours later.

The sudden disappearance of Chung Ling Soo's manager after his death was a mystery until it was discovered they were one and the same; out of costume, Billy had dealt with bookings himself. Suee was also revealed to have the real name of Olive or 'Dot' and was just one of several women romantically associated with Billy Robinson.

RIVAL CHINESE MAGICIANS
The Amenities between Chung Ling Soo at the Hippodrome and Ching Ling Foo at the Empire

At the Hippodrome: Chung Ling Soo, whom his rival declares to be a Scotch-American!

The picture shows Chung Ling Soo putting his wife into a cannon; the gun is turned towards the audience and a cannon ball put in; the gun is fired, the cannon ball comes out, but his wife has entirely disappeared from the gun, and appears in the front of the house among the audience

At the Empire: Ching Ling Foo, who claims to be the original and accredited Chinese magician

Ching Ling Foo was an interested spectator the other evening at the Hippodrome when the tricks of his rival were being prepared. The outcome of his visit was a challenge to Chung Ling Soo

The rivalry between Chung Ling Soo and Ching Ling Foo reported with relish in *The Bystander* magazine in January 1905.

> **Chung Ling Soo performs conjuring tricks with a quiet neatness that is delightful**
> The Tatler

Publicity photographs for Chung Ling Soo's act at the London Hippodrome in 1904.

Picturesque scene from *Joy Bells* in 1919, published in *The Tatler*, with Phyllis Bedells and chorus posed amid a gorgeous spring setting, which had prettily transformed from a 'Winter Fantasy.' Bedells and the cast performed a dance intended to represent the opening of spring, a popular theme in a post-war world, representative of new beginnings.

Ragtime and revue 1909-1919

> ## "The Vampire Dance at The Hippodrome is quite the most truly sensational thing to be seen in town"
>
> **The Tatler**

In the autumn of 1909, Bert French and Alice Eis were engaged to give an exhibition of their infamous 'Vampire Dance'. The dance's genesis lay in Rudyard Kipling's poem of the same name, which in turn had been inspired by a painting by Kipling's cousin, Philip Burne-Jones, in which a woman (purportedly modelled by the actress Mrs. Patrick Campbell) was depicted straddling an unconscious man. Playing the predatory femme fatale, Alice cavorted around the stage in a wispy costume split to the thigh, leaving little to the imagination. Deep red lighting added to the air of sensuality and menace, as she sank her fangs into her dance partner. Such an openly erotic performance unsurprisingly drew mixed reactions. "There were, it is true, a few hisses at the end of this performance," wrote *The Tatler*, "but the 'claps' were in a huge majority. The Vampire Dance at The Hippodrome is quite the most truly sensational thing to be seen in town."

One of the most talked-about acts to perform at the Hippodrome when it re-opened was 'Die Drei Schwestern Wiesenthal' from Vienna, a trio of sisters who were to personify a transitional moment in dance. *The Sketch* described the "striking novelty" of their carefree performance in its 28th July issue:

"These brilliantly accomplished ladies have a style distinctly their own... Their dances seek to embody the joy of life and the intoxicating influence of Spring on the emotions... In their act, they dispense with scenery in favour of a background and draperies of one or two colours, with which their dresses are in harmony. The result is most striking and is evidence of the guidance of a highly-endowed and artistic mind."

THE BEARS Come to TOWN.
The Arrival of *Seventy White Bears* in London for the Christmas Performance at the Hippodrome

THE BEARS AS THEY APPEARED ON THEIR ARRIVAL AT THE HIPPODROME

Seventy large white polar bears have just come to London from Hamburg to take part in the Christmas production at the London Hippodrome, *The Arctic*, in which fifty of the bears will plunge from realistic icebergs into a lake while the remaining animals will clamber about a deserted ship wedged between walls of ice. Their arrival in seven huge steel cages caused quite a sensation in the Leicester Square district. The animals are fed on biscuit, fish, and meat.

Page from *The Sphere*, 1909, showing the arrival of the polar bears at the Hippodrome.

"Seventy polar bears!! It sounds like the cry of an ancient showman who is boosting his benefit regardless of facts. Yet 'tis true," declared *The Stage* with a light-hearted incredulity.

While fifty of the polar bears capered around ice caps and ice-strewn water, the remaining twenty took over a wrecked ship caught between two icebergs. At one point, they slithered down a slide into the arena, an echo of Busch's elephants a few years earlier. The animals were trained by Willy Herkenrath, who told *Pearson's Weekly* how he considered polar bears, along with black panthers, the most difficult of animals to train, largely due to fact that a polar bear exhibited no warning signs if it was to attack. "I can read the eyes of any animal except the polar bear," he explained. "His narrow, slanting brown eyes betray nothing." During training, Herkenrath ensured he was accompanied by men with guns, poles and irons in case any of his pupils might suddenly turn on him. Over a number of years, Hagenbeck had bought cubs from whalers who captured them on fishing trips. Those that survived the journey and were considered trainable joined the troupe where the general principles of training were "kindness, patience and playing on their appetites".

> "The London Hippodrome has been swept and dusted, and several coats of paint have been laid on with a thick brush, so that it is now as good as new. Indeed, it is better; for the old arena, with its rather tiresome water effects, has been removed."

'Jingle' in The Bystander, 11th August 1909

For a decade, the London Hippodrome and its water spectacles had flourished. Over 5760 performances, it had dazzled its audiences with the best that variety theatre could offer, from strongmen and fearless divers to performing seals and escapologists. But in a move admirably lacking in sentimentality, the management sensed change in the air and decided that its famed water tank had had its day. Matcham's alterations increased not only the seating capacity with further stalls fitted over the arena, but, more significantly, the size of the stage was extended. The ruby red upholstery of old had been replaced by a softer green, echoed by green hues used for the act-drop, stage curtains and paper on the walls, all of which apparently gave the overall impression of added height to the auditorium. This remodelling and expansion would provide a more suitable setting for a refreshed programme of entertainment with an increasing bias towards music, dance and drama. By this time, Edward Moss, now Sir Edward Moss after receiving a knighthood in 1905 for services to theatre and charity, had taken a back seat in the business that bore his name and Oswald Stoll (who would be knighted in 1919) had taken over as managing director. Stoll's fingerprints are all over the Hippodrome's updated programme which was varied and entertaining enough to maintain the loyalty of its traditional customer base, but also forward-looking and edifying in order to appeal to a more demanding and sophisticated theatre-goer.

The final water spectacle, in March 1909, had been the 'The Motor Chase', which had run for just over a month until 3rd April 1909, and replaced plunging horses or elephants with the more modern choice of the motor car. Modernism was reflected elsewhere in new forms of expressive dance. In 1908, the American dancer Loie Fuller thrilled Hippodrome audiences with her 'Ballet of Light', the highlight of which was the 'Fire Dance' which, through clever use of low-level lighting and swirls of billowing silk, created the impression she was dancing in a ring of fire. In the same year, Mlle. Artemis Colonna was another among the vanguard of young women in togas who were skipping and twirling freely across the capital's stages. One of the most talked-about acts to perform at the Hippodrome when it re-opened was 'Die Drei Schwestern Wiesenthal' from Vienna, a trio of sisters who were to personify this transitional moment in dance.

Born into an artistic Viennese family, Grete Wiesenthal and her sister Elsa had studied at the Hofoper Ballet School, and were members of the corps de ballet at the Vienna Grand Opera, where Franz Mahler selected Grete to dance the role of Fenella in *La Muette de Portici*, a decision that eventually led to his resignation as his selection had undermined the ballet master. Grete, together with Elsa and another sister, Berthe, left the ballet and began to perform around Europe and America where they entranced audiences with their modern interpretation of the Viennese waltz. No film footage exists of Grete's dancing from these days so we can only go on contemporary descriptions, which suggest it was a breath-taking

DANCING IN TSCHAIKOWSKY'S "LE LAC DES CYGNES": RUSSIAN DANCERS WHO ARE APPEARING AT THE LONDON HIPPODROME.

1. MLLE. MUCHINA.   2. MLLE. ALEXIZIEWA.   3. MLLE. DEVELIERE.
4. MLLES. MENDES, MAKLIZOWA, MUCHINA, DEVELIERE, KURSC IINSKAJA, ALEXIEWA, ALEXIZIEWA AND PERIEKOWA.

At the Hippodrome Mlle. Olga Preobrajenskaja is accompanied by twenty other famous dancers from the Imperial Opera Houses of St. Petersburg and Moscow, every one of whom is a "star." The dancers at the Imperial Opera Houses in Russia, who are all paid by the State, are divided into three classes, and the dancers who are now appearing at the Hippodrome were selected from the First Class; that is to say, they could each individually fill the premier rôle should circumstances require it.

> **London is not yet tired of Russian dancing, and the latest form of it, to be seen at the London Hippodrome should at least give a fillip to any declining interest**
> The Sketch

In May 1910, the Russian State Ballet marked a significant moment in dance (and musical) history, when they performed Tchaikovsky's *Le Lac des Cygnes* for the first time in Britain at the London Hippodrome. *Swan Lake*, to give it its more familiar, English title, boasted twenty-one dancers from the top class of the Imperial Opera Houses of St. Petersburg and Moscow, including prima ballerina Olga Preobrajenska in the role of Odette (as a teacher later in her career, Preobrajenska would count Margot Fonteyn among her pupils). London was in the midst of a love affair with Russian dance. While audiences at the Hippodrome sighed at the soft grace of *Swan Lake*, the Empire was playing host to Lydia Kyasht and at the Coliseum, another troupe featured the extraordinary Tamara Karsavina. Serge Diaghilev's sensational Ballets Russes would take London by storm when they performed at Covent Garden the following year, sealing Russia's reputation as the world leader in dance. Among their number were some of the dancers who had performed in *Swan Lake* including Ludmilla Schollar and choreographer Mikhail Fokine.

Albert de Courville (1887–1960), mastermind behind the Hippodrome's run of successful revue shows before and during the First World War. George Robey greatly admired de Courville and wrote of him in his memoirs: "What he doesn't know about dancing, acting, singing, colour, music, costume, stage-grouping, scenic effect, the way to bring out the 'point' of the line, the moment at which to end a scene, and all the rest of the techniques of such productions, is simply not worth knowing."

Oriental dancer Sahary Djeli, whose 'La Danse des Bras' saw her contort her arms into sinuous and serpentine shapes – a task made easier, it was suggested in the press, by the fact she kept a number of snakes as pets.

experience. In response to Grete's dance to Strauss's 'Blue Danube' at the Hippodrome, *The Telegraph* enthused: "The flowing rhythm of their movements, the virginal poses, made a feast for the eye of rare quality."

It was a complete aesthetic experience where every detail had been considered in order to maximise the effect; even the fabric of their dresses was designed by the sisters. In the creative atmosphere of Vienna, where the Secessionist art movement was in full flow, there was a natural synergy between art, music and dance. Gustav Klimt had designed sets for Grete's debut shows and she had performed at the Fledermaus cabaret club in Vienna where artists traditionally congregated. In booking the Wiesenthal Sisters, with their unorthodox, unrestricted dancing and bohemian pedigree, the Hippodrome was clearly dipping its toe in culturally sophisticated waters. However, if anyone was concerned the theatre was losing touch with its diehard circus fan, sharing the bill were Monsieur and Mademoiselle X, a pair of 'educated baboons'.

Also part of the programme in July and August 1909 was a one-act play, 'Time is Money', starring leading comic actor Charles Hawtrey, and another drama, full of suspense, entitled 'The Flag Station', in which Fanny Ward played the wife of a signalman who was convinced his mistake was about to cause an inevitable rail disaster. These short plays filled the slot previously occupied by water spectacles, and as a consequence needed to be fast-paced, with a dialogue and plot that could hold the attention of a 2000-capacity theatre, as well as of a standard high enough to satisfy a cultured West End audience. The one-act play became a phenomenon of this period as the Hippodrome attracted big stars and expensive writers. In 1911, Lily Langtry, former mistress of Edward VII, appeared in a sketch written by Sydney Grundy called 'The Right Sort'. The following year, actress Irene Vanburgh, a real theatrical heavyweight, was the star of 'The Twelve-Pound Look' written by J. M. Barrie. It ran for five weeks during which time George Bernard Shaw visited and was struck by the lavish staging. "The dramatists get what they want," he marveled. "It must have cost enough to mount six Winters Tales."

Despite these new introductions, the Hippodrome had not entirely abandoned the performing animal genre. In fact, the end of 1909 was to bring an act that arguably eclipsed anything that had preceded it (except, perhaps, fifteen elephants sliding down a chute). In mid-December, a specially chartered steamer arrived at Tilbury Docks from Hamburg with a highly unusual cargo. On board were seventy polar bears from Wilhelm Hagenbeck's menagerie, bound for the London Hippodrome, where, when they arrived in seven immense cages, they caused quite a sensation around Leicester Square. The polar bears, who were housed in what *The Stage* described as "a big stone hall adjoining the London Hippodrome", were to star in the 1909–10 Christmas production. Written by Sydney Blow, 'The Arctic' was a snowy spectacular, complete with ice floating in the water tank, which had been temporarily resurrected for the season.

"All London is talking about the Christmas spectacle at the Hippodrome," reported the *Derby Daily Telegraph*. "In the arena of this popular West-End hall, seventy polar bears disport themselves twice a day amid scenes vividly realistic of the Arctic regions."

The grisly climax was a scene where the villain, played by Frank Atherley, suffered blindness after his gun exploded in his face. Unable to see, he was set upon by a polar bear that began to devour him in

Ragtime and revue 1909-1919

> **There arose a round of applause and cheering that made one's blood tingle**
> The Sketch

Another Great Composer
CUT DOWN AND ADAPTED TO VARIETY PURPOSES

SIGNOR MASCAGNI
The famous composer, who is now conducting a special orchestra at the Hippodrome, where performances of his world-famous opera, "Cavalleria Rusticana," are being given. Incisiveness in attack and temperamental treatment are the features of his conducting

As part of the Hippodrome's policy to pursue a more sophisticated, high-brow programme, in 1911 Albert de Courville travelled to Montecatini, Italy to track down the composer **Ruggero Leoncavallo**, whose opera *Il Pagliacci* was familiar to anyone visiting a restaurant and hearing it played by the house orchestra. De Courville had a hunch that bringing the actual composer to conduct his own work at the Hippodrome would have the desired effect on bookings.

Leoncavallo was tickled by the idea of his opera, which was about performers in a commedia dell'Arte troupe, being played in a 'circus', though de Courville tried to explain he would in fact be performing in one of the finest theatres in London. On the first night, when manager Fred Trussell led the composer through the stalls to the orchestra pit, de Courville recalled, "there arose a round of applause and cheering that made one's blood tingle". The house was full, many seats taken by members of London's Italian community, delighted to witness a musical genius from their homeland in their adopted city. Realising this formula of popular one-act operas had further potential, de Courville attempted to engage Puccini to conduct *La Bohème* (unsuccessfully) but then secured the Austrian composer Leo Fall, whose operetta *The Eternal Waltz* premiered at the Hippodrome on 22nd December 1911. The following spring, Pietro Mascagni came to the Hippodrome to conduct his *Cavalleria Rusticana*. It proved to be a nerve-shredding experience. Mascagni was temperamental, demanded £2000 a week, and persistently complained about the musicians in his orchestra, but on the night, was the consummate professional, so energetic and consumed in his performance he was obliged to change his sweat-soaked shirt during the interval.

Leoncavallo, who had clearly enjoyed both the appreciation of his work and the handsome fee paid to him by de Courville, returned to the Hippodrome in September 1912, this time to conduct *Zingari (The Gipsies)*, an operetta he had composed especially for the theatre.

A HIPPODRAMATIC APPEARANCE
"Hullo, Ragtime!" Will Never be a Frost as Long as there is a Thaw.

MISS EVELYN NESBIT (MRS. HARRY THAW), WHO IS APPEARING AT THE HIPPODROME WITH MR. CLIFFORD

Wynford Swinburne

The papers recently had much to say on the pros and cons of Mrs. Harry Thaw's (Miss Evelyn Nesbit) appearance at the Hippodrome revue. Mrs. Thaw, it will be remembered, was the Angel Child of the Thaw-White drama, which caused such a sensation in the States a few years ago. She says that she is unable to make a sufficient living for herself and little son as a sculptor and is thus returning to the stage. Above she is seen with Mr. Clifford, who partners her in the Hippodrome revue. Mr. Clifford is the originator of the turkey trot, grizzly bear, and kindred dances. He is in great request among society people as a teacher of dancing—even in this broiling weather

---

In June 1913, Albert de Courville booked Evelyn Nesbit to appear as dance partner to Jack Clifford, to appear in a special guest slot in *Hullo Ragtime!*. Nesbit possessed one of the most famous faces in America. As a young model and actress, she had appeared on countless magazine covers and was widely celebrated for her beauty, but her innocent involvement in a scandalous murder trial and 'crime of passion' gave the gossip columns one of their juiciest stories in years. She had married the wealthy but mentally unstable Harry Thaw who became increasingly consumed with jealousy about the prominent New York architect, Stanford White, who had allegedly seduced Nesbit some years earlier. Thaw murdered White on 25th June 1906, shooting him in cold blood in front of hundreds of people at a New York theatre. The resulting 'trial of the century' resulted in Thaw being incarcerated in an asylum, while Nesbit earned the reputation of being a 'lethal beauty'. De Courville met her on board the *Olympic* during one of his transatlantic trips, and booked her, the newshound in him recognising good publicity when he saw it, even though many American producers considered her old news. During her time at the Hippodrome, it was reported that her husband, Harry Thaw, had escaped from his asylum. Even if he had been of sound mind, his timing could not have been better.

---

front of the audience. Even the most expert trainer could not teach polar bears to the point where they could 'pretend' to eat a human so instead, Atherley was savaged by a fellow actor in a bear costume. Nevertheless, surrounded by plenty of actual polar bears, Atherley was pleased to survive each performance: "… what with the realness of the human bear, there being real bears being all around and the bare possibility of one or more of them getting at me, and the strength and horror of the scene, I can assure you that I 'live' every moment of my 'death'," he confided in an interview with *Pearson's Weekly*. 'The Arctic' was the last Hippodrome show to feature animals on such a scale. As grand finales go, it was a memorable effort.

Meanwhile, exciting and unconventional dance acts were continuing to proliferate. These modern and often risqué forms of dance were successfully drawing sizeable audiences, who were no doubt enjoying a degree of titillation under the mantle of artistic edification. Dance, or at least, dance music, would underpin what was to become the next big craze, and one of the Hippodrome's biggest successes. In 1911, a young journalist, Albert de Courville, had begun to work for Edward Moss, with the nominal title of assistant. Courville had been a journalist with the *Evening News* and *Daily Mail* and through mutual acquaintances had got to know Edward Moss, who was once again at the helm at the Hippodrome following the departure of Oswald Stoll from Moss Empires to concentrate on the Coliseum and other interests. De Courville's theatrical experience was minimal and his first foray into variety had been to book a young French boy who was a diabolo champion when the toy was at the height of its popularity in 1907. Edward Moss was intrigued by de Courville's confident optimism. De Courville recalls that around this time the Hippodrome's successes were sporadic, and that it was beginning to earn the name the 'Moss-oleum' due to an increasing number of periods where the auditorium was only half-full. This doesn't quite add up. Reports of the Hippodrome's shows across the press are consistently positive. It is possible de Courville rather exaggerated the theatre's problems to emphasise the role he would play in its rejuvenation. Whatever the case, it was clear the Hippodrome needed to proactively keep ahead of the competition. Moss didn't care about experience. He wanted ideas, and de Courville was the man to find them. In his first week of employment, de Courville suggested he travel abroad to scout for new talent. Moss wrote him a cheque from his own account to cover expenses. The first two contracts he secured and successfully promoted were dancer Sahary Djeli, and Max and Moritz the chimps. Both were big hits and an early indication of Albert de Courville's natural flair for discovering the next big thing.

As far as Albert de Courville was concerned, whether it was exotic dancers, brainy monkeys or Italian opera, he was proving himself to be a man with the Midas touch. But the perennial issue of finding sufficient quality acts to keep the Hippodrome's variety programme running *and* profitable was becoming increasingly difficult. De Courville suggested a new direction – one single show, which would have a long run, perhaps over months rather than weeks. As a new form of entertainment, revue was a natural heir to variety, consisting of separate sketches that combined drama, music, dance and comedy, but with topical skits on real-life events and impersonations of well-known figures as the binding agent. "The whole secret of revue lies in the blending of scenes in such a way that, though there is no definite story, there is an almost logical continuity," he explained to *The Observer* in 1920. A decade earlier, he had set off on another scouting trip to America, convinced he would find the perfect blend.

Hullo Ragtime! would come to define and popularise the sound and style of ragtime in Britain. Furthermore, the new format – revue – with its quickfire sketches, topical jokes, catchy songs and gorgeous spectacle, had huge appeal to an audience who not only enjoyed sharing in the worldly humour but embraced this fragmented and fast-paced delivery. For writers and producers, the other benefit of revue was its flexibility; it was entirely possible to add and omit sketches, insert new jokes or songs, even different performers, yet the essence of the revue remained. It was not unusual for people to go and see a popular revue several times, so refreshing and tweaking the programme kept repeat visitors engaged without serving them something completely different. The poet Rupert Brooke saw *Hullo Ragtime!* ten times in total, fully admitting his addiction when he wrote, "How those foolish melodies bite at one's heart!"

> **It struck me as being exceedingly smart and amusing, quite unlike anything I had seen before**
>
> Lord Northcliffe, The Daily Mail, January 1913

MR. IRVING BERLIN—FOR BEING THE FATHER OF RAGTIME WITHOUT BEING ABLE TO WRITE A NOTE OF MUSIC.

In July 1913, Irving Berlin, the popularly acclaimed 'genius of ragtime', heralded in the programme as 'the man who set the world ragging and swaying', performed for one week only in *Hullo Ragtime!*, rattling through a selection of his hits including 'Everybody's Doin' It' and 'Alexander's Ragtime Band'. Anyone who had either had their fill of ragtime, or had refused to be converted in the first place, was likely to have their opinions changed by seeing Irving Berlin, reasoned the *Guardian*, writing of his delivery, "Ragtime, as sung by Mr Irving Berlin, is delightful. He brings out all the dreaminess, the softness, the plaintive or humorous beauty of it, and the quality of the tunes appeals to the ear, perhaps for the first time."

Berlin famously did not learn composition until much later in life, hence the caption underneath this portrait of him, featured in *The Sketch* magazine's regular, 'We Take Our Hat Off To' section in its 25th June 1913 issue.

In 1912, ragtime was the music craze sweeping America and it seemed to de Courville that this could form the basis of his show. "The new rhythm fascinated me," he recalled in his memoirs. "It seemed to fit into the atmosphere of revue marvellously, as its tempo was so suitable for chorus work." He had already engaged the dancers Oscar and Suzette to perform a number of exhibition dances at the Hippodrome in February of that year, including the fashionable, if slightly scandalous, Turkey Trot – though Oscar purposely edited the choreography to omit "all the objectionable steps" (steps which had caused the teaching of it to be banned in New York). Listen today to some of ragtime's most famous tunes – Scott Joplin's 'Maple Leaf Rag' or Irving Berlin's 'Everybody's Doing It' – and we hear something light, jaunty, toe-tapping but essentially harmless. Yet in 1912, with its syncopated rhythms and unmistakable connection to American negro music, ragtime was a thrilling sonic departure, and one which in turn encouraged a new style of dancing. The Turkey Trot included moves such as the Bunny Hug and the Grizzly Bear. It was fun, it was carefree, but critics found it ugly and lacking in decorum. Even Oscar, despite appearing across the press performing the dance, considered it "idiotic and lacking in grace". Its detractors may have thought it shocking and morally dubious, but ragtime's many fans embraced its joyful rhythms. In New York, de Courville engaged Louis Hirst to compose the music for his revue, and identified American actress Shirley Kellogg as a potential leading lady, orchestrating a meeting the day before rival producer Andre Charlot in order to sign her up for the Hippodrome. She agreed to come to London providing she could star in a musical first. De Courville obliged, and Kellogg appeared in a one-act musical, 'The Blue House', in November 1912 at the Hippodrome. Before departing for home, he visited Coney Island where he found 'song pluggers' – men paid by music publishers to sing ragtime harmonies together in bars and cabaret clubs so that the public would become familiar with them and buy the songs.
De Courville selected eight of these men to form a singing group he christened the 'American Ragtime Octette' the purpose of which was to perform at the Hippodrome and whet the appetite of the public for the ragtime sound.

Hullo Ragtime! opened at the London Hippodrome on 23rd December 1912 and would run for 451 performances. It was one of a number of ragtime-inspired shows in London at the time; the Empire had *Everybody's Doing It*, the Alhambra was putting on *Kill That Fly!*, but the Hippodrome was the only revue to use the actual word ragtime in its title. Such a simple choice ensured the Hippodrome would be the first place to be associated with this fashionable new phenomenon. It must have been galling for the Empire to see a report in *The Sketch* about the Hippodrome's ragtime triumph mischievously headlined with the words, "Everybody's Seeing It!". The rehearsals for the show had been fraught with anxiety. Edward Moss was suffering with cancer and had undergone two operations. In his absence, the immense cost of the forthcoming revue was alarming the board of directors. De Courville, an upstart from nowhere, was apparently draining the Hippodrome's coffers in pursuit of a vainglorious project. The musical director Julian Jones found the music he was being asked to play abominable and Ned Wayburn, the American director de Courville had employed, was upsetting everyone by barking brusque orders through a megaphone. Edward Moss sent de Courville a telegram urging him to keep going, and advising him he had told the board to allow de Courville to continue with the production as he saw fit. De Courville persevered. He oversaw scenery, costumes, wrote the script with the novelist Max Pemberton and pulled in a favour with his friend J. M. Barrie who agreed to write one of the sketches.

The 'Hippodrome Beauty Chorus' quickly became an integral element of the Hippodrome's revue format during the de Courville years, especially when they marched down the gang plank (or 'joy plank'), a walkway leading from the stage, over the orchestra and down through the centre of the stalls. Shirley Kellogg made the gangplank walk her own. As a little girl of eleven or twelve, the novelist Barbara Cartland recalled going to see *Hullo Ragtime!* with her father, the highlight being the vision of Kellogg walking through the audience and distributing pink roses to the men, including Barbara's bemused father.

Music sheet for 'That Rag-time Suffragette' as featured in *Hullo Ragtime!*. Before the advent of radio and television, the stage was where people heard and enjoyed popular songs. Themes were often topical, and *Hullo Ragtime!* coincided with the increasing militancy of some branches of the suffrage movement. Its lyrics include the lines, "Ragging with bomb shells and ragging with bricks. Hagging and nagging in Politics."

"And threw flowers at the poor men"

Albert de Courville signed up a big name to work on costumes and scenery for *Hullo Tango!*. Leon Bakst, best-known for his work designing for the Ballets Russes, was at the height of his celebrity and charged accordingly. Each of his sketches cost de Courville £50 and he demanded the originals back so he could them sell them to collectors. Nevertheless, it was money well spent. The costumes he created, many with a Futurist appearance, marked out *Hullo Tango!* as the smartest show in town. "Bakst at His Best: A Glorious Spectacle in Hullo Tango at the Hippodrome", announced *The Tatler*. Ethel Levey, described by *The Sketch* as "an artist to her fingertips", belted out the show's most popular number, 'The Tango Girl', and wore Bakst's costumes with insouciant ease.

Ethel Levey (1870–1955), one of the stars of *Hullo Tango!*, wearing a costume designed by Leon Bakst.

Moss's gamble paid off. *Hullo Ragtime!* became a by-word for the new musical sound setting Britain's toes tapping. Attending the first night in January 1913 was Lord Northcliffe, proprietor of the *Daily Mail* where Albert de Courville had worked as a journalist. Northcliffe was impressed and gave his former employee a helping hand by ensuring a glowing review in the following morning's paper. *The Dancing Times* said of the show, "It struck me as being exceedingly smart and amusing, quite unlike anything I had seen before." There was much to admire about *Hullo Ragtime!*. Its two stars, Shirley Kellogg with her fair curls and beaming smile, and Ethel Levey, who in contrast was dark, chic and gamine, had their photographs printed in the illustrated magazines repeatedly, often pictured in costumes from the show. The songs were catchy with cute, playful titles like, 'My Honolulu Honey Lou', 'How Do You Do Miss Ragtime', 'Snooky Ookums' and, the hit of the show, 'Hitchy Koo'. The sets were sumptuous (though de Courville often achieved the most striking effects with clever and economical use of lighting), and the so-called 'Hippodrome Beauty Chorus', assembled by de Courville, introduced a new, modernised version of the Gaiety Girls who had been such a popular feature of 1890s London theatre. While in New York, de Courville had seen the Ziegfeld Follies, and fully understood the impact a large chorus of beautiful and identically dressed girls dancing in well-drilled unison could make in a show. Shirley Kellogg may have been one of the most admired women of her day but by June of that year, she was no longer on the marriage market. She had become Mrs. Albert de Courville.

There was a poignancy about the success of *Hullo Ragtime!*. Sir Edward Moss had died at his Edinburgh home, Middleton Hall, on 25th November 1912, aged 59, just a few days before the show opened. He left behind his second wife and a baby daughter, and would never witness his Hippodrome's glorious new phase. "It truly seemed a cruel trick of fate," wrote de Courville mournfully. Otto Twigg, another Hippodrome stalwart, who had been ringmaster in its first ten years, died in November 1913.

A sequel to *Hullo Ragtime!* opened in December 1913 and took its title from the tango, which was at the pinnacle of a widespread craze. The core team from *Hullo Ragtime!* re-assembled for *Hullo Tango!* – de Courville, Pemberton, composer Louis Hirsch, Ethel Levey and Shirley Kellogg, with the addition of music hall stalwart Harry Tate. J. M. Barrie even threw in another playlet, 'The Slice of Life'. It was a sideways step in terms of concept, but to keep ahead of the game, Shirley Kellogg roamed among the audience during her number 'Who's That Girl?', embarrassing men in the audience by asking if the lady accompanying them was their wife or sweetheart. Each unsuspecting victim would have the spotlight thrown onto them to add to their discomfiture and the general hilarity of the proceedings.

In August 1914, while *Hullo Tango!* was still drawing in the crowds, war broke out in Europe and within a short time, instead of displaying the usual advertisements for chocolates, restaurants and ladies' outfitters, pages in the Hippodrome's programme were given over to the call: "Your King and Country Need You – Another 10,000 Men Wanted." In the first few weeks of the war, the theatre-going public were temporarily reluctant to visit the theatre. Was it frivolous, even unpatriotic to enjoy a night of fun and laughter during such a crisis? It was a dilemma that was discussed at length in the press with the conclusion drawn that not only was the theatre good for national morale, but it was also important to ensure continuing employment in the entertainment industry. Theatres must follow the advice given to

Promotional postcard designed by John Hassall for *Business as Usual*, the Hippodrome's first revue of the First World War. British illustrators and cartoonists took every opportunity to lampoon the German enemy, pictured here as piglets in pickelhaube helmets. The other postcard, for the same show but in a more glamorous style, demonstrates the varied nature of revue and the Hippodrome's aim to appeal to all tastes.

Scene from *Business as Usual*, the Hippodrome's first revue of the Great War. Topicality defined wartime revue and here a vicar hosts a tea party for a group of well-dressed ladies who are sewing and knitting 'comforts' for the troops.

Shirley Kellogg, American revue star and mainstay of Albert de Courville's Hippodrome shows between 1913 and 1919, pictured with her Chow dog at the time she was appearing in *Push and Go*. She became Mrs. Albert de Courville in 1916 although the pair would divorce in 1924.

In 1915, the leading ladies and chorus girls of the Hippodrome took the rather unusual step of forming the 'Hippodrome Ladies' Home for Soldiers' Pets', with each one fostering a dog whose owner had gone off to fight at the front. Not only was it a worthy cause, it was a fantastic photo opportunity and foster mothers and their canine charges appeared in *The Sketch* magazine in this picture; guaranteed to tug on the public heartstrings.

the country in general; that life should carry on, and that everything should be 'business as usual'. If there were any silver linings to the country being at war, it at least offered fertile ground for a topical revue. *Hullo Tango!* had quickly adapted to wartime conditions, with the inclusion of songs such as 'Sister Susie's Sewing Shirts for Soldiers', but it was time for a completely new show with war-themed cheer to lift the public mood. Albert de Courville borrowed the phrase on everyone's lips and called his next revue *Business as Usual*.

Business as Usual opened at the end of November, and offered audiences topicality with a light-hearted touch. An opening scene showed haymaking in the French countryside, which was rudely interrupted by a German invasion; famous *Punch* military cartoons were re-imagined on stage and to end, a vicar hosted a tea party for ladies who were sewing those shirts for soldiers. *The Bystander*'s theatre critic in his review described how he arrived at the Hippodrome to find a huge queue snaking around the side of the theatre, and police officers drafted in to control the crowds. Having managed "an on-the-spot ticket" he concluded it was "certainly the show of the moment in Town". Following B*usiness as Usual* was *Push and Go*, a title this time borrowed from the popular description of the new prime minister, the dynamic and results-driven David Lloyd George. Around this time, wartime entertainers in Britain no longer felt an obligation to make the conflict their entire focus, and in fact, theatrical escapism was increasingly in demand as an antidote to the hardships of reality. De Courville delivered this in spades. Escapist fantasy was most definitely order of the day for his fifth Hippodrome revue, which opened in December 1915 and which he unapologetically named *Joyland*. A dazzling diversion from war stress, *Joyland* was notable for its lavish, spectacular scenes, many of which starred his wife, who for this particular show was dressed by the leading couturier Lucile (Lady Duff Gordon). Another *Joyland* leading lady was Violet Loraine, who was becoming a Hippodrome regular. She had first appeared in *Hullo Tango!* in a comedy routine de Courville convinced her to do, setting her on the path to being one of the West End's most celebrated comediennes.

The theatrical world was heavily involved in fundraising for various war charities during these years and the Hippodrome was no exception. On 15th November 1915, a charity matinee took place in front of a packed auditorium in aid of *The Daily Mirror* Nurse Cavell Fund, just a few weeks after news had reached Britain of the execution by the Germans of British nurse Edith Cavell for helping Allied prisoners to escape. The show included no fewer than thirty-nine performers including Gladys Cooper, George Robey, Irene Vanburgh and, of course, Shirley Kellogg. In the royal box, Queen Alexandra was accompanied by two of her daughters, as well as her grandchildren Princess Mary and Prince Albert, the future King George VI. Like most theatres, members of staff were personally involved in the war, among them Richard Winslow, the stage manager, who joined the Royal Navy as a lieutenant. Fred Trussell's son Arthur, who was in the armoured car division of the RNAS, received the Distinguished Service Medal for gallantry at the Dardanelles. It is highly likely there were many other men working at the Hippodrome, unrecorded, both staff and actors, who went off to fight. The pressure on young men to join up was intense, and the stage was frequently used as a recruiting platform. In its *Joyland* programme, the Hippodrome placed a special notice:

"The Management begs to announce that the members of the male chorus engaged in this production, have all been approached with

Promotional postcard for *Box o'Tricks* by Wilton Williams.

Left: Delightful cover of the programme for the 1918 revue *Box o'Tricks* designed by William Barribal. After seeing the show, *The Graphic* reported the experience was "to forget that a great war is raging".

> **The members of the male chorus engaged in this production, have all been approached with regard to joining His Majesty's Forces before being engaged, and in each case satisfactory reasons have been furnished for their not doing so**
>
> Notice in the Hippodrome's *Joyland* programme, 1916

Shirley Kellogg at a recruiting rally in Trafalgar Square, kissing a young boy who had mounted the stage to ask what he could do for the war effort. Theatre and stage stars not only played a role in boosting the morale of the nation during war, but more unsettlingly, were involved in encouraging men to join up.

regard to joining His Majesty's Forces before being engaged, and in each case satisfactory reasons have been furnished for their not doing so."

It is an unsettling indication of how young men who were not fighting for King and country were judged.

The Hippodrome's 1916 revue, *Flying Colours*, starred Gabrielle Ray and Little Tich, still going strong a decade and a half on from appearing in the Hippodrome's very first programme. Notable among the sketches was 'Bairnsfatherland', a theatrical adaptation of the popular cartoons created by Captain Bruce Bairnsfather in *The Bystander*.

Another hit West End production was *The Bing Boys are Here* at the Alhambra, whose main star was George Robey, the so-called 'Prime Minister of Mirth'. Robey was at the time Britain's most bankable entertainer, renowned and loved nationwide, and once his run at Alhambra came to an end, de Courville secured him for his 1917 revue, *Zig-Zag!*. Fresh from his *Bing Boys* triumph, Robey's involvement was a guarantee of success. He remembered, "We had crowded houses for months; with the war still raging. Considerably more than half the men in the audience would be in khaki, and the enthusiasm with which every patriotic allusion would be greeted was something not to be forgotten."

Box o'Tricks, which opened 7th March 1918, was the final Hippodrome revue of the war, but the public's appetite for revue entertainment showed no signs of abating, and de Courville's font of ideas showed no signs of running dry. In 'The Bee Hive' the Hippodrome's chorus girls, now re-christened 'The Joy Babes', appeared as worker bees in a hive while Dorothy Jordan sang 'The Bee Song'. Another sketch had girls appearing on stage wrapped in flags which they artfully unfolded to form a Union Jack with the words 'Mons', 'Haig' and 'Ypres'. As George Robey alternated between the Alhambra and the Hippodrome during these years, Harry Tate returned as the leading comedian, twirling his famous moustache (Tate expressed himself through his moustache, Robey through his incredibly mobile eyebrows). Tate's trademark act was 'Motoring' in which he showed mirth-inducing ineptitude in operating a car and he simply extended this incompetence to other areas; in *Box o'Tricks* a boating trip goes horribly wrong. "To hear the house screaming when Harry Tate comes on in *Box 'o' Tricks*, at the Hippodrome, is to forget a great war is raging."

The Hippodrome's trailblazing run of success during the war had attracted both imitators and critics. The great showman C. B. Cochrane told one interviewer that he had heard de Courville's revues cost £12,000, adding, with a superior air, that he was going to produce a less costly show at a smaller theatre, proving that wit rather than excessive expense could produce an equally good entertainment. De Courville let it be known he had in fact spent £17,000 on *Box o'Tricks* (he hadn't but he wanted to give the impression his audiences got value for money) but was secure in the knowledge that, after a month or so, each Hippodrome revue typically began to turn a profit of £3000 a week. The Hippodrome's management were also often at pains to point out how much they contributed to government coffers in entertainment tax.

Ragtime and revue 1909–1919

A cartoon by Bairnsfather, reproduced inside the programme for *Flying Colours*. This time, his famous soldier characters, Bill and Bert, find themselves outside the Hippodrome's stage door.

Promotional postcard, designed by Bruce Bairnsfather, for the 1916 revue *Flying Colours* which featured the sketch 'Bairnsfatherland'.

"We won't find a better 'ole than this, Bert."

Below: Front cover of *The Bystander* showing the Bairnsfatherland sketch in *Flying Colours*, with John Humphries playing 'Old Bill'.

The Bystander, October 4, 1916.—No. 670. Vol. LII

The Bystander

BERT: "'Ere, 'ave a look at this photo of my 'bit'"
OLD BILL: "Hum! Yer likes 'em plain, I see"

(Mr. John Humphries and Mr. Charles Berkeley in "Bairnsfatherland" at the London Hippodrome, the joint work of Captain Bairnsfather and Mr. B. Macdonald Hastings)

Bruce Bairnsfather had first submitted his comic impressions of trench life to *The Bystander* magazine while at the front, had his first cartoon published on 31st March 1915 and when recovering from shell shock in hospital was offered a contract to supply weekly cartoons. Bairnsfather's cast of characters, headed by 'Old Bill', a curmudgeonly old soldier with a walrus moustache, summed up the irrepressible spirit and stoicism of the British Tommy and Bairnsfather's fame escalated rapidly. His cartoons were published as complete sets in a publication called *Fragments* and disseminated around the world as postcards, jigsaws and china. It was only a matter of time before Old Bill and his chums would be adapted for the stage, and it is typical that Albert de Courville, who had collaborated with his friend Wal Pink on *Flying Colours*, should identify Bairnsfather's work as a hot property. Bairnsfather wrote the five-minute sketch together with Basil Macdonald Hastings (grandfather of the journalist and historian Max Hastings), and John Humphries was cast as Old Bill. The sketch received more attention than any other in *Flying Colours* and would lead to a complete show based on Bairnsfather's cartoons. *The Better 'Ole*, which was named after his most famous cartoon, opened at the Oxford Theatre in March 1917 and would become one of the longest-running and most popular shows of the Great War.

Joyland offered wartime audiences some much-needed escapism. "'Joyland' must surely appreciate the limit so far as expenditure on costumes and scenic effects is concerned," marvelled *The Referee* paper. "'Joyland' is the biggest thing the Hippodrome have given us," wrote *The People*. "The biggest and the most resplendent."

The Original Dixieland Jazz Band, formed of five white musicians from New Orleans led by cornet player Nick La Rocca, had recorded what is considered the first ever jazz record in 1917 ('Livery Stable Blues'). Their appearance in *Joy Bells* in 1919 marked the Hippodrome as an early adopter of the new jazz sound, but due to George Robey's intervention, their tenure at the theatre would last just one night.

Following the armistice in November 1918, London celebrated but although hostilities had ended, the residual effects of war lingered much longer. George Robey, back at the Hippodrome for *Joy Bells*, remembered entertaining a group of patients from the Queen's Hospital at Sidcup, where mending facial injuries was the speciality of the pioneering Sir Harold Gillies. In a large box at the Hippodrome, he noticed the men who had suffered the worst disfigurements sat concealed by a curtain or at the very back in the shadows, so they would be hidden from public view. Robey insisted on speaking with and entertaining all the men. One, who had endured thirty operations to rebuild his face, he nicknamed 'Merry-Eyes'. Robey believed the exchange had lifted the man's spirits. *Joy Bells*, as was becoming customary with Hippodrome revues, was deemed more magnificent than the last in terms of its production. One sketch, entitled 'The Bird Cage', was noted for its elaborate tropical bird costumes and the popularity of the show prompted jewellers The Goldsmiths and Silversmiths Company to place an advertisement for their 'Joy Bells' range of necklaces and charm bracelets. Also available to the *Joy Bells* audience was the 'Hippodrome Review', a newspaper-style pamphlet within the programme, "issued by the management of the London Hippodrome and printed at the theatre". On its front page, beside a photograph of the suave Albert de Courville, was a piece explaining his recent spat with various members of the press (though who precisely we don't know) regarding their snobbish views on revue.

"The truth is of course, is that the public have a very natural preference for the class of entertainment that pleases them most. We have just passed through a terrible, serious and difficult time. There is hardly a home in England to which sorrow or deprivation has not come… People want to be amused, they want to recover the old habit of laughter… so we shall go on being frivolous, and continue in our efforts to please the eye and charm the ear…"

It seemed characteristic of the Hippodrome to actually produce its own publication and use it as a vehicle to silence its critics. Audiences voted with their feet anyway, and Albert de Courville's reputation as an innovator and a showman kept them returning to the Hippodrome. And for *Joy Bells*, he had something new up his sleeve. Having claimed to have brought ragtime to the London stage in 1912, he was now about to introduce the next music craze sweeping America – jazz.

The Original Dixieland Jazz Band, formed of five white musicians from New Orleans led by cornet player Nick La Rocca, had recorded what is considered the first ever jazz record in 1917 ('Livery Stable Blues') and had quickly gained a following in New York where they appeared at fashionable nightspot Reisenweber Café. There were plenty of bands in London claiming to be playing jazz. In fact, the Octette, brought to London by de Courville in 1912, could arguably lay claim to have introduced the syncopated sound to the capital. But the 'ODJB' billed themselves as "the creators of jazz" and as nobody was going to argue, these apparent pioneers, and their wild, irreverent, almost anarchic sound, were brought to London by Albert de Courville where they would play for a fifteen-minute slot in the *Joy Bells* revue. The Hippodrome sent out its press releases to drum up attention. *The Bystander* magazine's reaction to the news was laconic but nevertheless tinged with curiosity:

"We are, according to the puff prelim, to hear at last, the REAL thing in Jazz Bands. Seems up to now we've had but a 'poor imitation' of what the jazzer can really do in terms of noise, speed and rhythm. This gets all previous J.B.'s beat to a frazzle."

Ragtime and revue 1909-1919

During 1915's *Push and Go*, theatre programmes carried photographs of every individual girl in the 'Beauty Chorus' and asked audience members to vote for who they considered the prettiest. Miss Juanita Symonds, with her dark hair and mournful eyes, emerged the winner in a landslide victory.

A zig-zag effect in *Zig-Zag!*: Shirley Kellogg seated on a silk cushion as Shir Lee in the 'Chinese Lacquer' scene. Behind her, ladies of the chorus march up and down the illuminated ladders, "with excellent effect".

Music sheet cover from *Joy Bells* designed by Arthur Ferrier, showing the star of the show, George Robey, with his expressive eyebrows, in his familiar garb of collarless jacket and bowler hat.

Programme cover for the 1917 revue, *Zig-Zag!* starring George Robey. The design is a nod to the show's highlight, a sketch called 'The Pre-Historic Man' in which Robey with co-star Daphne Pollard played Mr. Umph, a cuckolded Stone Age husband. Robey and Pollard's wigs alone were enough to provoke laughter, and audiences and press alike adored the concept, several decades before prehistoric marital harmony was tackled in Hanna-Barbera's Flintstones cartoons.

Unfortunately, *Joy Bells* had to open without the ODJB as a strike by New York harbour workers had delayed the band's voyage. By the time they did arrive in Britain, anticipation was at fever pitch. According to the actress Phyllis Monkman, writing in her 'Dancing Days and Nights' column in *The Sketch*, at the Press Rehearsal, "the noise was so tremendous people thought part of the roof had collapsed". It turned out the thundering vibrations were down to the muscular playing of drummer Tony Sbarbaro. Their first public performance had the desired effect, and the audience's reaction was as riotous as the music itself. It would have been a triumph except for one problem – George Robey. Robey's immense talent and fame were matched by a comparable ego and there were two things Robey did not like. One was being upstaged, the other was jazz. In his autobiography, on several occasions he makes his feelings about modern music known, describing with thinly veiled disgust, "semi-barbarous 'melodies' and blatant orchestration that set the brain throbbing and aching". He demanded that either the ODJB go or he would, leaving Albert de Courville with little choice. Robey was a solid box office draw, and would go on to appear in several more Hippodrome revues and pantomimes. The Original Dixieland Jazz Band were, in retrospect, a seismic cultural happening, but in 1919 their music divided opinion and there was no guarantee the ODJB's appeal would extend beyond an enthusiastic band of early adopters. Albert de Courville acquiesced and made an arrangement with Charles Gulliver at the Palladium where the ODJB were welcomed. They also played at Marten's and then Rector's nightclubs and even at a 'Joy Bells' fancy dress party thrown by de Courville at Prince's club. Did George Robey decline to attend, one wonders? Ironically, the ODJB were also invited to perform at Buckingham Palace in front of the deeply conservative George V (who apparently sat still throughout the set and then guffawed and clapped at the end of the performance of their hit, 'The Tiger Rag'). Afterwards the band had a successful residency at the Hammersmith Palais dance hall, where it was clear that the post-war youth did not share Robey's aversion to the new musical sound.

It may have been the briefest of flings, but the Hippodrome had brought to London the music form that would go on to define the next decade.

Programme for the Hippodrome's fundraiser of 30th April 1912 for sufferers from the *Titanic* disaster. Reflecting the epic production involving 150 different performers, the programme was equal in its lavishness, featuring illustrations by artists such as Bernard Partridge of *Punch* and Walter Crane.

Albert de Courville had a ticket to travel on the Titanic's maiden voyage, but was summoned to a meeting at the Hippodrome and cancelled his trip

Charity at the Hippodrome

Through the nineteenth and twentieth centuries, theatre and the acting community played a vital role in helping to lift up those less fortunate than themselves and in this respect, the Hippodrome was no exception. In June 1900, just a few months after the theatre's opening, Edward Moss staged a benefit show to raise funds for victims of the great fire in Ottawa of 26th April, which had left over 1500 people homeless.

The spirit of altruism continued through the decades. In the aftermath of the *Titanic* disaster, a special matinee was organised at the Hippodrome in May 1912, raising £900 for the fund for sufferers from the disaster. Coincidentally, Albert de Courville, its mastermind producer of revues through the 1910s, had a ticket to travel on the *Titanic*'s maiden voyage, but he was summoned to a meeting at the Hippodrome and cancelled his trip. The Hippodrome's history may have been quite different if de Courville had been on board that fateful voyage. Instead he helped to produce the show. No expense was spared with 150 performers including Marie Tempest, Lena Ashwell, the dancer Lydia Kyasht, and the three big stars of the era – Harry Tate, Little Tich and George Robey.

The Great War of 1914–18 saw the theatre industry galvanise and shift gear to raise funds for numerous war charities. A matinee at the Hippodrome in memory of Nurse Edith Cavell, who had been executed by the Germans for helping Allied soldiers escape, was held in October 1915 and featured a stellar line-up that included Gladys Cooper, Irene Vanburgh, Shirley Kellogg and George Robey (whose fundraising efforts during the war led to a knighthood). On a lighter note, the ladies of the Hippodrome chorus also volunteered to foster soldiers' dogs for the duration of the war, providing the papers with a golden photo opportunity. Charitable activity did not end in 1918. A 'Victory Peace Festival' in aid of the American Fund for French Wounded took place in 1919, and each year, theatres across the country staged charity performances in aid of Warriors Day, to raise funds for ex-servicemen. In 1921, the Prince of Wales attended the Warriors Day evening performance at the Hippodrome and provoked an enthusiastic display of patriotism from the audience, as described by *The Bystander*:

"When he entered a burst of cheering that shook the very walls, epitomised the feeling which no words could express how much the people love their Prince. Never in my life have I heard 'God Save the Prince of Wales' sung with such mighty volume, such enthusiasm. It was a thrilling, inspiring sight."

The first of a regular series of Royal Command Performances, held at the Hippodrome in 1921, raised an impressive £1200 for the Variety Artistes' Benevolent Fund, with £50 of that donated by the King himself. In 1925, George Robey again appeared in a variety show to raise money for the Education Aid Society; a special matinee performance of *That's a Good Girl* in 1928 was in support of the Journalists' Convalescent Home in Ipswich.

A sense of noblesse oblige prompted many high society women to take to the stage for fundraising events at the Hippodrome. One production, staged in May 1931, trod familiar territory when real-life debs took part in a tableau on the theme, 'A Day in the Life of a Debutante' in aid of the Highway Club for Boys and Girls in the east end of London – it was attended by the Duchess of York. Elsewhere, each year children from Madame Vacani's dancing school took part in a highly publicised matinee usually in support of hospitals or children's charities, typically Great Ormond Street Hospital for Sick Children. Vacani's was very exclusive; famously Princesses Elizabeth and Margaret took dancing lessons there, and so the participants in these events were the sons and daughters of aristocrats and celebrities. Both Margaret Elphinstone, niece of the Duchess of York, and Raine McCorquodale, daughter of Barbara Cartland, were among the children who took part during the 1930s.

By the 1970s, when the Hippodrome had become The Talk of the Town, it staged a number of charity gala evenings produced by Robert Nesbitt, most notably a fundraising event in November 1970 in support of the World Wildlife Fund, which entertained eighteen members of royalty. Today, the Hippodrome Casino continues the tradition of charity by donating around £250,000 each year to local community causes and national charities.

Cynthia Pratt (left) and Margaret Whigham taking part in a charity tableau on the theme of 'A Day in the Life of a Debutante' at the Hippodrome in May 1931 in aid of the Highway Club for Boys and Girls in the east end of London, attended by the Duchess of York. In a case of art imitating life, Margaret has been hailed as deb of the year in 1930 and was the darling of the society columns both before and after her marriage when she became Mrs. Charles Sweeney. She subsequently married the 11th Duke of Argyll and gained notoriety during their scandalous 1963 divorce case.

Page from the programme for the Hippodrome's 1921 Warrior's Day show attended by the Prince of Wales, signed by some of theatre's greatest stars including Lupino Lane, Harry Lauder, George Robey and Nellie Wallace. Also visible is producer Julian Wylie's autograph underneath the date.

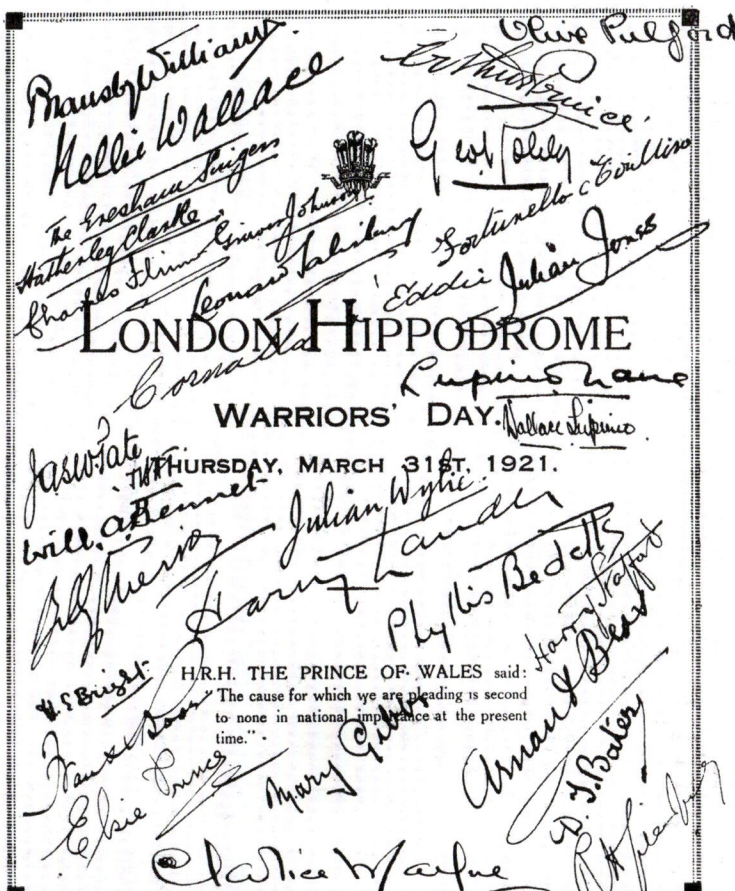

In 1915, the Hippodrome staged a production in memory of Nurse Edith Cavell. Cavell was a totemic figure of self-sacrifice and courage, her execution by the Germans widely considered in Britain proof of the enemy's moral deficiency. The press reported widely on the national reaction to Cavell's fate including this memorial service held at Christ Church, Westminster in the aftermath of the event. A state funeral at Westminster Abbey took place after the war, on 15th May 1919.

Children taking part in a Vacani matinee at the Hippodrome in 1937 in aid of Great Ormond Street Hospital. Among the young stars is Raine, daughter of the novelist Barbara Cartland (left) and future stepmother of Diana, Princess of Wales.

Ragtime and revue 1909-1919

Scene from *Sunny*, a light-hearted feast of song, dance, love and laughter and with no fewer than fifteen scene changes. *The Weekly Dispatch* noted how it was "a show of such magnificence of scenery and dresses that the audience constantly broke into applause as some new splendour came into view".

The comedy musical 1920-1939

Music sheet from *Jig-saw*, the Hippodrome revue that kicked the 1920s off in style. *The Bystander*'s theatrical correspondent, 'Jingle', described it as having "scenes of dazzling splendour with a quite amazing lavishness, and the humourists are as plentiful as currants in a pre-war penny bun".

> **Drug culture in the 1920s was wrapped in an aura of shady glamour, and 'Limehouse Nights' cannily tapped into the public fascination with 'dope girls' and their wild existence**

THE DOLLY SISTERS AND LADDIE CLIFF

The Dolly Sisters, who have hitherto been better known on the film than on the stage, have carried all before them in the new de Courville revue, "Jig-Saw," at the Hippodrome. Nothing much prettier than their "pony" dance (see lower pictures), in which they are driven by Mr. Laddie Cliff, has been seen on the revue stage for many a long day. They sent all the flowers that were showered upon them on the first night to the hospital for epileptics

The arrival of the 'delectable Dollies' on the London stage was another coup for the Hippodrome. Born Janszieka and Roszika Deutsch in Hungary in 1892, they had emigrated to New York with their parents where they began to perform on stage to make a living. With their sleek black bobbed hair, exotic beauty, effervescent personalities and chic sense of style, all in duplicate, they soon found success and became part of a celebrity milieu, rubbing shoulders with millionaires and playing recklessly at the gaming tables. Men wanted to possess them, the finest couturiers wanted to dress them, and by the time they arrived in London, both escaping from disastrous first marriages, they were well on the way to becoming icons of the jazz age. Edward, Prince of Wales admired them, and the ageing Gordon Selfridge proposed repeatedly to Jenny. *Jig-saw* would be their only Hippodrome appearance.

The Hippodrome's 1920–21 pantomime was, according to *The Tatler*, "more gorgeous than, and just as lovely to the eye as the best of the de Courville revues". Highlights included Phyllis Dare, as the Princess, singing the 'Bubble Song' while surrounded on-stage by thousands of soap bubbles, a curtain of diamonds concealing Aladdin's cave and Lupino Lane tumbling through a succession of trap doors. It was declared "worthy of Drury Lane", the ultimate accolade. Cover design by Hugh Willoughby.

> **This is the prettiest, jolliest, certainly the funniest pantomime that London has seen for years**
>
> The Bystander

1920 would see Albert de Courville produce his tenth and final revue for the Hippodrome. Always at the forefront of current trends, the sketches in *Jig-saw* seem to presciently sum up the 1920s even before the decade had got properly underway.

Early in the show, 'A Perfume Ballet' had the chorus dressed as various well-known fragrances from the period including Guerlain's L'Heure Bleu and Houbigant's Quelques Fleurs (a firm classic; Diana, Princess of Wales wore it on her wedding day in 1981). As Winnie Melville sang 'The Perfume Song', various girls moved among the audience to distribute vials of scent, a typically extravagant de Courville touch. In another scene, sweets were given out, bringing the scantily clad chorus into close proximity with the audience.

A further sketch, 'Limehouse Nights', set in what was then London's Chinatown in the East End, was "necessarily associated with opium dens and that sort of thing", and featured a song called 'Poppyland'. Drug culture in the 1920s was wrapped in an aura of shady glamour, and 'Limehouse Nights' cannily tapped into the public fascination with 'dope girls' and their wild existence.

Appearing for the first time on the London stage were the magnificent and beautiful Dolly Sisters, identical twins Jenny and Rosie, who performed what *The Guardian* called "an unusually spirited and graceful" 'pony trot' dance with Laddie Cliff at the reins, their white feathered costumes enhanced by a jet-black backdrop. Cliff also partnered with Rosie in an 'Apache Dance', a dramatic dance that was said to re-enact an argument between pimp and prostitute with the associated (mock) violence.

Sophisticated perfumes, drugs, darkly suggestive dances *and* the Dolly Sisters; it was a mix in perfect tune with the new relaxed mood of post-war Britain. And if there was any doubt, a cheeky scene called 'The Lingerie Store' confirmed the country had entered a rather more permissive era.

In December 1920, the Hippodrome's pantomime, *Aladdin*, received glowing reviews. "This is the prettiest, jolliest, certainly the funniest pantomime that London has seen for years," wrote *The Tatler*. The man behind the show was Julian Wylie, known as 'The King of Pantomime'. Born in Southport, he began a career as an accountant, briefly became a stage magician and then went on to act as agent for an illusionist called David Devant, before moving into theatre production. He had made a name for himself by producing pantomimes across the biggest theatres outside London, in Glasgow, Manchester, Newcastle, Leeds and Birmingham. The principles of pantomime and revue were interchangeable and Wylie could equal de Courville when it came to grand spectacles. He partnered with James W. Tate in 1913, producing their first Wylie-Tate revue, *I Should Worry*, at Alfred Butt's Palace Theatre, a partnership that lasted until Tate's premature death in 1922. He also regularly collaborated with his brother Lauri, who was a scriptwriter and librettist, often providing the 'book' (the story and script) for Julian's shows. Wylie, a large, reserved man with a fondness for ice cream, was a workaholic and visionary. Like de Courville before him, he was not afraid of technological progress, and fully embraced

The comedy musical 1920-1939

Julian Wylie (1878–1934), the 'King of Pantomime'. While some producers left the details of shows to others, Julian Wylie ensured he was involved in productions on every level, and during the annual period of pantomime rehearsals embarked on a relentless regime of travel, criss-crossing the country by rail to ensure all was in order at various theatres. It was not unusual for him to simultaneously present five or six pantomimes around the country in any given year and in between that time, work on revues. When he died suddenly, in December 1934, at the age of fifty-six, most papers ascribed the cause of death to overwork. He had been on the verge of presenting another pantomime at Drury Lane, and had stayed at the theatre past midnight the day before his death. Despite its tragic suddenness, it was thanks to the minute instructions he had written down that the show was able to open as if he had been there to conduct its smooth running in person.

Right: *Peep Show*'s programme cover featured a striking art deco-style design, similar in style to the work of the Russian graphic artist, Erté. It was by an artist called Hugh Willoughby who had honed his talent for drawing while a prisoner of war in Germany. Willoughby was also engaged to design costumes and scenery and would later find work as a designer for the *Folies Bergère* in Paris.

The Hippodrome stage packed to the gills as Julian Wylie auditions wave upon wave of hopeful chorus girls in a photograph published in *The Sketch* in 1927. The magazine claimed Wylie had eight hundred auditionees to select from.

In 1922, a group of prominent London figures had formed the 'Brighter London Society' with the aim of making London 'the magnet of the world'. Essentially, it was a glorified tourism marketing exercise aimed at making the capital as attractive as possible to visitors. Spearheaded by an interesting mix of people including Harry Gordon Selfridge, owner of Selfridge's, and Woodman Burbridge of Harrods, at the time the 'Brighter London' campaign had quite an impact; the *Pall Mall Gazette* even ran a competition encouraging readers to send in some brightening ideas. What better title then to choose for Julian Wylie's 1923 revue? *Brighter London* opened on 28th March and announced its arrival on the Hippodrome corner with a dazzling display of light adorning the building's exterior. Nobody could accuse the Hippodrome of shirking its responsibilities when it came to beautifying London.

Far left: Glamorous theatre-goers arrive at the Hippodrome during its run of *Round in 50* in 1922.

Front page of *The Illustrated Sporting and Dramatic News* featuring photographs of George Robey in *Round in 50*, a modern re-working of the popular Jules Verne novel *Around the World in 80 Days*. Julian Wylie was a huge fan of Verne's novel and, believing every child should know the story, printed a special edition with his own personal message inside, which could be ordered for free by any junior members of the audience.

The modern stage version of the story (written by Sax Rohmer) saw Robey as 'Phileas' or 'Phil' dashing around the world, while the staging of his extensive travels was facilitated by the use of the cinematograph to form an all-action backdrop in a number of scenes including one where he was attempting to catch up with an Atlantic liner and then motoring at speed from Portsmouth to London. Julian Wylie had seen the future, and rather than regard 'moving pictures' as the enemy, he embraced the new medium and only saw creative opportunities. "For the first time in the history of theatre, I believe an alliance has been formed between the two rival arts," commented *The Queen* magazine in its review. Robey remembers the effect always received thunderous applause, and in his autobiography concluded, "Altogether I think *Round in Fifty* was the best revue I ever took part in."

Left: Paul Whiteman and his band, bringing the latest jazz sounds to the Hippodrome in 1922.

developments in lighting and stage engineering. In an interview in *The Sketch* in 1922, with remarkably confident foresight he predicted, "actors and actresses will cease to appear in the flesh, and dramatic entertainments will be obtained at home by every subscriber to a State service."

Moss Empires now had R. H. Gillespie at the helm following the retirement of Frank Allen as managing director. Seeing the success of *Aladdin*, he contracted Wylie to produce its next revue. *Peep Show* was notable for its innovative use of lighting effects by a Russian specialist, Adrian V. Samoiloff, but despite this modernism, two of its biggest scenes were of a historical flavour. There was the nostalgic 'Song Shop', a recreation of the shop window of the leading music publisher Francis, Day & Hunter, with some 1890s music hall celebrities brought to life. Stanley Lupino played Dan Leno; Mona Vivian gave an excellent impression of Maggie Duggan. 'Down Dickens Street', the highlight of the revue, featured all the best-known characters from Charles Dickens, as well as several memorable Dickens locations, all cleverly assembled together on stage. Both sketches had previously featured in touring Wylie-Tate productions, *The Passing Show* of 1920 and *The Follies* of 1920 respectively, giving them a clear advantage over revues opening in London. Albert de Courville had to launch his revues cold, and would subsequently make tweaks and changes to address any problems during the show's early weeks, but Wylie-Tate picked proven sketches from their other shows, already tried, tested and polished to perfection. The only thing needed was some appropriately big names to fill the main roles.

George Robey would make a triumphant return to the Hippodrome stage for the 1921–2 pantomime season, taking on the role of Dame Trot in *Jack and the Beanstalk*. Although a veteran of playing pantomime dames in the provinces, it was his first London pantomime and consequently, something of an event. A British Pathé news clip survives showing scenes from this, including Robey larking about in a clumsy attempt to milk a cow. Even in this brief, flickering footage, it's easy to see what a charismatic, larger-than-life performer Robey was. *Jack and the Beanstalk* was blighted by the death of James Tate during its run. His wife, Clarice Mayne, renowned as one of the very best principal boys in the business, had been starring as Jack and was replaced by Dorothy Ward. In the final weeks of the run, Robey began rehearsals for a new Hippodrome revue, *Round in 50*, and so his part was taken over by Nellie Wallace, one of pantomime's few female dames.

With *Brighter London*, the Hippodrome once again tapped into the musical zeitgeist by signing up a big name from across the pond, the 'genius of syncopation', the so-called 'King of Jazz', Mr. Paul Whiteman and his orchestra. By 1923, jazz had permeated music halls, clubs, cabaret and hotel restaurants, most of which laid large dance floors to satisfy their patrons' desire to dance. Whiteman was the acceptable face of jazz and his appearance at the Hippodrome chimed in perfect synchronicity with the times, earning unanimous praise from the press. "Paul Whiteman's musicianship is equalled only by his showmanship," wrote the *Dancing Times*. "His great bluff personality fits our idea of the jazz musician completely."

Another transatlantic import would generate plenty of publicity for the Hippodrome's next revue, *Leap Year* (1924 was a leap year, but the show opened on 20th March rather than the 29th February). George Robey returned to the Hippodrome for *Leap Year* and recalled

COSTUME AND SCENE CHANGED BY COLOURED LIGHT: STAGE MAGIC.

DRAWN BY OUR SPECIAL ARTIST, CECIL KING.

First Scene — The Valley of Echoes.

Second Scene — The Indian Temple.

1. AS THE SCENE FIRST APPEARS, AT THE LONDON HIPPODROME: "THE VALLEY OF ECHOES"—A DAYLIGHT MOUNTAIN VIEW, WITH A BROWN-BEARDED MAGICIAN AND A DARK-HAIRED GIRL IN MODERN DRESS.

2. AN INSTANTANEOUS CHANGE: THE SCENE TRANSFORMED BY M. SAMOILOFF'S COLOUR-LIGHTING INTO AN INDIAN TEMPLE AT NIGHT; WITH WHITE-BEARDED PRIEST AND FAIR-HAIRED GIRL, IN EASTERN DRESS.

M. Adrian Samoiloff's wonderful new method of instantaneous scene-changing and costume-changing by an alteration of colour in the lighting, is demonstrated in "The Peep Show," at the Hippodrome. The transformation is effected without moving a scrap of scenery or requiring any changes of dress, and the characters move about as in an ordinary play. "The Valley of Echoes" opens with a daylight view in the mountains, with two characters, a girl with dark hair in a dark skirt and a sleeveless silk jumper; and a magician, also in dark clothes with a brown beard. Suddenly a different-coloured light is switched on, and the valley is turned into an Indian temple, with a fire and a hanging lamp, and in the background the moon-lit sky at night. The two characters are also transformed: the heroine now has fair hair, and her dress becomes an Oriental costume with light-patterned skirt, while the magician is seen in a striped gown, with a white beard. Other characters appear. The scene suddenly changes back to the valley, and they are all in modern dress. M. Samoiloff describes his method as a harmony between lines, lights, and colours. The changes depend on the colour-scheme plus the combination of coloured lights. The actual chemical composition of some colours — as opposed to others — contributes greatly to the effect. "Dazzle" camouflage, by which a form is altered by the direction of lines in a pattern, likewise comes into play. The method has been worked out scientifically by spectrum analysis.—[*Drawings Copyrighted in the United States and Canada.*]

> Page from *The Illustrated London News* demonstrating how the stage lighting of specialist Adrian Samoiloff could completely change a scene in *Peep Show*. The effects were achieved with a combination of coloured lights based on the principle of spectrum analysis.

> "*Peep Show* was notable for its innovative use of lighting effects by a Russian specialist, Adrian V. Samoiloff"

On 28th July 1921, the Hippodrome staged the *Royal Command Performance* (later known as the *Royal Variety Show*). Although there had been two command performances at other theatres in 1912 and 1919, this was the first of what would become an annual theatrical event. The news that the King's only daughter, Princess Mary, was to make her first public appearance since the announcement of her engagement to Viscount Lascelles meant swift trade at the box office and on the night, the engaged couple were enthusiastically applauded both by crowds who had gathered outside the Hippodrome, and by the audience as they arrived in the royal box. In total, £2000 was raised for the Variety Artistes' Benevolent Fund, with £50 personally donated by the King himself. George V, a man of simple tastes, enjoyed the comedian Milton Hayes and as an ex-sailor, was particularly appreciative of G. S. Melvin's hornpipe dance. The Hippodrome also hosted the *Royal Command Performance* again the following year. Illustration by Fortunino Matania in *The Sphere*.

WEBBERS WEBBING ON THEIR WEB: THE "HIT" OF THE LONDON HIPPODROME.

DANCERS AND GYMNASTS TOO: THE HOFFMAN GIRLS OF "LEAP YEAR," IN THE SCENE "WEBBING."

The eighteen Gertrude Hoffman Girls, who have come from the United States to appear in "Leap Year," the new revue at the London Hippodrome, have made a great "hit," and their Webbing turn is one of the stage performances which everyone in town is talking about. As our double-page photograph shows, the girls actually posture and turn on a series of webbing "ropes," and do clever acrobatic "stunts" which delight everyone with their neatness and grace. Their Webbing act is one of their best performances; but they also do some very entertaining dances, both as a team and separately. It will be remembered that in our last issue we gave portraits of nine of these girls from the "other side."

The Hoffman Girls pay tribute to the British Empire Exhibition, the major highlight of 1924 and a fertile source of inspiration for Julian Wylie who produced the Hippodrome's own *Leap Year* tribute. The Hoffman Girls performed an elaborate number inspired by the countries and cultures of Britain's dominions; dancing in front of a backdrop of Wembley (pictured here), dressing up as Maori villagers and in one part even as ostriches on a South African ostrich farm!

Stars of *Leap Year*, the Hoffman Girls were managed and choreographed by Gertrude Hoffman who, as Kitty Hayes, had been a popular, and somewhat notorious, vaudeville star in the United States, arrested on several occasions for the revealing costume she wore for her 'Salome' dance. The girls in her troupe danced with an athletic energy, and seemed, at least according to pictures in the press, to spend most of their lives leaping around in shorts and playsuits, or hanging from gymnasium bars – all good practice for their act, which involved striking poses and elegantly scaling webbing that hung the height of the proscenium. George Robey observed they were "as comely as they were bouncing… in one dance, they were so dressed that they seemed to have nothing on – yet, of course, they were perfectly all right." He took great pleasure in remarking to the audience how the girls were "a great credit to Mr. And Mrs. Hoffman".

Winifred Arthur, the nineteen-year-old conductor and central star of *The Jazz Mistress* in 1925. Arthur was fresh from the Trocadero where she and a ballroom dancing teacher called Vera Clarke had made a name for themselves conducting an all-male orchestra. As it had done for quarter of a century, the Hippodrome management moved quickly to sign up anything that was novel and newsworthy, including female jazz band leaders.

> **In one dance, they were so dressed that they seemed to have nothing on – yet, of course, they were perfectly all right**
>
> George Robey referring to the Hoffman Girls

that Prince Henry (later Duke of Gloucester) was in the audience on the first night, giving Robey the irresistible opportunity to crack what seems like a laboured joke about plums: "Doesn't His Majesty's own anthem ask us to send him Victorias?" As *Leap Year* ended, preparations were made for the Christmas pantomime of *Mother Goose*, starring Shaun Glenville as Dame Trot, Isobel Elsom as her daughter, Dorothy Ward (married to Glenville) in the principal boy role, Fred Conquest as the goose and music-hall stalwart Wee Georgie Wood as Dame Trot's son. It was Julian Wylie's eighth production for the Hippodrome, and in a special commemorative booklet to mark the theatre's twenty-fifth anniversary in January 1925, Wylie's photograph was printed, alongside those of de Courville and Frank Parker. "Press and public have acclaimed his work," it stated, "and the box office has sung its sweetest song. Need I say more." Most papers saved particular praise for the grand finale of the first act named 'Dream of Beauty' in which Dorothy Ward was surrounded by members of the chorus dressed as potions and brushes typically found on a lady's dressing table.

Halfway through the decade, the popularity of jazz music continued to inform and influence much of the London theatre. For 1925, the Hippodrome staged The *Jazz Master* revue, featuring Vincent Lopez and his band, which later morphed into The *Jazz Mistress* when nineteen-year-old South African violinist Winifred Arthur took over to conduct an orchestra of twenty-two male musicians.

In August 1925, the Hippodrome turned temporarily into a cinema for five weeks during which time it screened the film *Don Q, Son of Zorro* starring the dashing Douglas Fairbanks. Wylie's brother, George Samuelson, ran his own film production studio and it's possible that this family connection influenced the decision to show films at the Hippodrome when the art form was still regarded as an encroachment into theatre's territory.

In fact, the Hippodrome's stint as a cinema bridged the gap while preparations were underway for the next production, which for the first time would not be a revue, but instead, a musical comedy – *Mercenary Mary* – imported from America where it had run for 136 performances at the Longacre Theatre in New York.

For a start, there was a plot, albeit somewhat flimsy. It followed the story of an impecunious married couple who pretended to divorce in order for the husband to inherit a fortune from his rich uncle. It was a pleasant mélange of romance, muddled relationships ("for a time all parties are in a pickle"), light-hearted comments on wealth and class, along with some justifiable deception. Naturally, everything resolved itself satisfactorily in true happy ever after fashion. In shifting its focus to musical comedy, the Hippodrome went head to head with the Palace Theatre which was already enjoying a hit with *No, No, Nanette!*. *The Sketch*, commenting on this rivalry, wrote, "Henceforth, no doubt, there will be a race between the Hippodrome and the Palace, and as both plays are littered with stars in the cast, it will be difficult to say which best man will win, in the long, very long, run." In fact, both shows, which enjoyed equal success, were produced by the same team; Herbert Clayton and Jack Waller, who were responsible for a number of hit musicals in the 1920s including *Princess Cinderella* and *The Boyfriend*. Taking the main roles in *Mercenary Mary* were Sonnie Hale, June (aka June Howard Tripp, who was one of a long line of actresses to marry into the aristocracy when she became Lady Inverclyde) and the Irish-American actress

Peggy O'Neill, the Irish-American actress who played the title role in *Mercenary Mary* in 1925. O'Neill dithered over whether to take the part, wondering if she would be become typecast by taking another musical comedy role. Unable to make a decision, she even visited a clairvoyant near Oxford Street who advised her to take a golden opportunity that would be worth at least £50 a week. As she had already been offered £200 a week as well as a percentage of takings, O'Neill sensibly decided to take the role.

Mercenary Mary opened at the Hippodrome on 7th October 1925 following a month-long provincial run with the London cast at the Alhambra in Glasgow. The book and lyrics were by William B. Frielander and Isobel Leighton, with the score, a mix of "wild jazzing and sweet melody" according to *The Sketch*, also by Friedlander together with Con Conrad. In many ways, the show would typify the style of musical that came to dominate the West End stage over the next decade. "Mercenary Mary is a tip-top entertainment in its kind," concluded *The Tatler* in its review, "and the Hippodrome hasn't given us a brighter show in years."

SOME "SUNNY" CELEBRITIES.

The cast of *Sunny* pictured by the theatrical caricaturist Einar Nerman in *The Tatler*. Top left Nancy Lovat, top right, Elsie Randolph. In the centre Jack Buchanan and Binnie Hale. Bottom left Claude Hulbert, bottom right, Jack Hobbs.

SOME OF THE LEADING "SUNNY" RAYS

The London Hippodrome has a better winner than anyone had over the autumn double, and "Sunny" is likely to go on packing the famous Moss Empire establishment until further notice. It is an excellently named production. The cast is also a tremendously strong one. In this collection of portraits, the top left and right are Miss Nancie Lovat and Miss Elsie Randolph, in the centre are Mr. Jack Buchanan and Miss Binnie Hale, in the left-hand bottom corner Mr. Claude Hulbert, and on the right, Mr. Jack Hobbs

The comedy musical 1920-1939

After a long run at the New Amsterdam Theatre on Broadway the previous year, the British production of *Sunny*, produced by Charles Mast, opened at the Palace Theatre in Manchester on 21st September before moving to the Hippodrome from 7th October. The show's reputation preceded it and applications for first night seats were, according to the press, sufficient to fill the Hippodrome three times over with £600 of box office receipts, a record for the house. The show's programme, with a frolicking impression of Sunny against a radiant orange and yellow background, promised joyful optimism, which was by and large what the audience got.

> *Sunny* ran for 363 performances and its hit song, 'Who?', would become a classic, recorded by dozens of artists including Josephine Baker and Frank Sinatra

Binnie Hale in her dressing room at the Hippodrome, surveying her toy mascots and wearing her costume for the gymnasium scene in *Sunny*. The daughter of actor-comedian Robert Hale, and sister of Sonnie (who had been in *Mercenary Mary*), she came with an illustrious theatrical heritage but the potted biography of her in the theatre's programme stressed she had found fame independently, starting in the chorus before being 'spotted'. With her wide blue eyes giving her a permanent expression of faint surprise, she was undeniably pretty, but she also possessed comic timing, charm and was an excellent mimic, all of which made her a favourite of audiences and critics alike: "The greatest musical comedy of the moment," claimed *The Sphere*. When Binnie got a new puppy during the show's run, naturally, she named it Sunny.

Peggy O'Neill in the title role. O'Neill had been uncertain about accepting the role and rehearsals were considerably delayed by her prevarication. There was some arguing among the actresses about who would get to sing 'Honey, I'm in love with you'. O'Neill had it written in her contract that the song would go to her but eventually it was sung by June, who was the better vocalist and dancer, while O'Neill, whose knack for comedy was widely acknowledged, instead sang, 'I'm a Little Bit Fonder of You than I am of Myself', composed by Irving Caesar (who is best-known for writing the lyrics to 'Tea for Two' for *No, No, Nanette!*). The song was almost omitted until Caesar turned up at rehearsals and threatened to tear up the cheque he'd been given unless it was reinstated. Late at night, before the first performance, the song was rehearsed and perfected and the following day proved to be the highlight of the show throughout its long run of 426 performances.

If *Mercenary Mary* was a blazing success, then the next Hippodrome musical threatened to eclipse it, in more than just name. *Sunny* was another American import, with some serious musical muscle on board in the form of Jerome Kern as composer, with words and lyrics by Oscar Hammerstein and Otto Harbach.

When Barbara Cartland went to see *Sunny* at the Hippodrome, a decade after she'd seen Shirley Kellogg in *Joyland*, she loaded praise on its two stars, Binnie Hale, who she adored, and Jack Buchanan who she declared the 'Prince of Fashion'. While Shirley Kellogg and George Robey had repeatedly drawn the crowds during the war years and the early 1920s, Jack Buchanan now comfortably filled that slot along with Binnie Hale, and, later, their co-star Elsie Randolph. Both would go on to star in three more hit musicals each at the Hippodrome during the 1930s. Jack Buchanan was also an entertainer at the top of his game having enjoyed success on Broadway performing with Bea Lillie and Gertrude Lawrence in *Andre Charlot's Revue*, and then in London with *Toni* and *Boodle*. Jack, with his easy elegance, effortless 'soft shoe' dancing and confident yet unobtrusive stage presence, was the object of affection for an army of female fans who filled the upper circle night after night to see their favourite leading man. Whichever theatre Buchanan played at, the 'Gallery Girls' were sure to follow, vociferously showing their appreciation, yet his gift for comedy meant he was also admired by male theatre-goers. It was a rare balance to get right.

The storyline in *Sunny* was almost interchangeable with *Mercenary Mary*. Hale played Sunny Peters, a circus girl, who ran away to America, marrying Jim on board during her voyage in order to gain access to the United States. Despite being romantically linked to others, the show concluded with Sunny and Jim realising they were really in love, necessitating some good-natured swapping of partners until the show came to its happy conclusion. Some critics wondered if *Sunny* could quite match up to *Mercenary Mary*, but any doubts were washed away in the surge of ticket sales. *Sunny* ran for 363 performances and its hit song, 'Who?', would become a classic, recorded by dozens of artists including Josephine Baker and Frank Sinatra; Judy Garland also sang it in the 1946 film, *Till the Clouds Roll By*. The show also received the ultimate accolade when Binnie's father Robert, appearing in the revue *C.O.D.* at the Duke of York's Theatre, sent up his own daughter in his burlesque of *Sunny*. "Mr Hale is funny as his popular daughter, Binnie, and Mr Heslop hits off very cleverly the comical, slack-legged dancing of Jack Buchanan," reported *The Stage*.

On the bill of Shake Your Feet were the Ralli Twins, in real life the Hon. Alison and Margaret Hore-Ruthven, aristocratic twin daughters of Lord and Lady Ruthven and members of the 1920s 'it' crowd, the Bright Young Things. Cecil Beaton was an admirer of their unusual looks, their, "large full mouths, high cheek bones, and knobbly noses… as decorative as a pair of Assyrian rams… dressed like fairies in a circus design by Picasso, with their dark locks tied with little tinsel bows, their spangled ballet-skirts, and low-heeled shoes." *Shake Your Feet* was the one and only time Alison and Peggy would appear in a major show. Family pressure led them to give up their dreams of stardom. Marriage beckoned, as it did to even the most outré of high-born young ladies.

The Hippodrome temporarily returned to revue at the end of 1927 with *Shake Your Feet*. The Hoffman Girls appeared once more to the Hippodrome; and Gwen Farrar, recently split from her comedy partner (and lover) Norah Blaney, performed with pianist Billy Mayerl. There was dancer Janette Gilmore, and comic actors Milton Hayes and Billy Merson with Jack Hylton and his orchestra providing the music.

The Five o'Clock Girl **opened in March 1929** and was the only Hippodrome show to feature the popular George Grossmith.

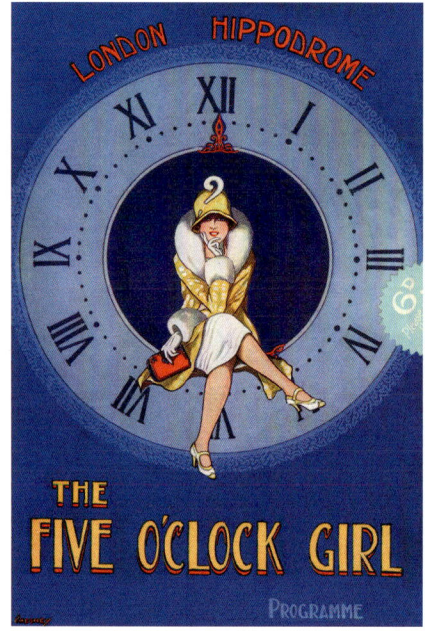

Frank Boor, general manager of the Hippodrome during the 1920s and '30s, hands his silk top hat to a bell boy on the first night of *Yes, Madam* in 1934. Boor began his career as an operatic tenor in the 1890s and was a member of the 'Mr. George Alexander Concert Recital Party' before moving into management. A genial and popular figure in theatreland, he was also a prominent member of the Stage Golfing Society. "The most immaculate theatre manager I ever set eyes on," wrote Gordon Beckles in *The Tatler* in 1951.

1927's *Hit the Deck*, starring Stanley Holloway and Ivy Tresmand, was unusual in that the core plot had the heroine pursuing the hero.

Father and daughter behind the scenes. Robert Hale and his daughter Binnie waiting in the wings, in the company of the production and stage director, Charles Henry, during a performance of the revue *Bow Bells* in 1932.

On 21st June 1927, at the annual Theatrical Garden Party, that year held at the Chelsea Hospital, 'Sunnyland' was recreated in the Hippodrome's enclosure, complete with cocktail bar, a flower garden, games of chance and a dance floor, on which dancers could sway to the tune of Geraldo's Hippodrome orchestra. True to form, the British weather did not cooperate that day and ironically, the rain drizzled intermittently on Sunny-land.

The revue *Shake Your Feet* was staged in 1927; *Hit the Deck* followed, a naval-themed musical starring Stanley Holloway and Ivy Tresmand, unusual in that the core plot had the heroine pursuing the hero, flipping traditional gender roles. But it was Jack Buchanan who would score the Hippodrome's next big success, with *That's a Good Girl* in 1928: a musical he devised, produced, choreographed and starred in. The book and lyrics were by his long-time collaborator Douglas Furber, with further lyrics by Ira Gershwin and Desmond Carter. As a home-grown show, it was instantly more profitable, with no hefty royalties due to the Americans. It was not without irony that Buchanan played Bill Barrow, an unsuccessful theatrical impresario. He also brought in Elsie Randolph as his co-star. She had already played second lead in a number of his shows, including *Sunny*, but this was the beginning of a more permanent on-stage partnership that was to be long-lasting, and much approved of by Jack's legion of fans. Randolph was a versatile performer; with expressive dark eyes and mobile facial features she was invariably cast as the comic foil to Jack, rather than the pretty ingénue who he eventually married. This probably mattered little to Elsie who was the undoubted female star of the show and at any rate was the one who was paid by Pond's Cold Cream to advertise their products in an advertorial called 'The Art of Being Captivating'.

The Co-optimists revue occupied the Hippodrome for a season in 1930 (during which time they held a party for the visiting Australian cricket XI on the Hippodrome's stage), before the return of Bobby Howes in *Sons o' Guns* – another American comedy, this time set during the Great War. He co-starred with Robert Hale as a man and his butler who join up together with inevitable humorous consequences. A revival of *Maid of the Mountains*, which had been popular during the First World War, was staged in the first half of 1931, followed by the return of Jack Buchanan and Elsie Randolph in *Stand Up and Sing*. With a vague plot centred on securing a contract for arable land in Egypt, there were inevitable sketches about dope and mesmerism, including a 'Dope Dance'. As well as its thirty-nine weeks at the Hippodrome, Buchanan took the show on the road before and after its London run, his pulling power guaranteed to fill theatres around the country.

Binnie Hale returned to the Hippodrome in December 1931, for another foray into revue with *Bow Bells*. Performing with Binnie was her father Robert Hale and Nelson Keys, although the press took an intense interest in Harriet Hoctor, a member of the glamorous Ziegfeld Follies whose beauty was carved into posterity by the sculptor Jacob Epstein during her time on the show. Next came *Out of the Bottle*, with cabaret star Frances Day in the lead role. Her suggestive shows at London nightspots like the May Fair Hotel and Ciro's, in which she notoriously wore very little, had sealed her daring reputation and bestowed sex symbol status upon her. She had also already appeared on the Hippodrome stage, in the chorus of *The Five o'Clock Girl*, and separately partnered with John Mills, just setting out on his career, in a double act called Mills and Day. A year before being cast in *Out of the Bottle*, Day had caused quite a sensation when

By the mid-1920s, 'Buchananism' had reached fever pitch. At the first night of *Shake Your Feet*, rather than performing, Jack was among the celebrities filling the auditorium. Florence Roberts, in her regular 'Fashions from the Stage and Stall' column in *The Illustrated Sporting and Dramatic News*, described the reaction: "And I need hardly tell you that countless eyes and opera-glasses were fixed on Jack Buchanan, who made his way to a gangway seat in the front row of the stalls to the accompaniment of loud cheers from his admirers in the gallery and energetic clapping from all parts of the house. He was, as usual, immaculate and attractive, and he was one of the few men to wear a buttonhole, his choice being a white gardenia." In the opening of *That's a Good Girl*, the male chorus entered with their backs to the audience, wearing top hats and tails. When the line turned around and it was revealed Jack Buchanan was in the centre, the audience erupted with a roar of approval.

Right: *That's a Good Girl*, starring Jack Buchanan and Elsie Randolph, featured on the cover of *The Play Pictorial* with a photograph epitomising the pair's natural comic partnership.

Jack Buchanan signing records for fans in the company of his *Sunny* co-stars, Elsie Randolph and Claude Hulbert. Jack's fan base was famously loyal. On the first night of *That's a Good Girl*, one enthusiastic gallery girl insisted on repeatedly shouting out, "Jack, you're more wonderful than ever." Two more well-known Gallery Girls, Nan and Dora, had seen *Sunny* eighty-four times, such was their dedication.

> **It was Jack Buchanan who would score the Hippodrome's next big success, with *That's a Good Girl* in 1928: a musical he devised, produced, choreographed and starred in**

Jack and Elsie's on-stage rapport was based on an intuitive knowledge of the other's strengths and weaknesses, and their dance routines together reflected this creative bond. According to Binnie Hale, "Jack was so tall and elegant and marvellously contrasted with Elsie – just the right height for him, so pert, lively and vivacious." It was a recipe for success, though any show starring Jack Buchanan could be relied on to do well. Caricature by Sallon in *The Illustrated Sporting and Dramatic News*, 1928.

"THAT'S A GOOD GIRL."
AN IMPRESSION OF ELSIE RANDOLPH AND JACK BUCHANAN AT THE HIPPODROME.

Stand Up and Sing ran for a total of 604 performances and was universally loved (apart from one critic who ungraciously dubbed it, "Shut Up and Sit Down").

In the cast of *Stand Up and Sing* was a young Anna Neagle, in her first non-chorus West End role. She was encouraged by Buchanan, who was always generous and supportive to his female co-stars, including those just embarking on their careers. She was spotted by Buchanan's film director and business partner, Herbert Wilcox, who cast her in her first film, *Goodnight, Vienna* in 1932.

Mr. Cinders starred Bobby Howes and Binnie Hale, another popular partnership that would be reprised for future Hippodrome productions. A role reversal re-telling of Cinderella, with Bobby as Jim, the downtrodden eponymous Mr. Cinders and Binnie as Jill, the heiress turned fairy godmother, the show transferred to the Hippodrome from the Adelphi, just as it was celebrating its 200th performance. Binnie Hale sang the hit song of the production, 'Spread a Little Happiness', recorded by Columbia Records. Listen to it today and although Hale's crystal clear soprano is old-fashioned, it remains delightfully uplifting.

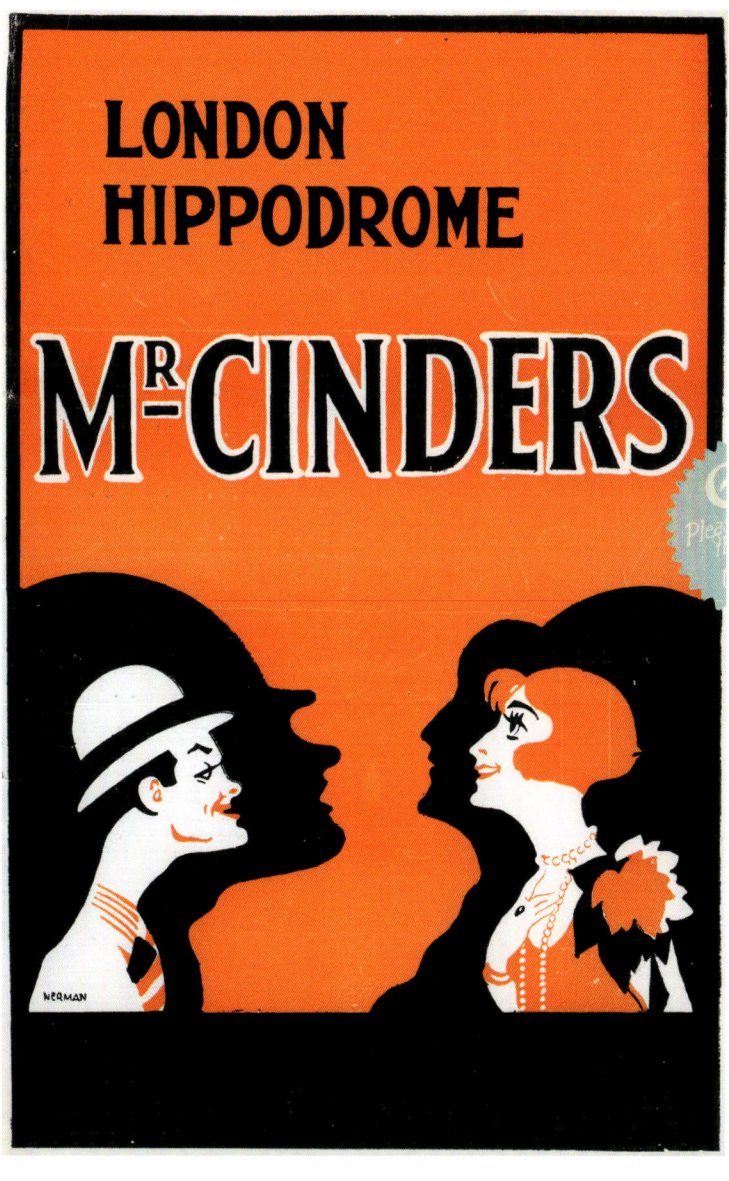

she arrived at the Hippodrome as a member of the audience to see *Maid of the Mountains*, "in a gown of cloth of silver, so closely fitting that she looked as if molten silver had been poured over her slender, supple figure."

A string of shows during the 1930s selected from the tried and tested pool of top-flight West End stars, including a number of Hippodrome regulars. Jack Buchanan returned for his final Hippodrome show in 1934 in *Mr. Whittington*, a modern take on the Dick Whittington tale. A year earlier, Fay Compton had taken the lead role in the actual pantomime of *Dick Whittington*; 1933's *Give Me a Ring* starred Evelyn Laye, dressed by Norman Hartnell for the show, whose cool and class were not deserving of a part as a "mere telephone girl", thought *The Bystander*. Among her co-stars were Flanagan and Allen and John Mills, stepping up the career ladder a little further after his stint at the New Cross Hippodrome with Frances Day. By the mid-1930s, Bobby Howes was dominating Hippodrome productions. He was reunited with Binnie Hale in 1934 in Jack Waller's *Yes, Madam* based on the novel by K. R. G. Browne.

Unlike Jack Buchanan, whose debonair dash had earned him adoration from female audiences, Howes was short and boyish. Women swooned over Buchanan; they wanted to mother Bobby Howes. After *Yes, Madam* he would appear again in *Please Teacher* (1935–6), *Big Business* (1936) and *Hide and Seek* (1937) where his co-star was Cicely Courtneidge. In most shows, he was ably supported by the comedienne Vera Pearce, who had appeared in as many Hippodrome musicals as Howes and whose larger frame always meant she was destined for character roles as wealthy spinster aunts or imperious opera divas. Invariably there would be a comedy dance routine between the pair, a winning combination due to "Miss Pearse being Zeppelinesque as to her figure, and Mr Howes being tiny", explained *The Bystander* in its review of *Please, Teacher*.

The pantomime for 1936 was *Mother Goose*, produced by Tom Arnold who was working under the auspices of the late Julian Wylie's company and who assembled a more unexpected cast. Florence Desmond was the star, in the role of Robbie; Chilli Bourchier played Jill, with Alicia Markova and Anton Dolin performing a ballet dance as a finale to the first act. The second act featured another star at the height of his popularity – Mickey Mouse, in a scene called 'Mickey Mouse's Xmas Party' by arrangement with Walt Disney.

By the time *The Fleet's Lit Up* opened at the Hippodrome on 17th August 1938, George Black was now joint managing director of the London Hippodrome (with R. H. Gillespie) as well as being credited as responsible for production and direction of the show itself. With control of Moss Empires Ltd. as well as the General Theatre Corporation and the London Palladium, Black was one of the most powerful figures in live entertainment, and would be responsible for the Hippodrome's shows until his death in 1945. *The Fleet's Lit Up*, a naval extravaganza, had Stanley Lupino and Adele Dixon joining the vivacious Frances Day and drew from the very best talent for its scenery and costumes. Erté designed costumes for some scenes, while Professor Ernst Stern provided costume sketches for the pirate scene. For the programme cover, the renowned poster and graphic artist Tom Purvis was drafted in. Accompanied by Geraldo's orchestra, Frances Day sang the musical highlight, Cole Porter's 'D'Lovely'. She had another hit song in the next show, *Black and Blue*, which opened in March 1938. Billed as 'George Black's Intimate Rag', *Black and Blue*'s producer was Robert Nesbitt, presenting his very first

The comedy musical 1920-1939

Two portraits by Angus McBean of the female leads in *The Fleet's Lit Up* are given his typical surrealist treatment – with a nautical theme – for the front cover of *The Sketch* magazine. Adele Dixon appears as a 1930s version of the eighteenth-century pirate Mary Read, whereas Frances Day is shown on the sea bed. *The Sketch* wrote of Day in the show: "She gives her usual delightful, elusive, naughty performance, and sings charmingly."

The Sketch

No. 2382—Vol. CLXXXIII.   WEDNESDAY, SEPTEMBER 21, 1938.   ONE SHILLING.

PHOTOGRAPH BY ANGUS MCBEAN.

PIRATE AND DICTATOR - RANEE : ADÈLE DIXON.

In "The Fleet's Lit Up," at the London Hippodrome, ADÈLE DIXON adds to the amusingly unusual rendering of the Dictator-Ranee of Zabolon a spirited study of Mary Read, the eighteenth-century pirate.

The Sketch

No. 2379—Vol. CLXXXIII.   WEDNESDAY, AUGUST 31, 1938.   ONE SHILLING.

PHOTOGRAPH SPECIALLY TAKEN FOR "THE SKETCH" BY ANGUS MCBEAN.

A DAY DREAM.

FRANCES DAY'S brilliant personality and vivid charm are responsible for much of the success of the new London Hippodrome musical play, "THE FLEET'S LIT UP," which is a big hit and is likely to run for months and months. Miss Day plays the part of Polly Brown, a character who goes through a series of chameleon-like changes, and is seen to great advantage in the part. Here she is somewhat surrealised as the centre of a strange seaside Day dream!

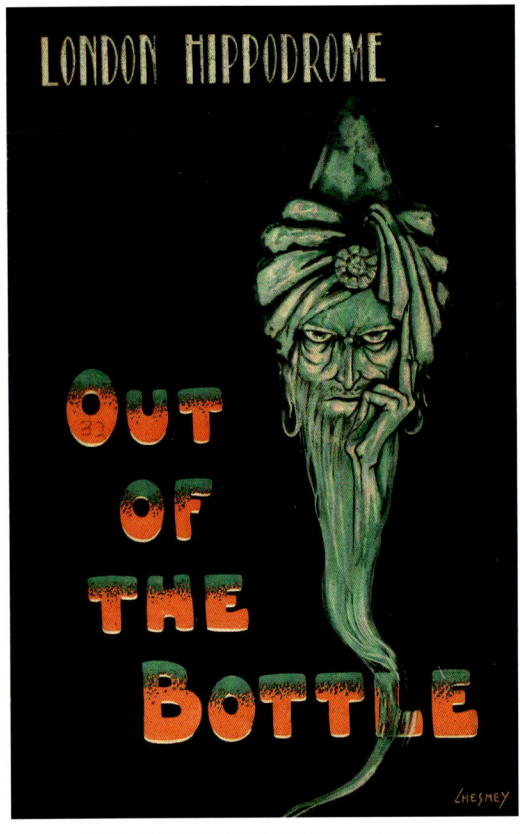

In June 1932, Julian Wylie was back at the Hippodrome as producer. *Out of the Bottle* was a new musical comedy, with book and lyrics by Fred Thompson and Clifford Grey based on 'The Brass Bottle' by F. Anstey, a story written thirty-two years earlier. Music was by Vivian Ellis and Oscar Levant. As the name suggested, *Out of the Bottle* was about a grateful genie who tries to help out his releaser in ways comically at odds with the show's modern surroundings; in one scene, a cocktail party is transformed into an ostentatious Oriental Palace and in another, the four main characters find themselves in the awkward position of being conjured into a bedroom scene together.

The artist drafted in to provide the exotic scenery for *Out of the Bottle* was Anna Zinkeisen, one of a rising number of female artists and designers working in a number of disciplines during this period, and through colour photographs printed in *The Sketch* of some scenes, including Oriental Palace, and the Kat's Kradle Klub (shown above), we get a good impression of how the show looked.

In what would become a career spanning nine decades, Sir John Mills (1908–2005) made one of his first stage appearances at the Hippodrome as part of the chorus in *The Five o'Clock Girl* in 1929. He returned to take the part of Jack Brookes, manager of the Porchester Hotel in *Give Me a Ring* in 1933. This brooding photograph appeared in the programme.

Far right: Evelyn Laye, elegant in a Norman Hartnell dress, enacts a love scene with co-star Ernest Verebes in *Give Me A Ring*, staged at the Hippodrome in the summer of 1933.

The 1930s introduced another innovation to Hippodrome audiences – the 'glowgramme' with its luminous text could be read when the theatre lights plunged the auditorium into darkness.

Frances Day, star of *Black and Blue*, on the cover of *Theatre World*. She was a dazzling presence, with feline features, a halo of platinum-blonde hair and a mischievous puckishness. "She was what in those days was what one called a knock-out," recalled Sir John Mills in later life. She remains an intriguing character. The toast of London in the late 1930s, she was remembered by Vic Oliver, her co-star in *Black and Blue*, as "one of the gayest and most volatile artists I know". She had a reckless reputation of arriving at the theatre with just a few minutes before she was due to go on-stage. Often she threw her costume on over riding breeches, and she had a 'photogenic complexion' so could dispense with the usual stage makeup. Off-stage, she was said to be generous with her sexual favours; among her alleged conquests were Anthony Eden, Denholm Elliott and several royal princes. Yet in her final years, she became a recluse, living anonymously in Maidenhead. When she died she left her house and all her money to a neighbour she barely knew, with firm instructions that there should be no publicity or announcement about her death.

> **She was what in those days was what one called a knock-out**
> Sir John Mills recalling Frances Day

show at the Hippodrome, beginning an association that would last over forty years. Day's breathily seductive rendition of 'My Heart Belongs to Daddy' was a show highlight, but there was much else to tempt audiences. Among the cast were Vic Oliver, who had married Winston Churchill's actress daughter Sarah in 1936, comedian Max Wall and a young starlet called Carole Lynne (who would also go on to form a close connection with the Hippodrome), and if Frances Day's singing had not fully seduced the audience, then a scene in 'History is Made At Night', where she appeared in a crinoline only to remove it layer by layer in a kind of Victorian strip tease, was surely bound to satisfy. Audience participation was also encouraged. In the show's programme the words to three of the rag's songs were printed under the encouraging instructions: "You know the tunes, here are the words – Sing Them with Frances Day."

But on 3rd September 1939, the singing came to an abrupt halt. When Britain declared war on Germany it would affect the British theatre far more profoundly than the previous war. With fears of immediate air raids, any places where large groups of people gathered were considered targets and the government issued instructions that all theatres should close. Frances Day packed up her kit bag and travelled to France to entertain the troops and, for the first time in four decades, the Hippodrome temporarily fell silent.

The comedy musical 1920-1939

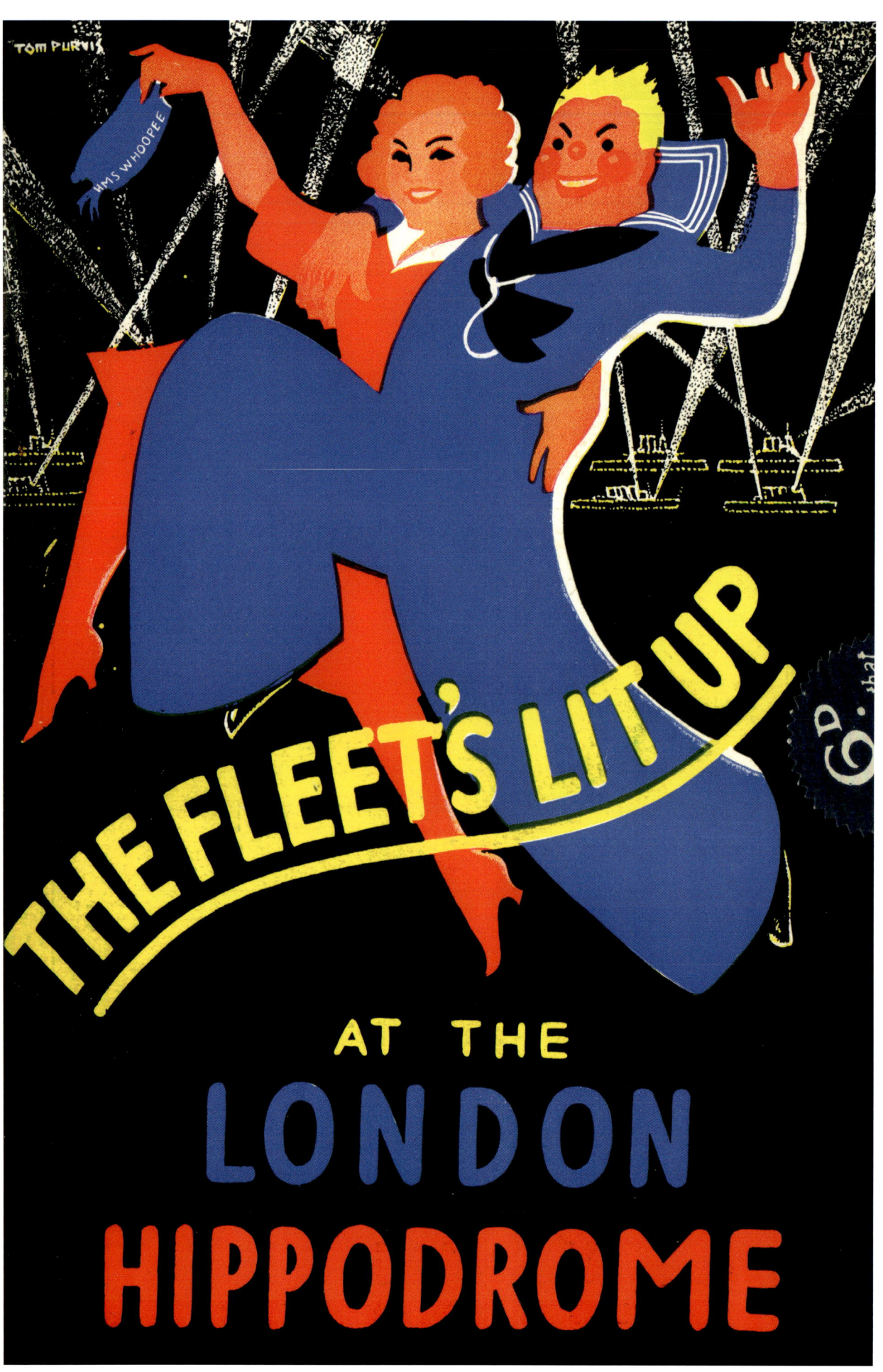

Programme cover for *The Fleet's Lit Up*, designed by the great commercial artist Tom Purvis. The show, a naval-themed extravaganza, opened on 17th August 1938 starring Frances Day, Adele Dixon and Stanley Lupino.

Dancers waiting to go on-stage during a performance of *Black and Blue*. Photograph taken by Tim Gidal for *Picture Post*, June 1939.

Pantomime at the Hippodrome

When Edward Moss opened the London Hippodrome in January 1900, his ambition was to offer a bill of entertainment that would appeal to all generations, including children. Pantomime, therefore, was an annual event on which Moss lavished a generous budget, allowing his stage director, Frank Parker, free rein to produce what was one of London's most splendid and spectacular Christmas shows. The Hippodrome's first pantomime, *Cinderella*, fired a salvo to the competition by boasting a fairy-tale coach lit with electricity and a glass slipper made of silver and Abyssinian brilliants ("more than possible that no living person has ever worn so valuable a shoe", whispered *The Illustrated Sporting and Dramatic News*). The following season, the Hippodrome's publicity campaign was working at full capacity to promote *Aladdin*, which opened on Boxing Day 1901. *The Illustrated Sporting and Dramatic News* again declared, in a statement brimming with superlatives, "This will be the most expensive version of the fairy story ever put on stage. The children will be delighted to hear that the wonderful Cinderella carriage of last year will be outshone by a palanquin of gorgeous beauty, and an Aladdin lamp which will in point of value and brilliancy far surpass the wildest dreams." To add atmosphere and ensure visitors to the Hippodrome that year enjoyed the full immersive experience, the Hippodrome was festooned throughout with Chinese lanterns.

In this first decade, Hippodrome pantomimes did not exist as a single show but instead were, at around an hour long, the highlight of a variety bill, which continued to offer the usual animal, acrobatic and novelty acts in support of the main event. Accompanying the 1901–2 production of *Aladdin* were fourteen new acts, occupying the stage and arena. And in 1908 alongside the production of *Honeyland* was a potted version of *A Christmas Carol* featuring Bransby Williams as Scrooge.

When Julian Wylie, hailed as 'The King of Pantomime', took over the Hippodrome's pantomime productions (as well as many of its revues) during the 1920s, the theatre's productions continued to captivate audiences with their extravagance and imaginative ideas. For the 1923 production of *Cinderella*, *The Tatler* reported, "The scene of the ball; the scene outside the palace; during which the chorus descend into a lake of real water and disappear; the last scene of all – these are not only costly, but extremely beautiful from the artistic point of view."

But a good pantomime is nothing without its comedy stars and the Hippodrome consistently secured some of the best names in the business for its season. In 1922, George Robey appeared in *Jack and the Beanstalk*. Although Robey was a legendary pantomime dame at theatres outside the capital, this was his first role in a pantomime on a London stage. He did not disappoint. "If laughter is good for the health, the Hippodrome ought to join the ranks of the other advertising patent medicines," wrote 'Jingle', *The Bystander*'s theatre critic. Likewise, when Nellie Wallace appeared as Widow Twankey in the Wylie-Tate production of *Aladdin* in 1921, *The Graphic* hailed her as a triumph for playing the dame "with a greater sense of grotesque fun than any man I have seen in the role". In the same production, Lupino Lane, who was renowned for his athleticism on stage, played the role of Pekoe and jumped through seventy-four traps in the space of just six minutes. Some actors, such as Clarice Mayne and Dorothy Ward, specialised in principal boy roles and were regulars in Hippodrome pantomimes, but other big stars often showed their versatility by dabbling in panto. Fay Compton appeared as Dick Whittington in 1932–3 alongside the comic actor, Leslie Henson, as Idle Jack. Florence Desmond was a multi-talented performer and impressionist, whose star was in the ascendent during the 1930s as she embarked on a successful film career. In 1937, at the height of her fame, she was cast as Jack in the Hippodrome's production of *Mother Goose*, bringing extra star quality to that year's show, not to mention impressions of Marlene Dietrich, Katharine Hepburn and Donald Duck.

> **The children will be delighted to hear that the wonderful Cinderella carriage of last year will be outshone by a palanquin of gorgeous beauty, and an Aladdin lamp which will in point of value and brilliancy far surpass the wildest dreams**

Poster for the 1901–2 pantomime, *Aladdin*, at the London Hippodrome.

Programme covers for *Jack and the Beanstalk* (1921–2), *Cinderella* (1922–3) and *Mother Goose* (1924–5). The pantomimes were all Wylie-Tate productions. In 1913, Julian Wylie had formed a partnership with the composer, songwriter and musician James Tate, who was married to singer, actress and principal boy par excellence Clarice Mayne. The pair produced numerous revues and pantomimes until Tate's premature death from pneumonia in 1922 at the age of forty-six. Wylie continued to produce under the Wylie-Tate name until 1931.

Ruth Lytton in the role of Dick Whittington, featured in *The Tatler* in 1903, with Fred Farren Jnr. as Dick's faithful cat.

Despite being a seasoned pantomime dame, George Robey's role as Dame Trot in the 1921–2 Hippodrome pantomime, *Jack and the Beanstalk*, was his first time in pantomime at a theatre in London.

Frank Parker's perfectionism revealed in this caricature by **Thomas Downey** in *The Illustrated Sporting and Dramatic News*, 7th February 1903, at the time the Hippodrome was staging its magnificent production of *Dick Whittington*.

On the cusp of greatness, chorus girl Audrey Hepburn waits in the wings during rehearsals for *High Button Shoes* in 1948, together with another dancer, Daphne Young, known as 'Blondie'. Hepburn had appeared in revue at Ciro's nightclub, but *High Button Shoes* was her West End theatre debut. She had just one line to say but it was enough to get her cast in a slightly more prominent role in Cecil Landau's revue, *Sauce Tartare* at the Cambridge Theatre later that year, and its follow-up, *Sauce Piquant* in 1950. From there, she landed a first leading role in *Gigi* on Broadway and by 1953, had been cast opposite Gregory Peck in *Roman Holiday*.

From blackouts to rock 'n' roll 1939-1958

Page from *The Daily Mail*, 28th November 1939, the day after the King and Queen, along with the Duke and Duchess of Kent and the Duke and Duchess of Gloucester, went to see *Black Velvet*, their first theatre trip of the war. Those observing in the audience were delighted to see the Queen teaching the King the words to one of the songs, 'Run, Rabbit, Run'. *Black Velvet* itself ran until August 1940 after which it toured around the country.

THE KING GIVES THEATRE PARTY

Learns Words of "Run, Rabbit, Run" from the Queen

H . . . H . . . . . (STAGE VERSION) CAUSED THIS ROYAL LAUGH

DUKES CELEBRATE THEIR FIRST LEAVE

By GRAHAM STANFORD, Daily Mail Reporter

THE Queen taught the King the words of "Run Rabbit Run" at the London Hippodrome last night when they went with the Duke and Duchess of Gloucester and the Duke and Duchess of Kent to see George Black's revue "Black Velvet."

Teddy Brown, 18-stone xylophonist, appealed to all members of the audience to join in. The two dukes—home on their first leave from the fighting Services—knew the words perfectly and immediately joined in. So—it seemed to me near the royal box—did the Queen.

But the King was not sure of the later lines, so the Queen leaned across and prompted, and the whole royal box joined in the chorus.

It was the most informal, intimate royal theatre party for years. The box was booked through a theatre ticket agency; the King and Queen were insistent that there should be "no fuss."

There was no fuss at all.

All the jokes—and some of them were pretty "blue"—stayed put. Vic Oliver cracked a couple as soon as the royal party arrived. And they rocked with laughter and settled in their seats.

"Patience Exhausted"

Vic said, "My patience is exhausted" when they wouldn't let him fiddle. The King—in the full uniform of an Admiral of the Fleet—roared with laughter, leaned forward in the box, and slapped his sides. The Queen wiped the tears from her eyes.

Vic said: "Commandeering! You talk of commandeering. They have commandeered my underwear for black-out curtains." Again the royal box rocked with laughter, and I thought the Duchess of Kent would never stop laughing.

And what about those Hitler jokes?

The Queen nudged the King and he leaned back and laughed when Mr. Jack Morrison—playing the part of Mr. Hitler as a masked intruder at the "Mystery of Information"—said, "Please I look for a job."

And we all joined in when this Hitler said, "I have painted and I have interior decorated too, and also I am a bit of a fiction writer. Have you not read the book 'Mein Kampf'?"

Altogether the "Mystery of Information' was a great royal hit. And the Duke of Gloucester particularly enjoyed that Vic Oliver crack when, chiding a subordinate for failing to censor "It's a Long Way to Tipperary," he says:

"Don't you know that is giving information away to the enemy?"

The Queen's Favourite

I know that before she came the Queen hoped that she would see some acrobatic dancing. She loves it. It was always a favourite of hers. It did me good to see her rock with laughter when Jack and John Bredwin gave "Achtung, Achtung, All Fall Down."

After the National Anthem had been sung at the end of the show there was a storm of applause in which members of the company, assembled on the stage, took part.

The King had turned to leave the box just before the cheering began, but the Queen, touching his arm, beckoned him back to make acknowledgment.

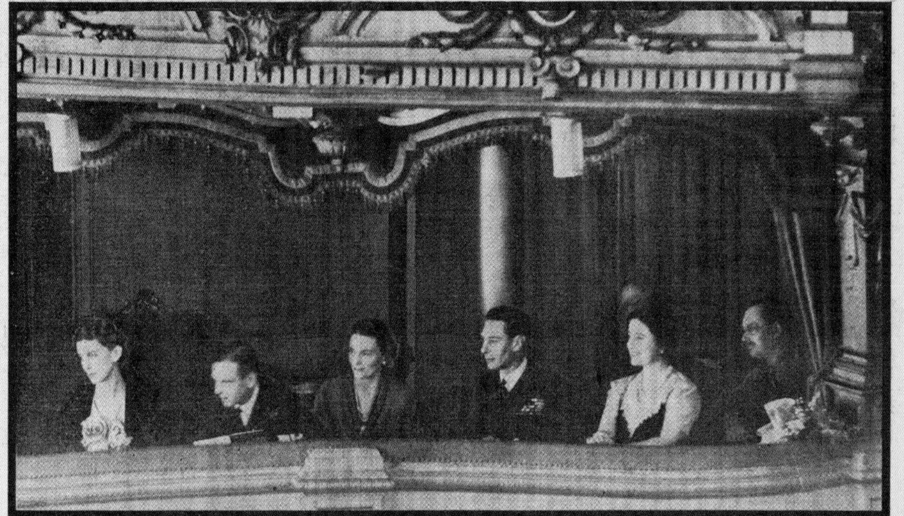

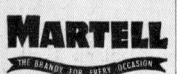

UNIFORMS and laughs in the royal box—seen by a "Daily Mail" camera at the London Hippodrome last night. The laugh—and the reason—are told in the story. During the show the Duke of Gloucester (right) wore these spectacles.

LADY BURGHLEY INJURED

By Daily Mail Reporter

LADY BURGHLEY, wife of Lord Burghley and sister of the Duchess of Gloucester, and a £2-a-week L.C.C. ambulance driver, fell and broke her collar-bone hunting with the East Sussex pack on her weekly day off last Saturday.

Her horse stumbled, threw her, and rolled on her.

The huntsman, Mr. Charles Lavender, jumped from his horse and went to her aid. He managed to drag the horse away, but was kicked on the leg

"Off Duty for Months"

Lady Burghley was taken to Chelwood Gate, Sussex, the home of Lord and Lady Donoughmore. Last night *The Daily Mail* was told that, although Lady Burghley was progressing comfortably, it would be several months before she could resume her A.R.P. duties.

Since the war Lady Burghley, whose husband is the athlete and M.P. for Peterborough, has done eight hours' duty daily with the ambulance service.

BOOKS FOR TROOPS

All books and magazines for the Army and R.A.F. should now be sent to the City of London Territorial Army and Air Force Association, Finsbury Barracks, City-road, E.C.1.

Brandy has so many uses

▼

MARTELL
THE BRANDY FOR EVERY OCCASION

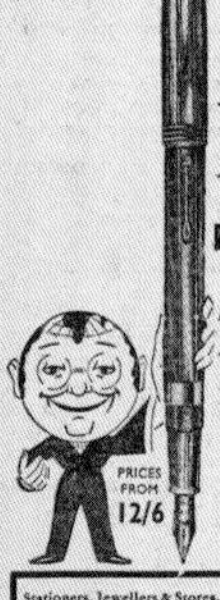

If seeking gifts appropriate for charming femininity, a Waterman's *will plead your case of "faithful to infinity".*

PRICES FROM 12/6

Stationers, Jewellers & Stores.
Waterman's Ink prevents Ink-clog.
L. G. SLOAN Ltd. 41 Kingsway, London, W.C.2.
Waterman's

Hibberd's Hindustani

Mr. Stuart Hibberd, the B.B.C.'s chief announcer, is to broadcast in Hindustani to-day at 3.45 p.m.

He is to introduce the first talk in Hindustani to be given by the B.B.C. It will be by Sir Muhammad Zafrulla Khan, in the overseas service, to millions of listeners in India.

Sir Muhammad, whose talk is "Some Observations on the War," is India's chief delegate to the conference in London between Dominion representatives and the Cabinet.

Mr. Hibberd learned Hindustani during his eight years' service in the Indian Army.

U.S. Club Wants the Quins for Duration

From Daily Mail Correspondent

NEW YORK, Monday.

Hawthorn Democratic Club, of California, to-day sent a resolution to President Roosevelt urging him to use his good offices to have the Dionne quintuplets transferred to California for the duration of the war, so that they would be safe from possible air raids over Canada.

The President has not yet replied, but Dr. Allan Dafoe, who brought the quins into the world, telegraphed: "The quintuplets are subjects of the King, and will take their chance along with the rest of the Dominion when the Empire is at war."

BLACK-OUT TO-NIGHT
4.25 p.m. to 7.11 a.m.

Sun rises, 7.40 a.m.; sets, 3.55 p.m. To-morrow: Sun rises, 7.41 a.m.; sets, 3.55 p.m.

Moon rises, 5.48 p.m.; sets, 9.39 a.m. to-morrow. Rises to-morrow, 6.52 p.m. Next full moon, December 26.

Lights on, 4.25 p.m.

Aged 4, She Tried to Save Boy

From Daily Mail Correspondent

BRIDGWATER, Somerset, Monday.

SHIRLEY YOUNG, a little girl evacuee from Bromley, Kent, who will be four years old next Sunday, jumped into a five-feet-deep stream of flood water into which her two-and-a-half-years-old brother, David John, had fallen.

She failed to help him and was rescued by another evacuee, John Henry Curtis, of Kennington-road, Becontree.

The children had been evacuated with their mother to Sutton Mallet, near Bridgwater. Shirley's father is serving in France.

John Curtis, describing the accident to-day to Mr. Leslie Rutter, the coroner for South-East Somerset, said he took the two children out in a pram. They asked to get out and walk. A dog with them ran into a field.

"I called the dog," said John, "and when I looked back David was in the water. Shirley went in after him, and I pulled her out. I picked up a stick and put it out for David to cling on, but the stick fell in.

Mr. Rutter: "Did Shirley fall in?"—John: "No, she went in after David."

The verdict was Death by Misadventure.

M.P. Rebukes Methodists

Mr. F. Seymour Cocks, Labour M.P. for the Broxtowe division of Nottinghamshire, received the following resolution from the Ripley Methodist Circuit Council:—

"That no person having children under 21 years of age should be allowed to be a licensee of any public-house."

He replied: "I consider that the resolution you have sent me is ridiculous and, by implication, grossly insults a perfectly worthy class of the community. I have no sympathy whatsoever with such narrow-minded views.

"In all reverence I suggest that your council should study the example of One who consorted with publicans and sinners and turned the water into wine at Cana in Galilee."

★ *IN ERROR*

The Board of Trade have explained that an asterisk was placed in error against "Baskets and Basketware" in a notice to importers issued on November 15, and that consideration would be given for licences to import these articles.

JACK PETERSEN HAS JOINED UP

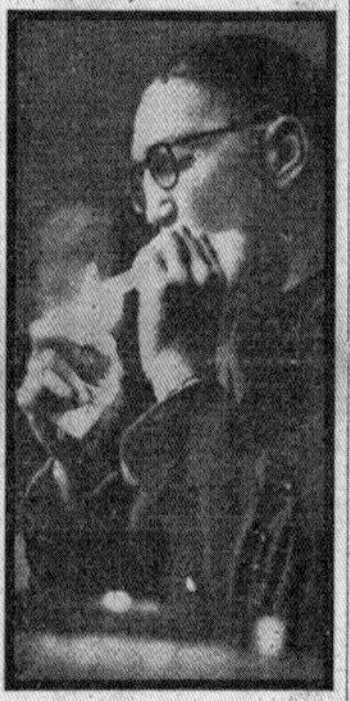

LAST night's picture of Jack Petersen—now an Army officer—wearing his uniform at the Empress Stadium, Earl's Court, where he saw Danahar outpoint Roderick over ten rounds.

MRS. BEST GOING TO FRANCE

MRS. MAY BEST, Dutch wife of Captain Sigismund Best, now a prisoner of the Gestapo, is planning to go to France.

She fled to Britain from Holland to escape the Gestapo, but now she wants to see if she can do anything to help her husband, who, with Captain Stevens, was kidnapped by Nazis on the Dutch frontier at Venlo, accused of plotting against Germany.

Resting in Country

Mrs. Best, who is still very distraught, is resting in the country at the house of friends. She hopes to leave England in a few days.

Captain and Mrs. Best were married 19 years ago and became prominent in the social life of the Hague.

Captain Best is a keen golfer and bridge player, a brilliant linguist and conversationalist. His wife is an accomplished painter.

When he first settled in Holland Captain Best became interested in the import business,

This work brought him into contact with many important British firms. He went into partnership with two Dutchmen and they acted as agents for a number of British goods.

Woman to Check Profiteers

EIGHT men and one woman have been appointed to check profiteering under the Prices of Goods Act. They will form the Central Price Regulation Committee.

The Board of Trade announced last night that the committee will be as follows:

Mr. Raymond Evershed, K.C. (chairman).

Sir Sydney Chapman.—Chief economic adviser to the Government from 1927 to 1932.

Mr. O. H. Forst.—Director of Messrs. Robinson and Cleaver, Ltd.

Mr. Joseph Hallsworth.—Industrial secretary-general of the National Union of Distributive and Allied Workers since 1916.

Lt.-Gen. Sir George Macdonogh.—Past-president of the Federation of British Industries and a director of a number of banking and other companies.

Mrs. Newman.—L.C.C. Alderman and member of the Woolwich Borough Council.

Mr. R. A. Palmer.—Secretary of the Co-operative Union, Ltd.

Mr. Ernest Evans Spicer.—Member of the firm of Messrs. Spicer and Pegler, chartered accountants.

Mr. W. S. Walters.—Chairman of the Fore-street Warehouse Co., Ltd.

Home!—With 14 Evacuees

A woman, summoned at Brighton yesterday for permitting a light to be shown at her house, burst into tears and told the magistrates that:

Her husband had left her for another woman;

Twins born to her three weeks ago were dead;

She had had 15 evacuee boys at her house and still had 14.

"They have broken up my beds," she added, "and when the prefect with them says anything they swear at him."

The summons against the woman, Mrs. May Welsh, of Beaconsfield Villas, Brighton, was dismissed, but the Bench advised her to see that she observed the black-out.

The woman explained that the light showed because one of the boys took a candle to a room not normally used.

'Murder on the High Seas' Charge

Patrick McGonigle, a 45-years-old seaman, was charged at Glasgow yesterday with murder on the high seas and ordered to be detained for observation.

The charge against him is that on October 19 on board the s.s. Delilian he assaulted a man and murdered him.

A COUNTRYMAN'S DIARY

November 27 The Singing Thrushes

The missel-thrush is a bold singer. There is nothing subdued about his effort, as in the case of the song-thrush, which at this season often seems to be singing for his own pleasure.

The missel-thrush has been said to shout his notes, an impression easily gained when he is singing on a wild, windy day and a fragment comes to you on a gust with a sudden vehement loudness when distance or the erratic wind softens or scatters the rest.

But he is naturally a loud singer, and we have been hearing much of him and his fellows as they have sung against each other from garden to garden and across the wet meadows these past days. All through this November both thrushes have been singing at least as much as ever I have heard them at this time of year.

PERCY W. D. IZZARD.

GIRLS SURPRISED THE BRIGADIER

A RETIRED brigadier, who said that his drawing-room had to be used as a bedroom, applied to Eastbourne billeting tribunal yesterday to have three schoolgirls moved from his house.

"We people who volunteered to take evacuees are the mugs," he said.

"I know lots of people with large houses at Eastbourne who have not anyone. Some of them are my friends, though I will not mention their names."

The Chairman (Mr. R. A. Gordon, K.C.): "We did not get as many children as we expected, so some people were overlooked."

The Brigadier: "I say nothing about these kids. They are very good except that they are difficult with their food. They will not eat fresh vegetables, but only things out of tins.

"Yet they have all put on a lot of weight since they have been with me."

He added that owing to the overcrowding in his home he found it very difficult when his son, an officer, came home on leave.

The tribunal agreed to move the children.

1889-1939

Married 50 years: Mr. and Mrs. John Baker, of Whiteleaf, near Princes Risborough, Buckinghamshire.

MEN OF COOL COURAGE . . .

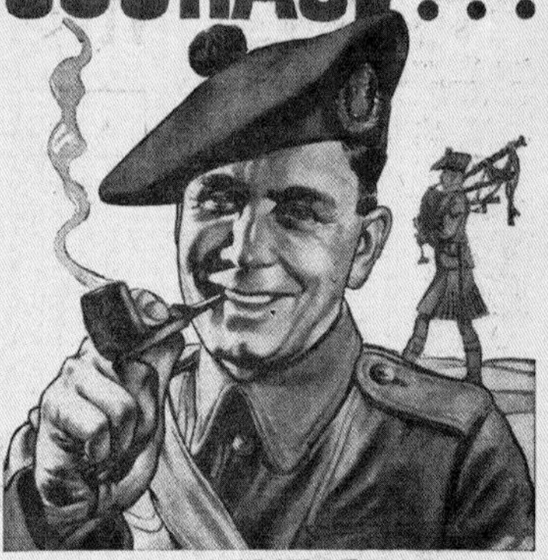

. . FIND BONDMAN THE COOLEST SMOKE OF ALL

In a world of surprises Bondman never changes. Tin after tin contains the same even textured, slow burning tobacco; puff after puff is clean, satisfying and *cool* from start to finish.

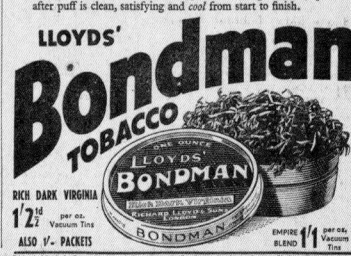

LLOYDS' Bondman TOBACCO

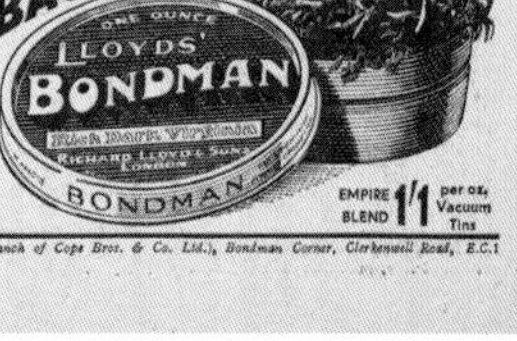

ONE OUNCE
LLOYDS'
BONDMAN
BONDMAN

RICH DARK VIRGINIA 1/2½d per oz. Vacuum Tins
ALSO 1/- PACKETS
EMPIRE BLEND 1/1 per oz. Vacuum Tins

Richard Lloyd & Sons (Branch of Cope Bros. & Co. Ltd.), Bondman Corner, Clerkenwell Road, E.C.1

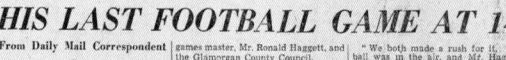

HIS LAST FOOTBALL GAME AT 14

From Daily Mail Correspondent

CARDIFF, Monday.

HOWARD BRINLEY JENKINS, a 14-years-old Pontypridd schoolboy whose leg had to be amputated after a football game, hobbled on crutches into a chair in the witness box at Glamorgan Assizes, Cardiff, to-day.

Howard, through his father, sued a games master, Mr. Ronald Haggett, and the Glamorgan County Council.

He began by describing how he had played football for his school and run in races at school sports.

Telling of his last game, Howard said: "We were playing on the concrete playground, and Mr. Haggett was refereeing and playing. We had been playing for 20 minutes when the ball dropped between Mr. Haggett and me.

"We both made a rush for it. The ball was in the air, and Mr. Haggett swung his foot, but missed, and kicked my right leg slightly below the knee. He asked me if it hurt.

"I said 'No,' because I did not like to say it did. I went to the line and did not play any more."

Counsel said the knee swelled and ten operations were performed.

It was denied that the football was under the supervision of Haggett. The hearing was adjourned.

Souvenir programme for *Black Velvet*, the Hippodrome's first show of the war, described as an 'intimate rag' but in fact serving up liberal quantities of glitz and glamour for a wartime audience. On the cover is actress and model Iris Lockwood wearing a monochrome costume in keeping with the show's title.

The theatrical impresario George Black (1890–1945), who controlled the Hippodrome during the Second World War, and collaborated with the brilliant producer and director Robert Nesbitt. Along with Nesbitt, and like Albert de Courville before him, he had an innate sense of what his audiences not only wanted but needed. Illustration by Molly Bishop in *The Bystander*, 1937.

"A master stroke of unimaginative stupidity." That was how George Bernard Shaw described the government directive to close theatres on the outbreak of war. The decision had been made with the best intention of protecting lives, but it also had inevitable side-effects on the West End economy and when the anticipated enemy action failed to materialise, rules were relaxed and theatres began to cautiously open for business again.

George Black was the first to re-open his theatres, the Palladium and the Hippodrome, and at the latter, he launched a new intimate revue named *Black Velvet*, a title that, like *Black and Blue*, referenced his own surname, but also the cocktail blend of stout and champagne. That it also suggested the cloak of inky darkness that had necessarily descended on blackout London was perhaps no coincidence. One of the show's songs, a tune by Harry Parr Davies, was 'Crash, Bang, I Want to Go Home', all about the increasingly familiar blackout experience. *Black Velvet* opened on 14th November 1939. "Just as there are shows for gallery girls, so there are also shows for girley boys," announced *The Bystander*, alluding to the show's unapologetic "song-and-dance-and-leg-stuff".

George Black's name was all over the Hippodrome's new revue but the creative force behind it was Robert Nesbitt. In many ways, *Black Velvet* was yet another typical review with pretty dancers, comedy sketches and catchy songs, but just as Albert de Courville's revues had offered escapism during the Great War, so George Black and Robert Nesbitt served up a superior dish of frivolity and fun during this conflict with a tasty side order of pure glamour, the perfect distraction from war's realities. Vic Oliver was drafted in as compere and anchor of the show, delivering an easy, good-natured patter and intermittently playing the violin. He was surprised to hear Black ambitiously describe his show as a luxury musical, at a time when most theatres were "reflecting wartime drabness with utility shows in which they risked nothing". Black had an instinctive grasp of what was required to lift wartime London out of its gloom and defiantly told Oliver, "I'm going to give the public colour, gaiety and pretty girls."

Among those pretty girls was eighteen-year-old Pat Kirkwood, who, on arriving for the first of twelve days of rehearsals, found everything planned out to perfection by Nesbitt and thought Vic Oliver a "suave and charming presence". To her surprise, she was selected to sing several solos including the opening number, 'Bubble, Bubble', for which Hartnell designed her a black velvet dress with white fox fur Cossack hat and muff; a fashionable metaphor for the drink after which the show was named. She was also one of four of the starlets who sang Cole Porter's 'My Heart Belongs to Daddy', one of the show's most popular hits. The first night was nerve-wracking for the young actress, not helped by her Hartnell dress catching on a nail on the stage with an audible ripping sound. Her response was to throw her head back and laugh, transforming the gasp of shock that had rippled through the audience into laughter also, and then tumultuous applause. The show was a triumph and Pat Kirkwood, according to the next morning's newspapers, was "Britain's first Wartime Star".

From blackouts to rock 'n' roll 1939–1958

Sketches by Rouson

Leading ladies: Carol Lynne, Roma Beaumont, Pat Kirkwood, Iris Lockwood

> **I'm going to give the public colour, gaiety and pretty girls**
> George Black

STARLETS AND SHOW-GIRLS OF "BLACK VELVET."

Eight super-lovely show-girls are included in the "Black Velvet" attractions. DAWN LAZARRE is one of the octet.

IRIS LOCKWOOD, starlet of "Black Velvet," is one of the most pictured photo fashion models in the country, and none brings her fascinating features and brilliant smile to the stage. She's known to the whole country as a thousand tea-shop "Nippy" advertisements.

PAT KIRKWOOD, Lancashire-born starlet, makes her début on the West End stage in "Black Velvet." She has appeared in North Country panto—was discovered by George Formby at a Newcastle Press concert, and became his leading lady in "Come On, George." She's had film experience, too, in "The Band Waggon."

George Black promises a "sparkling brew" in "BLACK VELVET," his new, intimate rag to succeed "Black and Blue" at the London Hippodrome on November 14. VIC OLIVER is one of the stars and is here posed with the quartet of starlets for the production—CAROL LYNNE, PAT KIRKWOOD, ROMA BEAUMONT, and IRIS LOCKWOOD.

ROMA BEAUMONT, principal starlet of "Black Velvet," was an Italia Conti Girl. Against advice she gave up dramatic study and joined a theatre chorus, but was proved right, for Ivor Novello wrote her in a special part in "Dancing Years," and now she's on the road to stardom.

ROBERTA HUBY is a beautiful young show-girl for the forthcoming production.

Left: And here is NORMA DAWN, another of the eight fascinating and beautiful "Black Velvet" show-girls.

Instead of one, well-known female lead in *Black Velvet*, five young actresses, described in the programme as 'The Starlets', shared the limelight: Roma Beaumont, Carole Lynne, Iris Lockwood, Roberta Huby, and eighteen-year-old Pat Kirkwood. For this clutch of young actresses, romance would blossom within the tightly knit network of figures connected to the Hippodrome. Roma would later marry Alfred, George Black's son, and in 1946, Carole Lynne married Bernard Delfont, a figure who came to play a pivotal part in the Hippodrome's history. Iris Lockwood, friend and muse of Norman Hartnell (who designed the costumes for *Black Velvet*), became Robert Nesbitt's wife in January 1943.

PAT KIRKWOOD

Pat Kirkwood, a sparkling brunette from Salford with two films already under her belt, had caught the attention of George Black after a pantomime appearance in *Cinderella* at the Theatre Royal, Newcastle. Summoned in front of Black, Robert Nesbitt and Joan Davis, the choreographer, at their offices, she was asked if she would like to be in a Hippodrome show and how much she thought she should be earning. She replied £25 a week, a slight increase on the £23 and 10 shillings she had been earning in pantomime. With that, the matter was settled. She was in the show. Pat and her mother "floated out into Leicester Square on our beautiful balloon".

Female members of the cast picking members of the audience to dance the polka down the central aisle of the stalls, a highlight of *Black Velvet*. In an auditorium filled with men in uniform, there is no shortage of partners.

Vic Oliver and the starlets of *Black Velvet* raise a toast with a drink of the same name.

Vic Oliver, the front man of several Hippodrome shows during the late 1930s and 1940s, surrounded by chorus girls from *Black Velvet*. Born in 1898 into a Viennese Jewish family as Viktor Oliver von Samek, Oliver planned to become a doctor until the Great War interrupted his studies. Instead he pursued his first love of music, studying under Gustav Mahler for a time. Multi-talented, he had an engaging and diffident comedy style, and soon found MC roles on stage that combined his presenting talents with playing the violin and piano. His fame rose further in 1936 when he married Sarah Churchill, the daughter of the future Prime Minister (who considered Oliver "an itinerant vagabond") although the couple divorced in 1946. As a high-profile entertainer – and being Jewish – he was among the 3000 prominent people listed in Hitler's 'Black Book' meaning he would have been among the first to be arrested in the event of a German invasion of Britain. Beyond the stage, Oliver had success as a conductor and radio comedian, notably in 'Hi, Gang!', and starred in a number of films. If a barometer of his fame at the time is needed, he was Roy Plomley's very first castaway on 'Desert Island Discs' in January 1942.

> **If an air raid warning be received during the performance the audience will be informed from the Stage. The warning will not necessarily mean that a raid will take place and in any case it is not likely to occur for at least five minutes**
>
> Notice in *Black Velvet's* programme

Dress design by Norman Hartnell for his friend and muse Iris Lockwood to wear in *Get a Load of This* (below). The Tatler described her appearance in the show as "the handsomest wench I've set eyes on for many a long day, does Mr. Norman Hartnell credit every time she enters in a new confection".

After a period of closure due to the Blitz in London, *Get a Load of This* opened in November 1941. Critics were divided about the show which had a gangster storyline climaxing in a sensational murder scene. 'Playbill', the theatre critic for *The Illustrated Sporting and Dramatic News*, found it "peculiarly crude and sordid... [an] orgy of murder, bullying, assault, blood and all the rest of it," and found it made him nostalgic for the revues of old starring Harry Tate. In contrast, *The Tatler* declared it "a triumph of ingenuity", reasoning that "the sub-current of brutality through the evening is, no doubt, in the spirit of the time."

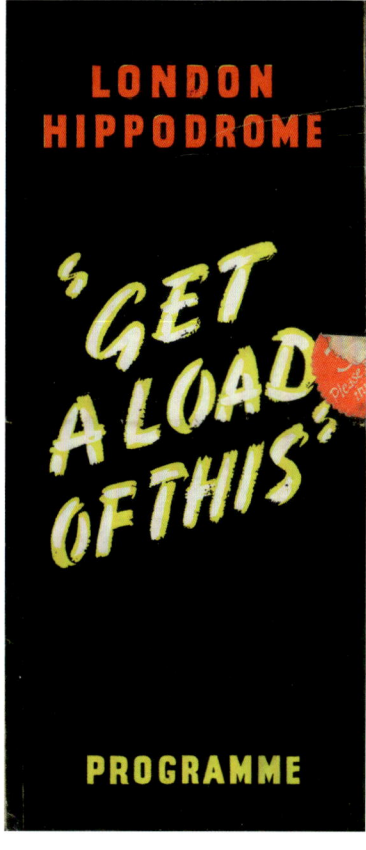

Black Velvet ("richly flavoured with the 'on leave' cachet – pretty girls" according to *Britannia & Eve* magazine) was a magnet for soldiers on leave in London. Every man must have hoped, as the dancers sashayed down the aisle among the stalls at the end of the show, looking for audience members to dance a polka with them, that they would be the ones to be picked, although Pat Kirkwood remembered the men who were there with their wives were more reticent about dancing. One night, the response was so poor, she and Roma Beaumont gave up and went back to their dressing-rooms for a cup of tea, behaviour that resulted in a fine from the Hippodrome management.

During air raids, *Black Velvet*'s cast and audience were often locked in the theatre together for several hours after a performance, and Vic Oliver would oversee an impromptu entertainment of songs, jokes and community singing, inviting audience members up on the stage to play the piano or tell stories.

"And I would accompany the eager amateurs on the piano or they would tell their stories – very badly, but very sincerely. The significance of it all was that we never stopped having fun, and with a seven-hour air-raid going on outside what more could we ask or hope for? As often as not it was 2:30am before the doors opened, and before long half London came to realise that a trip to 'Black Velvet' would mean a night's entertainment with as many laughs in it *after* the show as during it. George Black's calculations were dead right."

Black Velvet ran for sixteen months. With performances at 5:45 and 8:40 nightly, and matinees on Thursdays and Saturdays, it was a relentless routine for the cast. At the Hippodrome alone it clocked up a total of six hundred performances, and it was estimated around one million people had seen *Black Velvet* by the time it came to the end of its run. To celebrate its 550th performance, George Black and the Hippodrome announced they would be donating all admission receipts towards the purchase of Spitfires to be named *Black Velvet* and *Black Vanities* (the name of Black's follow-up revue, staged at the Victoria Palace Theatre).

Most theatres were forced to pause their activities at the height of the Blitz, which began in September 1940 and lasted until the spring of 1941, with the exception of the plucky little Windmill Theatre, whose by-line was, "We never close". Several theatres in London and around the country fell victim to the Luftwaffe, including a number of Matcham theatres, the Holborn Empire and Stratford Empire among them. In *Black Velvet*'s programme, the following notice was printed:

"If an air raid warning be received during the performance the audience will be informed from the Stage. The warning will not necessarily mean that a raid will take place and in any case it is not likely to occur for at least five minutes. Those desiring to leave the theatre may do so, but the performance will continue and members are advised in their own interests to remain in the building."

As air raids became more commonplace, people usually stayed put during shows, although writing in an article, 'The Theatre in Shadow' in *The Tatler*, Anthony Cookham acknowledged the difficulty of holding an audience's attention, "while they were being rocked in their seats by explosives". In such precarious times, theatre managers, led by George Black, brought in new systems for paying artists. Most headline acts were paid either a percentage of receipts or received part of profits on a syndicate system. In fact, once the Blitz was over

View of the Hippodrome's Royal Circle from the Stage Box by Walter John Bayes (1869–1956), done around 1940 during the run of *Black Velvet*.

In common with most London theatres, the Hippodrome closed during the worst of the Blitz. Mercifully, the building was left relatively unscathed by the air raids, but one bomb blast blew away hoardings to reveal a link with the past: original posters from 1900 (see page 12), flanking a larger one advertising Madame Arnotis, the strongwoman, who had been among the first acts to perform at the theatre forty years earlier.

From blackouts to rock 'n' roll 1939-1958

Perchance to Dream **ran for 1022 performances over two years.** Although this does not compare to the lengthy runs of West End musicals today, until *Salad Days* in 1954 *Perchance to Dream* was London's longest-running musical. The familiar design of the programme cover references the show's most well-known song, 'We'll Gather Lilacs in the Spring Again'.

Ivor Novello and Roma Beaumont in *Perchance to Dream* on the cover of *Theatre World* magazine. Roma played the lead female role, having risen in the six years since *Black Velvet* from starlet to leading lady. Adding to the attractions, Novello cast himself in the romantic male lead, although his character did not sing. He was fifty-two at the time but retained a youthful magnetism. With his dark mournful eyes and a finely sculpted profile, it is difficult to imagine anyone else in the part. *The Tatler* agreed, writing, "Ivor Novello is the soul of romance in every reincarnation." On VE Night, the Hippodrome played to a packed house, which cheered Novello and the cast for half an hour at the end of the show. Just a few weeks before Novello's death in 1951 from a heart attack, Noël Coward wrote of him, "The reward of his work lies in the indisputable fact that whenever and wherever he appears the vast majority of the British public flock to see him."

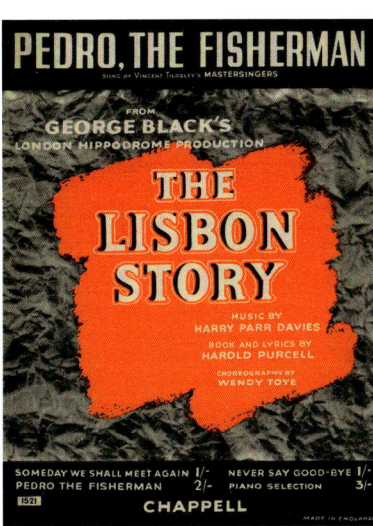

'Pedro the Fisherman', a song composed by Harry Parr Davies, was the big hit of 1943's *The Lisbon Story* and was famously recorded by the Austrian tenor Richard Tauber.

and theatre went through a boom period, performers found they were earning far more than pre-war days. With costs for everything from costumes to scene shifters spiralling, a coupon system was introduced where a producer would apply to a committee who in turn advised the Board of Trade on what was needed. Generally, the authorities were mindful of the morale-boosting role of theatre in war, so recommendations were accepted and the resources were found to keep shows to a high standard.

After a period of closure throughout most of 1941, the Hippodrome opened in November with a new musical, *Get a Load of This*. Written by James Hadley, the show was set in the fashionable Orchid Room nightclub, Park Avenue, New York, with tables extending into the stalls to give the audience an immersive experience. Vic Oliver, as Vic Vandyke, was once more in charge, and was joined by dancer Jeanne Ravel, teenage pianist and singer Celia Lipton, clowns, the Cairoli Brothers (a nod to the Hippodrome's circus days; they had also appeared in *Black Velvet*) and Iris Lockwood – "the handsomest wench I've set eyes on for many a long day, does Mr. Norman Hartnell credit every time she enters in a new confection" (*The Tatler*). There were two shows daily, one at 2:30pm and one at 5:15pm. Wartime theatres were keeping odd hours, mainly due to a concerted effort to stagger exit times, so underground stations were not overwhelmed at any one time of the day.

After the disruption of the Blitz, the Hippodrome settled into a pattern of staging a new show each year. Veteran Bobby Howes and Pat Kirkwood appeared together in *Let's Face It*, a fast-paced American musical with music and lyrics by Cole Porter, much resembling the romantic capers of the 1930s. In 1943, *The Lisbon Story*, billed as "a patriotic spy-drama", was the first time the Hippodrome had strayed from its traditional blend of light-hearted and amusing entertainment, which was "no bad thing", thought Philip Page in *The Sphere*, "particularly in these days when so many London theatres are littered with tedious revivals." He also admitted that the complicated plot with twists and turns featuring spies and Nazis in occupied Paris was almost impossible to follow, but it mattered little when it had a hit song ('Pedro the Fisherman' composed by Harry Parr Davis) and was beautifully dressed. Hartnell was again on board to dress the leading lady, Patricia Burke, while another high-profile London designer, Digby Morton, designed the suits worn by the principal ladies.

1944's musical, *Jenny Jones* starring Carole Lynne, was another unusual departure. Based on the stories of Rhys Davies, it was set in a Welsh mining town and its heroine was one of nineteen children who stages an operetta in the local theatre in a bid to prevent the local factory desecrating the site of an ancient abbey. In terms of style and plot, it sounds an improbable choice for the Hippodrome, a world away from its usual glitz and glamour. Perhaps the single most significant legacy of *Jenny Jones* was that its leading man, Ronald Miller, went on to become the speech writer for Margaret Thatcher; the immortal words, "The lady's not for turning," were down to him.

The cool reception of *Jenny Jones* was a minor blip, for in a few months, the Hippodrome would enjoy one of the biggest theatrical successes London had ever seen. Between the closure of *Jenny Jones* and the opening of the new show, the Hippodrome staged a revue starring 115 serving men and women of the Royal Canadian Navy, which proved to be a surprisingly rich pool of talent, including as it did members of the Montreal Repertory Company. *Meet the Navy*

Staff of the London Hippodrome, on the stage set of *Perchance to Dream*, pose for a photograph prior to the staff outing of 1947. The photograph belonged to Doris Benton, nee Bodie (seen seated in front of the column, third from right), who, aged twenty-two, worked at the Hippodrome as an usher. During her time there, she was delighted to have been selected to show the Queen to her seat during one performance. Doris moved to Canada with her husband shortly afterwards.

From blackouts to rock 'n' roll 1939-1958

Starlight Roof programme cover, 1947.

> **There was a hush – then the audience went absolutely wild. People rose to their feet and would not stop clapping. My song literally stopped the show**
>
> Julie Andrews recalling her childhood fame at the Hippodrome

Twelve-year-old Julie Andrews acknowledges the audience's response to her singing the 'Polonaise' from Ambrose Thomas's opera *Mignon*. A member of the audience at the time, Marion Clapson, recalls Andrews was a radio sensation and remembers going to see *Starlight Roof* aged fifteen: "Her range was phenomenal, amazing top notes and to me, she seemed a very small girl to have such a wonderful voice." Anthony Cookham in *The Tatler* commented presciently that "presumably more will be heard" of this "infant prodigy of trills". *The Sketch* called her "a demure infant in plaits with a sudden soaring jet of song".

Julia Wells, aka Julie Andrews, at home with her mother and stepfather Ted Andrews at the time she was causing a sensation in *Starlight Roof* at the Hippodrome.

Planted in the audience, Julie Andrews is invited on-stage by Vic Oliver (right) and balloon-modeller Wally Boag.

Maurice Chevalier performed his sell-out show at the Hippodrome in 1948 and again in 1952. Youngman Carter, who wrote the 'Limelight' column in *The Tatler*, was at the first night in 1952 and gave an honest appraisal of the sixty-year-old crooner's performance: "He is older, fatter, slower and he nurses his voice sadly, but his is still the greatest one-man show of his age."

felt like the familiar Hippodrome show: it was a novel idea, it was spectacular, and of course, it was topical. At the end of February 1945, the King and Queen came to see the show, accompanied by their daughters, Princesses Elizabeth and Margaret Rose.

On 21st April 1945, less than three weeks before VE Day, *Perchance to Dream* opened at the London Hippodrome, devised, written and composed by Ivor Novello, at the time Britain's most successful and sought-after popular composer, who had already scored a hit with the war's leading show, *The Dancing Years*. Set in a crumbling mansion, romantically named Huntersmoon, *Perchance to Dream* followed star-crossed lovers through Regency, Victorian and modern times, through tragedy and missed opportunities until eventually finding each other in the present day. With its lush production, abundant yet bittersweet romance and a score gracefully threading its way through the plot, it was exactly what London's post-war audiences wanted. Its most popular song, 'We'll Gather Lilacs in the Spring Again', had been written by Novello during the war and tested out while performing touring concerts for the troops. The lyrics by Christopher Hassall, full of hope and optimism, not only fit snugly into the show, but genuinely touched people, effectively stoking the hope and optimism of the post-war population.

"We'll gather lilacs in the spring again/And walk together down an English lane/Until our hearts have learned to sing again/When you come home once more/ // And in the evening by the firelight's glow/ You'll hold me close and never let me go/Your eyes will tell me all I need to know/When you come home once more."

In 1947, a new Hippodrome revue, *Starlight Roof*, introduced a twelve-year-old girl with an extraordinary voice to the world. Her name was Julie Andrews. Three years earlier, Julia Wells' stepfather, Ted Andrews, who performed a vaudeville act with her mother, had decided to pay for her to have singing lessons, and after discovering she had a real talent, began to act as her manager. Val Parnell was now managing director of Moss Empires Ltd. following the retirement of R. H. Gillespie (George Black had died in 1945 aged just fifty-four). During a chance meeting with Val Parnell at a golf club, Ted Andrews told him about his step-daughter's prodigious talent, and invited him to their home, calling Julie in from the garden to sing in an informal audition. While recognising her talent, Parnell was sceptical about the success of including a child singer in a sophisticated revue, but Robert Nesbitt knew star quality when he saw it and insisted on her inclusion. She was given a contract for a year to appear in *Starlight Roof*.

Each evening, one of the acts, Wally Boag, would model balloons and invite children in the audience to come to the stage. Planted in the stalls, Julie would be among the children. Vic Oliver, back in his familiar compere role, would ask her what she liked doing, at which point she would announce that she sang. It was clearly a set-up but once the little girl got on stage and began to sing the 'Polonaise' from Mignon, the audience were transfixed. In her memoirs of her early years, Julie Andrews explained the difficulty of the piece as, "a real coloratura tour de force, finishing with a high Fabore top C... I belted it out, leaping octaves and ripping off cadenzas and changes of key with bravura and dash." As she came to the end of the performance: "There was a hush – then the audience went absolutely wild. People rose to their feet and would not stop clapping. My song literally stopped the show."

From blackouts to rock 'n' roll 1939-1958

The original West End production of *High Button Shoes* opened at the London Hippodrome on 22nd December 1948 and ran for 291 performances. With music by Jule Styne and lyrics by Jimmy Cahn, the book was by Stephen Longstreet and adapted from his novel, *The Sisters Liked Them Handsome*.

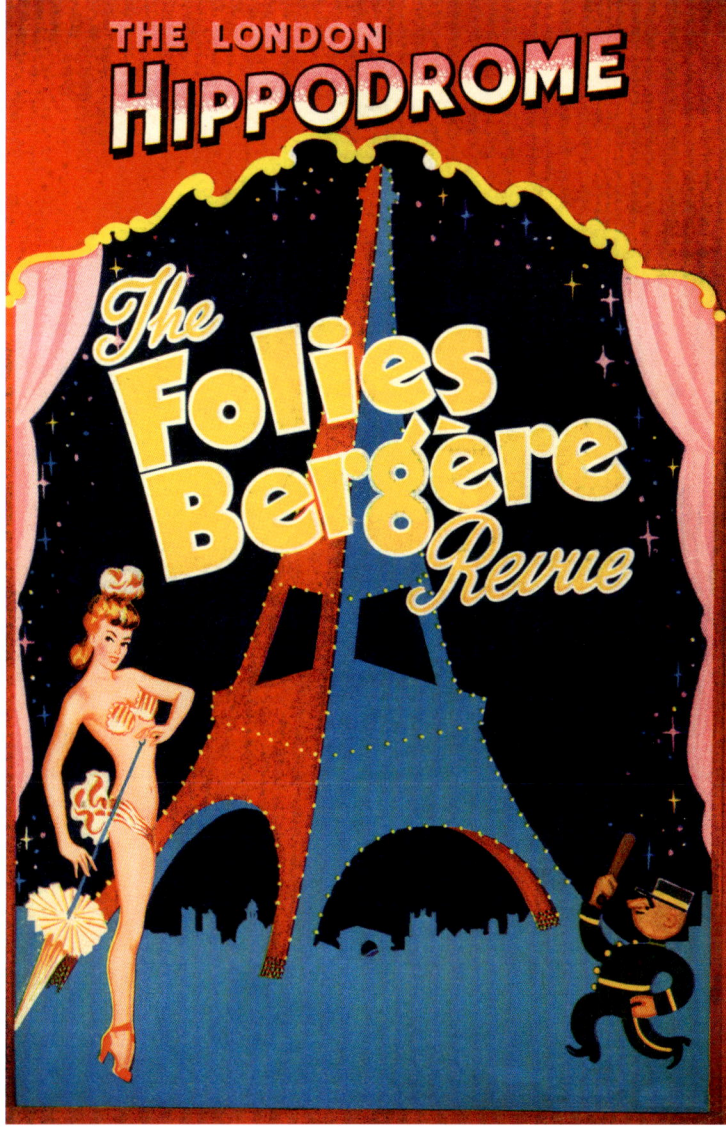

Folies Bergère programme cover.

> "It is speedy, extravagant, gorgeously staged, and, of course, chock-a-block with girls. Girls dressed as panthers, as ostriches, as candelabra. Girls wearing little more than a smile and a pair of cat's whiskers"
>
> The Daily Express reviewing the *Folies Bergère*

Julie Andrews adored performing in *Starlight Roof*. London County Council ruled that, as a juvenile, she should have a tutor in order for her to keep up with lessons. She was also looked after by a series of chaperones and because of the late hours, could not appear on stage for the final curtain. But she fell in love with the glamour of the Hippodrome, the magic of the production and felt at home among the talent. She admired Robert Nesbitt the producer ("a dignified gentleman with dark, brilliantined hair") and had a teenage crush on Vic Oliver. When it was all over, she admitted to crying inconsolably. The Hippodrome had been the place that had set her on the road to stardom.

1949 brought a new American musical, *High Button Shoes*, and other starlets on their way to becoming fully fledged stars. "A fast-moving and exhilarating entertainment," was how *The Tatler* described the show, with the recommendation, "if we are willing to drop the comparisons and to receive it as pre-Oklahoma and pre-Annie." *Oklahoma!*, the first of the new American musicals from the dream team of Rodgers and Hammerstein, had opened in 1943, beginning a golden age that set the bar high for musicals. Everything afterwards would be compared to *Oklahoma!* or *Annie Get Your Gun*. *High Button Shoes* was fun but was definitely pre-*Oklahoma!*. The show was more significant for the fact that among the chorus girls were Alma Cogan and Audrey Hepburn. Alma Cogan turned to singing and during the 1950s was Britain's most successful female singer, topping an NME readers' poll four times between 1956 and 1960, and appearing on television with Morecambe and Wise before hosting her own show. She would return to the Hippodrome, by now The Talk of the Town, as the headline act in 1964. Within a few short years, Hollywood had come calling for Miss Hepburn, transforming her from a chorus girl to an iconic film star.

One more musical, *Her Excellency*, starring Cicely Courtneidge and produced by her husband Jack Hulbert, ran for a modest two months before transferring to the Saville, allowing the Hippodrome to once again undergo a re-invention. Bernard Delfont, brother of Lew and Leslie Grade, was the ultimate impresario with a career spanning everything from agency work and management to film, television and theatre production, but up to 1949, he had suffered his fair share of failures; his first show at the Hippodrome was to mark his earliest commercial success. Delfont had ambitions to bring to London the famous Parisian *Folies Bergère* show, devised by Paul Derval. But he needed a suitable venue and set his sights on the Hippodrome. It was central, roughly the same size as the home of the *Folies Bergère* in Paris, and was, according to Delfont in his autobiographical account, "in need of a show". But Val Parnell, Delfont's arch rival, controlled the Hippodrome and would need convincing, especially as Parnell was well aware of how protective and domineering Paul Derval could be where his beloved show was concerned. But Delfont persisted. He signed up the designer Michel Gyarmathy, a Hungarian Jew whose talent was considered so important to the show, he remained working at the *Folies Bergère* in Nazi-occupied Paris throughout the war. With the director Dickie Hurran also on board, the show was planned to open at the Hippodrome after a trial run in Birmingham. Two thousand girls were auditioned for one hundred places ("We were looking for style and charm and beauty – and we found all three in abundance."). Delfont was visited by representatives of the Lord Chamberlain's office, keen to ensure the nudity on stage would be done in the best possible taste. Nudity was allowed, providing the girls remained completely motionless and wore a 'cache-sexe', the theatrical equivalent of a fig leaf. It was also advised that the

Gallic glamour in a format imported directly from Paris, The *Folies Bergère* continued the Hippodrome's reputation for the spectacular. Two thousand girls were auditioned for one hundred places. "We were looking for style and charm and beauty," recalled Bernard Delfont, "and we found all three in abundance."

Dancer Marqueez, befeathered and bejewelled, photographed backstage waiting to perform in *Folies Bergère*, 1950.

From blackouts to rock 'n' roll 1939-1958

Double trouble: Sally Ann Howes and Joel Riordan (Belita's husband) come down with a thump, and Barry Barczinski—one of the *Champagne on Ice* cast—dashes up to help.

Thump! But it doesn't take the smile off Terry-Thomas's face. Belita (*right*) helps Doreen Russell Roberts (*left*) and Al Earl (*centre*) to haul him back to the vertical.

Frankie Howerd can't skate, so no one knows how he was in at the finish of "Musical Chairs on Ice" with Lizbeth Webb!

Impresario Bernard Delfont has a lesson from Doreen Russell Roberts and Al Earl, both of *Champagne on Ice*.

His partner Jane Conlan is down, but Val Guest is making a valiant effort to stay on his feet.

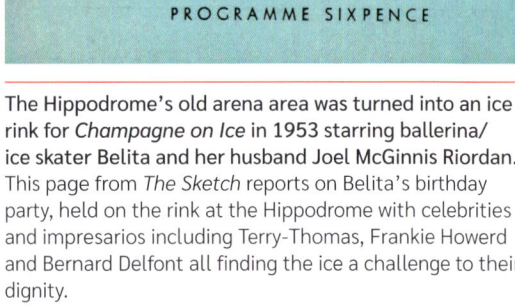

LONDON HIPPODROME
The Incomparable BELITA
Champagne on Ice
PROGRAMME SIXPENCE

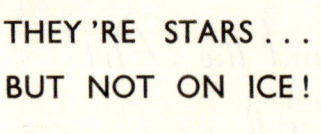

THEY'RE STARS... BUT NOT ON ICE!

It wasn't only the champagne that was on ice at Belita's birthday party at the London Hippodrome on October 21st. Stage, screen and radio stars, agents and impresarios "took the floor" one after the other—and most of them repeated the process every time they endeavoured to stand. For Belita, scintillating star of *Champagne on Ice*, had issued all her guests with skates. Apart from the cast of the show, the only guest who seemed to know skates from flying saucers was lovely Lizbeth Webb, star of *Guys and Dolls*.

Right: Belita holds a slice of her birthday cake for Lizbeth Webb to take a bite, while Mary Naylor, behind Belita, Bruce Trent (*right*) and other guests look on.

The Hippodrome's old arena area was turned into an ice rink for *Champagne on Ice* in 1953 starring ballerina/ice skater Belita and her husband Joel McGinnis Riordan. This page from *The Sketch* reports on Belita's birthday party, held on the rink at the Hippodrome with celebrities and impresarios including Terry-Thomas, Frankie Howerd and Bernard Delfont all finding the ice a challenge to their dignity.

Right: *The Blue Lamp*, a show based on the 1950 film directed by Basil Dearden, ran for thirty-two performances at the Hippodrome in 1951 and starred Jack Warner, who actually played Chief Inspector Cherry in the stage version but would famously reprise his film role of PC George Dixon (above right) in the long-running TV series, *Dixon of Dock Green*. The show ran from 1955 to 1976, with Warner continuing to play Dixon into his eighties.

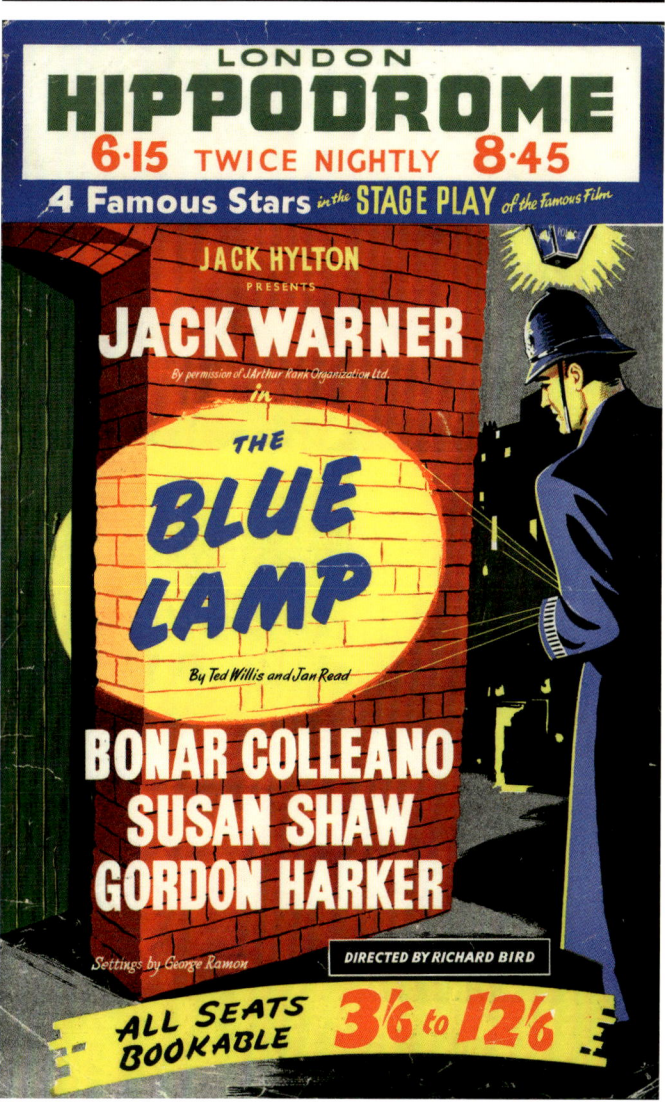

programme should not be entirely focused on nude girls. Therefore, for balance, Dickie Hurran signed up Michael Bentine (who had already appeared at the Hippodrome in *Starlight Roof*) and Tommy Cooper. "Who's this Tommy Cooper? Is he any good?" Val Parnell barked at Bernard Delfont. "Yes, Val. He's first class." "Well I've never heard of him," was Parnell's curt reply.

The show was coming together, but there were some set-backs. The costumes, sent over from Paris in crates, smelled so offensive when opened, an entire new set had to be made in a short space of time. And after seeing the show in Birmingham, Val Parnell dropped a bombshell by dismissing it as not good enough for the Hippodrome. Lord Delfont recorded his dismay at this decision: "My career and the livelihoods of some hundred and fifty performers and stage-hands were on the line." The only course of action was for Delfont to call Val Parnell's bluff. He allowed rumours to circulate that he would stage the *Folies Bergère* at his one remaining theatre, the Saville. Val Parnell called him to ask for a meeting. He had changed his mind. The *Folies Bergère*, presented by Val Parnell and Bernard Delfont, opened in October 1949.

With the *Folies Bergère*, the Hippodrome was spectacularly back to what it did best, although the number of topless girls positioned around the stage may well have caused Edward Moss and Oswald Stoll to turn in their graves. The press reviews were effusive enough to be printed in subsequent show programmes: "It is speedy, extravagant, gorgeously staged, and, of course, chock-a-block with girls. Girls dressed as panthers, as ostriches, as candelabra. Girls wearing little more than a smile and a pair of cat's whiskers," wrote *The Daily Express* with a nudge and a wink. "Gorgeous feast of girls and singers... extremely well-undressed show," said *The Sunday Dispatch*. "The nudes are beautiful to behold," declared Logan Gourlay in *The Sunday Express* with the air of a connoisseur.

After a British musical, *Bet Your Life* with Arthur Askey, Julie Wilson, Brian Reece and Sally Ann Howes in 1952, the Hippodrome looked towards France again for its next booking. Maurice Chevalier had already appeared at the Hippodrome in 1948, taking a month-long slot between *Starlight Roof* ending and *High Button Shoes* beginning. At sixty years old he had proved a surprising hit. "Getting Maurice Chevalier out of the London Hippodrome stage-door and into a car is an operation which makes the storming of the Bastille... seem quite gentle little skirmishes," wrote *The Sketch*, as it described the crowds of female fans waiting for him outside the theatre each night. More than thirty years earlier, when Chevalier was visiting London for the first time and trying to carve out his own career, he had stayed in a rather down-at-heel digs just opposite the London Hippodrome and remembered going to see George Robey perform, never dreaming he could attain such success. And yet there he was standing on the same stage in a critically acclaimed one-man two-hour show. This was indeed a Robeyesque level of success. In 1952, Jack Hylton brought Chevalier to London again, paying him £10,000 for a three-week residency. Accompanied by Fred Freed on the piano, Chevalier once again held the audience spellbound for the full two hours, mixing songs of old, mostly sung in French, with stories and anecdotes.

For most of its existence, the Hippodrome had had a well-defined brand of entertainment, from the circus and variety of the first decade, its revues through the 1910s and the comedy musicals of the 1920s and 30s, each period presided over by a producer who successfully stamped their personality all over the productions and

Anna Lucasta, written by Philip Yordan, was originally meant for a white cast but the American Negro Theatre Company in Harlem staged it, resulting in a long and popular run when it transferred to Broadway in 1947. It came to His Majesty's Theatre in London later that year. Isabelle Cooley's performance as Anna in the 1954 revival at the Hippodrome received good reviews.

Right: Rock 'n' roll came to the Hippodrome in 1955 in the form of teen heart throb Johnnie Ray, seen (above right) basking in the adoration of three members of his fan club on arrival in London for a two-week residency. Ray's blues-inflected songs and melodramatic stage performances were influential for a number of rock 'n' roll performers including Elvis, and guaranteed him a legion of adoring female fans, particularly in the United Kingdom.

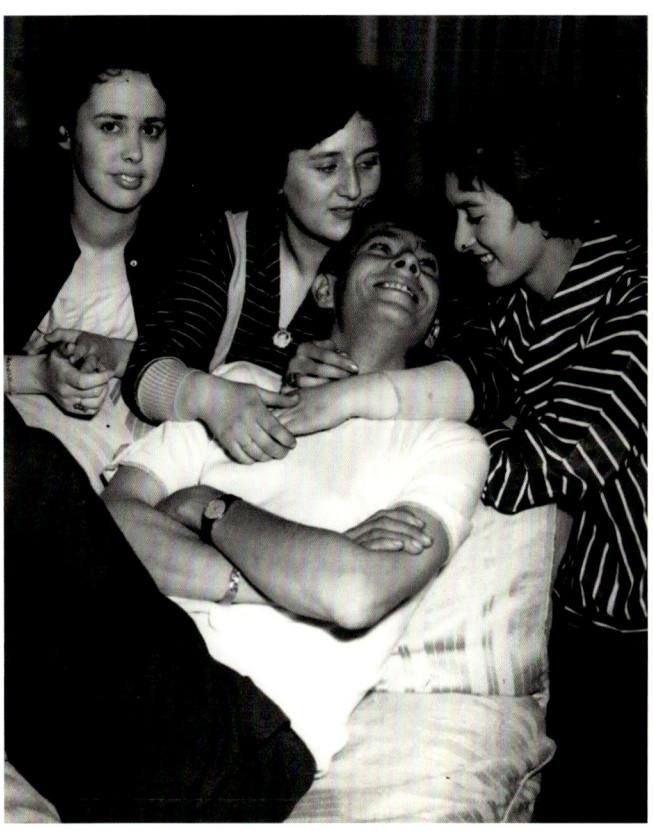

showed confidence in predicting their audience's tastes. In contrast, the post-war period brought what might be described as a mild identity crisis for the London Hippodrome. It continued to put on successful shows, but there were more acute fluctuations in the different entertainments on offer. As Bernard Delfont had recognised, rather than proactively blazing a trail during this decade, sometimes it was simply a matter of being the right-sized venue in the right place for a particular show. Through the mid-1950s it staged a series of light musicals, such as *High Spirits* (1953) and *Wild Grows the Heather* (1956 – based on J. M. Barrie's *The Little Minister*) alongside more serious plays such as *The Blue Lamp* in 1952 starring Jack Warner, a stage adaptation of the 1950s film. There were few flops – far from it. In fact, most productions had definite merit. But in retrospect, only some of them seemed to reflect the heart and soul of Matcham's building. In *Wedding in Paris* (1954–5), a British musical set on an ocean liner, Evelyn Laye returned to musical comedy for the first time in nine years, in what was considered a triumphant comeback. That was followed by a revival of *Anna Lucasta*, the story of a Brooklyn street-walker with an all-black cast. There were more thriller-style plays such as *Desperate Hours* starring Diana Churchill, and *The Caine Mutiny Court Martial*, which were well received but seem incongruous in their flamboyant host theatre. In amongst these productions, music and dance acts ranged from the Ram Gopal Ballet to Johnnie Ray, who played in 1955, to a host of screaming teenage fans. *Meet me on the Corner* starring Max Bygraves tapped into people's nostalgia for the Hippodrome (and its corner) and the idea of old London town, wrapped together in a variety-revue style which would have been more familiar to Hippodrome audiences.

From 1956 to 1957, another likeable TV celebrity, Dave King, hosted his own eponymous show at the Hippodrome, following a successful run at the Winter Gardens in Blackpool. Produced by George and Alfred Black (sons of George Black senior), King was joined by Shani Wallis, best-known for her role as Nancy in *Oliver!* the following decade, and supported by a cast of comic actors, singers and dancers. King himself was a versatile performer. He would mimic Bing Crosby when he sang and in later life, took on a number of serious acting roles. But *The Dave King Show* got off to a shaky start due to an unresponsive first-night audience who, when King asked, "Do you want me to sing?" remained resolutely silent. *The Daily Herald* noted how Shani Wallis "stomps the stage with less grace than a young elephant" and reported that King had quipped, "What's the name of this church?" in response to the audience's lack of reaction. During the run of *The Dave King Show* the matinee slot over the Christmas period was filled by a children's performance of Enid Blyton's 'Famous Five'. Blyton and her books were at the height of their popularity and the programme, packed with advertisements for Blyton books and merchandise including Noddy toothbrushes, shows that brand Blyton was cashing in on this popularity.

In July, a young woman who was making waves, not only with her hit single 'The Banana Boat Song' but also her glamorous, figure-hugging costumes and fiery performances, took to the stage at the Hippodrome. The critics were bewitched by Shirley Bassey, the 'Tigress from Tiger Bay', who, at the age of just twenty, commanded the stage and the audience as if she were already the veteran diva we know today. Shirley Bassey would have been a fitting finale for the Hippodrome, as the public of the past fifty-seven years knew it. Val Parnell, and the chairman of Moss Empires, Prince Littler, were beginning to wonder if the refurbishment the large theatre clearly needed was worth the investment. At the same time, Bernard Delfont

In the summer of 1956, the Hippodrome staged a children's matinee stage show based on Enid Blyton's popular series of books. Blyton herself was heavily involved (the programme contained countless advertisements for Blyton books and merchandise including a Noddy toothbrush!). Grazina Frame played the part of Anne and remembers the author seated in the audience wearing a smart navy suit. Performing alongside her co-stars was, she recalls, a delight. Grazina had an early ambition to perform and with the support of her family, attended Aida Foster's theatrical school, making her debut in *A Time to be Born* starring John le Mesurier in 1951. She would return to the Hippodrome, by that time The Talk of the Town, in 1969, to perform in Robert Nesbitt's *Fine Feathers*.

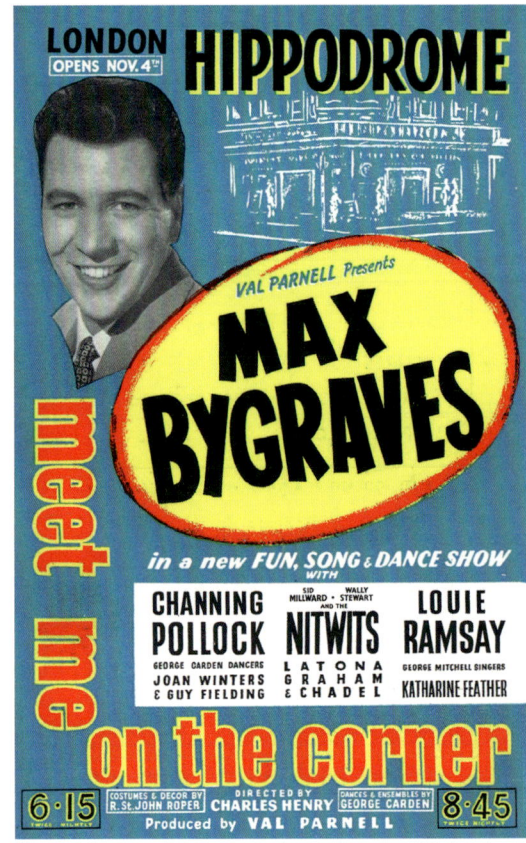

By the mid-1950s, the growth of television saw an exchange of stars between the stage and the small screen. "Mr Val Parnell is a showman who knows his business. What he gives the public is something appropriately big and dazzlingly bright, and part of the brightness he has come to feel, and probably with good reason, had better be a television star." Max Bygraves was that star, though he was helped by a number of acts including comedy musicians The Nit-Wits, Wally Stewart and his eccentric dancing, and the suave magician Channing Pollock, who kept pulling doves from "goodness knows where".

The Dave King Show, a revue starring the TV star Dave King along with Shani Wallis, ran at the London Hippodrome from 1956 to 1957.

Right: Cecil King in *The Daily Mail* was dazzled by Shirley Bassey, the 'Tigress from Tiger Bay', when she performed for the first time at the Hippodrome in 1957: "The clinging shimmer of her dress, the hungry stretch of her arms, the close, immaculate cut of her gold-tipped black hair and the blaze of her rolling, snapping eyes all fit seductively into a completely professional and ferociously vital act."

was developing a new business idea that had been fermenting for some time. The Hippodrome was just the kind of venue he needed and although performers continued to take to the stage each night, negotiations were underway for the building to change hands. On the final bill in August 1957 was Charlie Gracie, the rhythm and blues guitarist whose technique would be admired by the Beatles and other rock greats. Gracie's top billing offended Dorothy Squires who was also scheduled to perform each evening, so she quit the show in a fury. During this very public squabble, both artists obstinately refused to admit they had heard of the other.

Dorothy Squires would eventually return to perform at the Hippodrome four years later, by which time the theatre had changed beyond recognition. It would even be given a new name – The Talk of the Town.

Programme—Cont.

8   LES MALLINI   ...   ...   Knockabout Comedy

9   NORMAN EVANS   "Over the Garden Wall"

10   THE FABULOUS **SHIRLEY BASSEY** BRITAIN'S SEPIA SONGSTRESS

Shirley Bassey's gowns by Darnell of London

SMOKING PERMITTED

Next Attraction

AUG. 5th—For Two Weeks

THE 'FABULOUS' YOUNG AMERICAN SINGING SENSATION

CHARLIE GRACIE

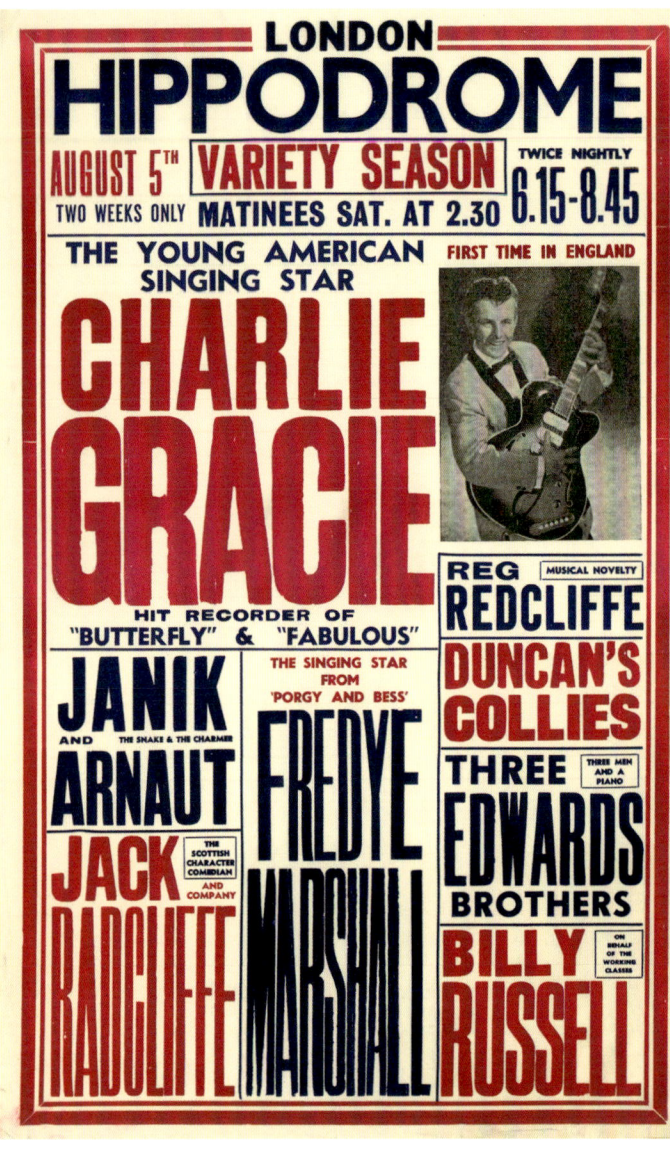

Charlie Gracie was the last act to play at the London Hippodrome in 1957 before it closed for its transformation. Gracie's top billing had infuriated Dorothy Squires, who was also on the bill, causing her to pull out of her contract.

Gracie entertains some of the theatre's cleaning ladies in a golden photo opportunity. He is recognised as one of the pioneers of rock music; Paul McCartney and George Harrison are among a number of musicians who cite Gracie, and his guitar style, as an influence.

From blackouts to rock 'n' roll 1939-1958   123

Fashion over the Footlights – Style at the Hippodrome

Ethel Levey in Hullo Ragtime!, wearing a stunning Lucile creation (1912).

There was a synergy between the worlds of fashion and the stage that saw some of the leading designers of the period create costumes for theatrical productions, a mutual arrangement which brought additional revenue and high-profile publicity to the designer, and an injection of glamour and sophistication to a show. Even during the austerity of wartime, the stage was one place where fashion fantasies could be played out; to dress leading actresses in West End shows gave fashion houses the oxygen of publicity and ensured a stream of well-heeled clients eager to sample a diluted version of styles seen at the theatre. From its earliest revues, the Hippodrome, always renowned for the lavishness of its productions, drafted in some top-flight names to dress its leading ladies. Ethel Levey and Shirley Kellogg in *Hullo Tango!*, and other revues around this time, wore outfits by Lucile, aka Lady Lucy Duff Gordon, at the time one of the world's most famous couturiers. Paquin and Redfern were two more designers credited with providing costumes.

During the 1920s, the couture house Idare et Cie predominated. Florence Roberts, who wrote a regular 'Fashions From Stage and Stalls' column in *The Illustrated Sporting and Dramatic News*, gave readers mouth-watering descriptions of costumes in *That's a Good Girl*, judging that "each beautifully staged scene has its own special fashion display". Elsie Randolph's gowns, one in hyacinth blue and another "of softly green chiffon with a coatee of silvery-green shimmering sequin", garnered particular praise. Reville, perhaps better known as a court dressmaker favoured by debs, dressed Ivy Tresmand in *Hit the Deck* as well as Binnie Hale in *Yes, Madam*, although Binnie also wore a gown by the Italian designer Elsa Schiaparelli – renowned for her daring, and often surrealist glamour. Frances Day was dressed by Jacqmar in 1939's *Black and Blue*, and in *The Lisbon Story*, Digby Morton provided the suits worn by the principal ladies. But the designer who dominated inter-war productions at the Hippodrome was Norman Hartnell, well established and much favoured by smart society, though further greatness via royal patronage was yet to come.

Even pantomime attracted some well-known clothing designers. In the 1936 production of *Mother Goose*, Florence Desmond wore costumes by Teddy Tinling (better known for his tennis fashions in the 1960s and 70s) and hats by Aage Thaarup, milliner to both the present Queen and the Queen Mother. Men were not forgotten; the Jermyn Street tailor Hawes and Curtis regularly supplied immaculately tailored suits for leading men, in particular Bobby Howes during the 1930s. It is interesting to note that for *The Caine Mutiny Court Martial* in 1956 all the men's shirts were instead supplied by a familiar high-street name – Marks and Spencer.

> *It frequently happens that women will adopt a costume or an accessory of the toilette, no matter whether it is becoming or otherwise, providing it has been worn by a celebrated person*
>
> The Tatler, 16th April 1913

Women behind the scenes

In a trail blazed by Lucile there were a number of women producing brilliant work in both costume and stage set design after the First World War. Dolly Tree (1899–1962) provided witty costume designs for Julian Wylie's productions during the 1920s including *Peep Show* and *Brighter London* before departing to work in America in 1926. There was also a woman behind Idare et Cie (Eileen Idare), a label that provided gorgeous contemporary gowns for the stage's leading ladies. Gladys Calthrop is best known for her collaborations with Noël Coward, but worked on *Dick Whittington* with Doris Zinkeisen, who, in turn, along with her sister Anna, was regularly credited for lending creative flair to Hippodrome productions including *Black and Blue*, *Mother Goose* and *Get a Load of This*.

Lucile, aka Lady Duff Gordon.

Revues frequently underwent a refresh, leading to a new set of publicity photographs of costumes and cast members. These costumes are by the celebrated designer Dolly Tree for 1923's *Brighter London*. Tree designed costumes for four other Wylie-Tate productions at the Hippodrome during the 1920s.

Dolly Tree in 1924.

Eileen Idare of Idare et Cie.

Norman Hartnell

Sir Norman Bishop Hartnell (1901–1979) was born in Streatham on 12th June 1901, the son of a publican. His talent for costume design first attracted attention when he joined the famous Footlights dramatic club while at Cambridge University, leading him to abandon his ambitions to be an architect in favour of pursuing a career in fashion. In 1923, with the backing of his father, he set up a salon in Bruton Street, London, showing his first collection the following year. Business initially came from the sisters and mothers of university friends but after showing in Paris where he pioneered a longer skirt length and earned good reviews in the fashion columns, he began to attract a wealthy clientele as well as a number of well-known actresses including Elsie Randolph, an early customer, and Evelyn Laye. Although closely associated with the productions of Charles B. Cochran and Andre Charlot, Hartnell had known Robert Nesbitt since he was a journalist for Fairchild's magazines and the pair were firm friends. He was frequently the designer of choice for numerous shows at the London Hippodrome including *Bow Bells*, *Love Laughs*, *Give Me a Ring* and *Let's Face It*. He also provided the costumes for Nesbitt's wartime revues *Black Velvet* and *Get a Load of This*, bringing a sense of romance and sparkling luxury in perfect tune with these most glamorous of shows. While designing for the stage, his career trajectory continued upwards. He was selected to design the wedding dress of the Duchess of Gloucester in 1935, which in turn introduced his work to the Duchess of York (later Queen Elizabeth, the Queen Mother). In 1947, he made the wedding dress of Princess Elizabeth, and six years later he created the new Queen's coronation gown, arguably his masterpiece. Despite his status as royal dressmaker, Hartnell continued to design for the stage into the 1970s.

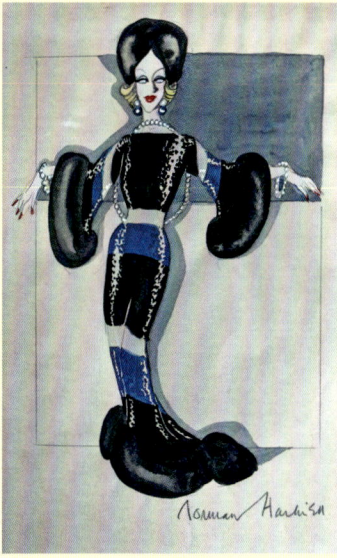

Original costume designs by Norman Hartnell for Iris Lockwood and (probably) Carole Lynne to wear in the wartime Hippodrome revues, *Black Velvet* and *Get a Load of This*.

Opened in 1958 after an extensive modernisation of the old London Hippodrome, The Talk of the Town offered evenings filled with glamour and good times in a venue that was, according to management, "the pinnacle of modern entertainment". This sparkling graphic interpretation of the venue's famous logo dates from the 1970s.

The Talk of the Town 1958-1982

From left, Robert Nesbitt, Bernard Delfont and Charles Forte toast their joint venture at the opening of The Talk of the Town in September 1958.

Artist's impression of the interior of The Talk of the Town, described as "vibrant and modern-minded" in its brochure. Guests could enjoy the full spectrum of fun on a night out, from the spectacular floor show and dancing to the house orchestras to enjoying a cocktail in the more intimate Topaz Room.

Left: *Illustrated* magazine front cover, 30th August 1958, recording the old Hippodrome's facelift and it's dramatic transformation into the modern, glamorous Talk of the Town, shortly before the venue's opening night on 11th September.

> "At the turn of the century, the first West End Moss Empire presented what was, in those days, a completely original type of show; today The Talk of the Town offers Londoners a form of entertainment that is unique in the history of the metropolis."

The Talk of the Town brochure, 1958

After the final performance at the Hippodrome on 17th August 1957 ended, the builders moved in and proceeded to demolish Frank Matcham's exquisite Edwardian interior. In its fifty-seven-year history, it had staged circus, variety, revue, musicals and plays, but now it was about to go through its most dramatic transformation yet and a drastic facelift was a necessary part of the process. The Talk of the Town opened on 11th September 1958 as a theatre restaurant; a venue offering the ultimate big night out comprising a meal, two floor shows and dancing to the in-house orchestra. It was new, exciting, state of the art and brought unprecedented, high-voltage glitz and glamour to the West End. Very quickly, living up to its name, 'The Talk' became the place to see and be seen.

The concept for The Talk of the Town was dreamt up by Bernard Delfont and Robert Nesbitt, who together had visited a number of London theatres before setting their sights on the Hippodrome, which was beginning to struggle for the first time in its history. But it had size, and potential for installing the mechanics that Nesbitt had in mind to help realise his creative ambitions for the place. Crucially, Moss Empires were willing to draw up a very satisfactory twenty-one-year lease.

Delfont had been involved in supplying acts for the Pigalle, a more intimate cabaret club on Piccadilly owned and run by Al Burnett where Robert Nesbitt produced the floor shows. Nesbitt, of course, had already scored successes at the Hippodrome with *Black and Blue, Black Velvet, Starlight Roof, Get a Load of This* and the *Folies Bergère* revues, as well as other popular shows at the Palladium. He had also spent time in America where the budgets were considerably bigger than in wartime London. In particular, he was pivotal at the Dunes Hotel in Las Vegas, where he was the first to introduce a new type of lavish floor show to a city that positioned itself as the entertainment capital of the world. Nesbitt envisioned this type of glamorous entertainment transferring to London's West End and knew what it cost to stage the best cabaret shows – he told Delfont the overhaul of the building would cost up to £275,000. Together, the pair hatched a plan for the Hippodrome. Delfont worked on the financial side, hoping to pique the interest of potential shareholders after receiving some well-placed press attention for the project, while Nesbitt made detailed drawings of how the venue should be re-modelled to suit his requirements. Joining them in the venture was hotelier and restaurateur Charles Forte who was so enthused by the idea, he put up the entire capital required. The project was green lit.

Looking back on the changes made to the Hippodrome sixty years ago, it is difficult not to feel a twinge of regret at the ruthless excision of the original interior. The plasterwork was removed, the gallery covered over with a false ceiling and the dress circle became a mezzanine dining area. Staircases led down on each side to the main

Talk of the Town 1958-1982

A feature of the West End for almost a quarter of a century, The Talk of the Town's illuminated façade became as familiar as the old Hippodrome, the still-visible chariot atop the dome a reminder of its former incarnation.

As the creative force behind the new venue's entertainment, Nesbitt was canny when it came to employing the very best backstage management and technicians to join his team at The Talk of the Town. Michael Haymen, previously at the Pigalle, came to work as stage manager, Ken Thomson was chief engineer, and for the music, he eventually brought in Burt Rhodes as musical director when his predecessor Sidney Simone departed. Billy Petch, a Canadian, was choreographer, already with an established reputation and a CV that included television work and several dance companies bearing his name. Tod Kingman, a top set designer, was responsible for the glittering stage sets, initially with Edward Delany who was already a veteran of many Hippodrome shows. Robert St. John Roper, who had been associated with the revues at the Prince of Wales Theatre, was in charge of costume design. Ensuring the front-of-house arrangements ran with the precision of a military campaign was the general manager, Lt. Col. Colin Gray, whose efficiency was as precise as his neatly trimmed and waxed moustache.

Diners watching the floor show from what had once been the Hippodrome's dress circle.

restaurant and dance floor and the stage was re-built to allow for a lift to rise up from below. In total, the venue could seat eight hundred. It had been given, concluded *Illustrated* magazine in a feature published not long after it opened, "the gaudiest facelift ever given to bricks and mortar". But Robert Nesbitt and architect George Pine had little time to be sentimental about a faded Edwardian interior. This was 1958. The old Hippodrome was a tired shadow of its former self and punters wanted smart, modern venues with all the latest technical innovations. Mid-century Britain was not always kind to its more ornate architectural past.

"Buildings move on," says Rosalyn Wilder, who worked at The Talk of the Town for two decades, from 1959 to 1979, as Robert Nesbitt's right-hand woman. She had visited the Hippodrome before its closure and saw Shirley Bassey's blazing performance in July 1957. She points out that at the time, the Hippodrome was no longer a state-of-the-art theatre, but it had the size and flexibility to become a state-of-the-art something else – an entertainment venue in tune with the times. The building had other benefits. The Hippodrome's structure, and its capacious water tank area, known as the 'elephant run' after some of its previous inhabitants, allowed builders to dig down and build lifts that would raise and lower the stages, an essential component of Nesbitt's vision. "The Talk of the Town hit London at *exactly* the right moment," Rosalyn explains. "Top cabaret artists were available and there were deals to be done." For much of its existence, The Talk of the Town's annual schedule tended towards American acts during the summer months, with British performers over the winter period. For those stars travelling to the UK, a two- or three-week residency could coincide conveniently with doing the Sunday night show at the Palladium, appearing on popular television shows and fitting in other engagements, which altogether made the trip worthwhile. The pay was nothing to write home about, but artists who performed at The Talk of the Town were aware of the prestige associated with the place. And they were treated very well, not least because of the Hippodrome's excellent orchestra, headed, for most of the venue's life span, by Burt Rhodes. If stars wanted to bring in extra musicians, the Hippodrome's musical director would smoothly adapt to their requirements. And he was adept at writing orchestral arrangements to any score, often at painfully short notice.

Rosalyn, who had started work aged sixteen in 1955 at ABC television, had then moved to working for Lew and Leslie Grade, the older and younger brothers of Bernard Delfont. While there, she was told, "Bob Nesbitt wants someone to do his office while his secretary has a baby." She went along, and, despite confessing she had no experience of either typing or switchboards, was given the job, and stayed for the next twenty years in a role that required her to have a working knowledge of every aspect of The Talk of the Town, from artist liaison and planning royal visits to stage cues and backstage mechanics. Working closely with Robert Nesbitt, she had the privilege of witnessing his genius first-hand. He was, she confirmed, "one of the most visionary men of the era".

Behind his old-fashioned charm and panache was an innovator who knew how modern technology could be harnessed and pushed to give the ultimate spectacle. Stage technicians were a vital part of The Talk of the Town's productions, ensuring lights and smooth transitions enhanced the glamorous costumes and sets. Between them, stage director Michael Haymen and the chief engineer, Ken Thomson, headed up an expert team who worked control panels that remotely operated stage curtains, lifts, slides and bridges, all at a flick of a

"The Pinnacle of Modern Entertainment" – The Talk of the Town's colour brochures fizzed with glitz, energy and optimism, reflecting the glamour of the shows, the costumes, sets and beautiful girls.

Grazina Frame at the time she starred in *Fine Feathers* at The Talk of the Town in 1968–9. Grazina's association with the venue stretched back to 1956 when, as a teenager, she had appeared in the role of Anne in *The Famous Five* at the Hippodrome. One of Robert Nesbitt's favourite leading ladies, by the time of *Fine Feathers*, Grazina was a fully-fledged West End star having appeared in *Blitz!* in 1962. She had also starred in several films and sung with Cliff Richard on hits including 'The Young Ones'.

> **Princess Margaret stood in the foyer, tapping her feet. A table was found, and a free bottle of wine was discreetly offered to the guests who had kindly cooperated**

With its reputation for glamour and top-flight entertainment, The Talk of the Town frequently attracted a starry clientele with many famous regulars among the audience. Joan Collins and husband Anthony Newley are pictured at The Talk of the Town, 18th May 1962. Performing that night was Lisa Kirk, the Broadway musical star.

The Talk of the Town's opening show paid tribute to the Hippodrome's glorious past with sketches that were a modern interpretation of its landmark moments including the grand opening in 1900 and its first water burlesque, 'Giddy Ostend', as well as the arrival of ragtime and jazz.

Trisha Money, sultry and sizzling in *High Life* in 1963.

switch. A six-way talk-back sound system allowed communication between different parts of the building, from the lighting operators to the dressing rooms. Two more panels, one for lighting and another for sound, controlled 176 lighting lanterns and fifteen microphones and thirty-four loudspeakers, respectively. By twenty-first century standards, this equipment has the quaint, primitive appearance of a console from a 1950s science-fiction TV show, but it had come on leaps and bounds from its predecessor, an adapted Wurlitzer organ, used at the Hippodrome, the Stoll Theatre and the Palladium. For the time, these consoles were sophisticated pieces of equipment, putting The Talk of the Town at the forefront of modern stagecraft innovation.

What then, could guests expect during an evening at The Talk of the Town? The entertainment on offer was a glamorous, slickly produced revue show, split into two parts, one at 9:15pm and the next at 11:15pm; the big cabaret star slot would be introduced two years later, in 1960. The old Hippodrome may have been gutted and modernised beyond recognition, but those first shows paid tribute to its heritage, with dance and music sketches giving a potted history of the past five decades, including the opening of the Hippodrome in 1900, and a spicy scene recalling the first water spectacle, 'Giddy Ostend', with dancer Jean Muir taking centre stage and disrobing to reveal a corset and black stockings. Steve Arlen and 'the girls' performed *Hullo Ragtime!* and Maggie Fitzgibbon was a dancing flapper for 'The Jazz Age' with, at one point, the looming and unmistakable figure of jazz band leader Paul Whiteman forming part of the scenery. There was a set-piece homage to the comedy musical era and Valerie Walsh, later to have a career as a TV comedy actress, even sang the popular Hippodrome tune of the war years, 'My Heart Belongs to Daddy'.

The Talk of the Town boasted two orchestras in those early days: Geraldo's Orchestra (with the famous Geraldo in an advisory capacity, leaving Harold Collins to conduct), and the Hermanos Deniz Caribbean Latin-American orchestra. After the show, the two orchestras combined to play a 'Cha-Cha-Rama', at which point the apron stage used for the show would lower, and diners could take to the dance floor. As well as the floor shows in the best Nesbitt tradition, there was the food, described as "international-classic as prescribed by Escoffier and Savarin", served with well-drilled and unobtrusive efficiency by a cohort of one hundred waiters. Dishes were classic with a touch of luxe; smoked salmon, Normandy pâté, or clear turtle soup for starters, steaks and salmon for mains, while Beluga caviar, prawn cocktail, parma ham or the exotic-sounding avocado pear vinaigrette were charged as extra. This was a night out to remember, an occasion to dress up, to splash out, drink in the glamour, dance the night away, and enjoy what The Talk of the Town's management called "the pinnacle of modern entertainment".

In September 1960, The Talk of the Town's show format changed as a succession of major stars were introduced into Nesbitt's lavish show in what became known as the 'star slot' of each evening's entertainment. Eartha Kitt had the honour of being the first headliner, beginning her eight-week residency at The Talk of the Town in style by making a grand entrance in a Rolls-Royce which rose up onto the stage via the lift system. Edward Goring in *The Daily Mail* reported that Eartha Kitt's debut at The Talk of the Town, at reputedly £1,000 a week was, "the latest salvo in the new battle of West End night-spots". Douglas Sutherland in *The Tatler*'s 'Going Places Late' column decided that if forced to choose, he would opt for The Talk of the Town, "as much for gastronomic as artistic considerations". He considered it a more wallet-friendly option: "There you can have a

An army of chefs preparing chicken for diners in 1959.

Illustrations in the programme echoed the décor of The Talk of the Town which, it claimed, "strike[s] an entirely new note in contemporary decoration". In parts of the venue, including the vestibule, and across The Talk of the Town's marketing material, a motif of a glamorous woman on the phone alongside a cockatoo emphasised the notion that this new, glitzy venue would indeed live up to its name, and everybody would be talking about it. The resulting brand image took its cue from some real live cockatoos in a cage in the foyer, by the entrance to the auditorium.

In 1960, The Talk of the Town introduced a star slot, with internationally renowned entertainers engaged to perform for between two and four weeks; Eartha Kitt was the first. Declared by Orson Welles as "the world's most exciting woman", a byline pounced on by the press, she was interviewed by Neville Nisse for *The Stage*, whose report described her lounging with ease on the long settee in the manager's office at The Talk of the Town, while Lt. Col. Colin Gray fetched her a "cup of English tea". She had first performed in London in 1948 with the Katherine Dunham Dancers, brought over from America by Val Parnell and Robert Nesbitt, and more recently had appeared on *Sunday Night at the Palladium* and on the bill at the Royal Variety Performance. Bernard Delfont had booked her just as her star was reaching its zenith, but also at the same time Shirley Bassey was appearing at the Pigalle, provoking some speculation in the press about rivalry between the two venues.

Talk of the Town programme from September 1960, introducing Eartha Kitt in what was "her first engagement in London for five years".

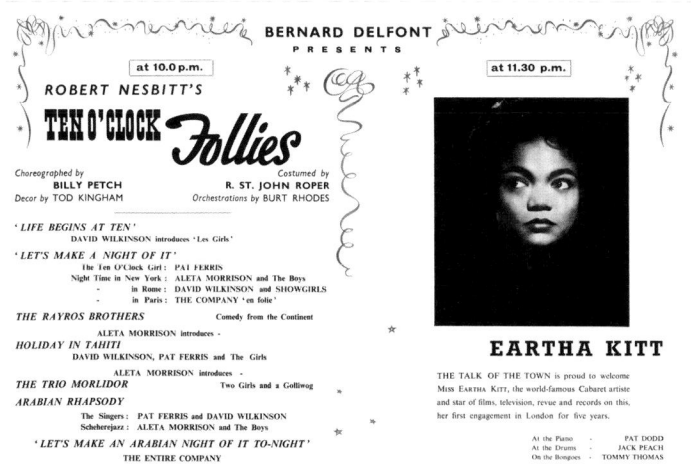

three-course dinner and a five-and-a-half hour entertainment for 47s. 6d a head. The cabaret starts at 10pm with 45 minutes of the Follies followed by 45 minutes of Eartha Kitt. You can then dance until 1:30am." He neglected to mention the added attraction of the Topaz Room, the "ideal rendezvous for cocktails" according to the in-house brochure. A night at The Talk of the Town was not particularly cheap, but it was excellent value for money. It was, according to *Illustrated* magazine, "within reach of a docker (on overtime) who wants to turn a night 'up West' into a night to remember."

This value for money approach, along with a star-studded line-up of entertainers, meant the audience at The Talk of the Town was an egalitarian mix ranging from couples treating themselves to a special night out, perhaps to celebrate an anniversary or birthday, to customers who were as famous as the performers themselves. Celebrity spotting was all part of the fun, wrote *Everywoman* magazine in its 1959 report underneath a photograph of Denis Lotis, a heart-throb singer of the 1950s, who was a member of the audience. It was not unusual to see Cliff Richard checking out the competition at The Talk of the Town; the singer and actress Elisabeth Welch was another regular, noting in her diary the nights she had visited The Talk of the Town to see Eartha Kitt (10th October 1960), Lena Horne (11th April 1961), Ethel Merman (19th February 1964) and Pearl Bailey (20th September 1972). One evening, Jonathan Aitken, a friend of Princess Margaret, called The Talk of the Town and announced Her Royal Highness wished to come to see Pearl Bailey perform. As the entire place was fully booked, Rosalyn Wilder politely told Aitken she would see what she could do, but before anyone had a chance to shuffle around seating arrangements, the royal party arrived. A few frantic minutes ensued while the front-of-house team apologetically moved customers. Meanwhile, Princess Margaret stood in the foyer, tapping her feet. A table was found, and a free bottle of wine was discreetly offered to the guests who had kindly cooperated.

The new format worked well. Among the stars occupying the star slot after Eartha Kitt were the Andrews Sisters, the 'Queen of Cabaret' Julie Wilson and Sophie Tucker, accompanied by her long-standing pianist Ted Shapiro. Tucker was no stranger to the venue, having originally appeared alongside George Robey in *Round in 50* in 1922 when jazz was in its excitable infancy. Almost forty years on, Tucker, known as the "original red hot momma", took the audience through her life and career in song, beginning with 'Monkey Rag' and ending with the deep and resonant 'Some of These Days'. Not content to wallow in the past, the seventy-five-year-old Tucker also sang some country and rock 'n' roll numbers, making it "a truly wonderful performance by one of the all-time greats", as *The Stage* concluded in its review. Tucker's status at the venue meant she was the only artist who was ever allowed out the front to chat to customers and to sign autographs. Dorothy Squires was another to perform in The Talk of the Town's early days, returning again in 1971. The spat over top billing over Charlie Gracie in the Hippodrome's dying days was not an isolated incident and Squires had a reputation for being argumentative. On one occasion, her insistence on singing a number that Robert Nesbitt knew would not suit her, provoked him to say, with measured exasperation: "Well Dorothy, darling – if you must sing it, why not do so in the taxi on the way home?"

The first revue, *Ten o'Clock Follies* – with the addition of the cabaret star – lasted until the spring of 1962 after which Robert Nesbitt designed a new show at regular, annual intervals, each one with an enticing and increasingly psychedelic title. *Fantastico* followed

'Meet the stars' at The Talk of the Town. A number of popular performers had already cut their teeth on the stage at the Hippodrome including Max Bygraves, Shirley Bassey, Sophie Tucker and Alma Cogan, who had been in *High Button Shoes* in 1948 alongside Audrey Hepburn.

> " **The Talk of the Town hit London at *exactly* the right moment, top cabaret artists were available and there were deals to be done** "
>
> Rosalyn Wilder – Robert Nesbitt's right-hand woman, 1959 to 1979

Below: Bruce Forsyth, one of Britain's most popular all-round entertainers, was also one of The Talk of the Town's most frequent stars and appeared in the star spot on eight separate occasions.

Below left: Sammy Davis Jr.'s exacting standards made him a demanding performer, but this multi-talented star always brought audiences to their feet with his barnstorming act.

Shirley Bassey pictured in a publicity shot to promote her appearance at The Talk of the Town in September 1962. She had already given a blistering performance at the old Hippodrome in 1957 and would go on to become one of the venue's regular and most popular stars.

A number of artists released albums of their live performances at The Talk of the Town. 'Shirley Bassey, Live at Talk of the Town', accompanied by the Burt Rhodes Orchestra, was released by United Artists Records in 1970.

the *Follies*, *High Life* opened in 1963 after which there was *Roman Holiday*. As the sixties progressed, revue themes ranged from the Wild West to outer space. There was the seductively named *Dangerous Curves*, *Out of this World* (in 1969, the year of the moon landing), *Jet Set 1970*, *Magnifique*, *Dream Machine*, *A Touch of Venus*, *Razzle Dazzle*, *Tonight's the Night* and *Sweet Temptation*. Each show was a feast for the senses – towering, befeathered showgirls, flamboyant, sequin-studded costumes, toe-tapping tunes, seamless scene changes and dazzling finales. It was entertainment on a grand scale, and because it was music-led, it had broad appeal. With neither conversation nor an understanding of English required, a night at The Talk of the Town was the ideal destination, whether entertaining business clients from overseas or celebrating a special occasion.

Each of Nesbitt's revues lasted a year during, which time the star slot was filled by the biggest names in show business, who generally were contracted to perform for a period of two to four weeks. The list of names to have stood on The Talk's stage during its twenty-four years acts as a crib-sheet for the most popular light entertainment and music stars of the period. Sandie Shaw, Stevie Wonder, Sammy Davis Jr., Dusty Springfield, Cliff Richard, Lulu, Paul Anka, Sacha Distel, Diana Ross and The Supremes, Roy Orbison, Lonnie Donegan, Engelbert Humperdinck, Tom Jones, Howard Keel, Neil Sedaka, Cleo Laine, The Three Degrees, Lena Horne, The Temptations, Des O'Connor, Val Doonican, Frankie Vaughan, Tony Christie, Liza Minnelli and, perhaps most famously, her mother, Judy Garland, were just some of the stars to perform at The Talk of the Town. For Judy Garland, her run of Talk of the Town shows in 1969, in which her performances lurched unpredictably between disaster and brilliance, would be the last before her death just a few short months later at the age of forty-seven.

While vocalists predominated, not all entertainers at the Hippodrome were singers. There were comedians too, like Jackie Mason, Jimmy Tarbuck, Dave Allen and Dick Emery. Impressionist Mike Yarwood appeared in 1974. There were also the all-rounders, those who could sing a bit, dance a bit, banter and joke; the likes of Roy Castle, Max Bygraves and Bruce Forsyth. Forsyth appeared at The Talk of the Town no fewer than eight times, a feat equalled by Matt Munro, and beaten by Frankie Vaughan who was The Talk of the Town's most frequent performer having appeared on ten occasions in total. Booking and looking after the famous came with its own particular challenges, all of which Rosalyn Wilder took in her stride. She recalls how demanding Sammy Davis Jr. was, insisting everything should be exactly as he wanted it, and bringing in his own musicians, but she concedes, "he was such an enormous talent". On another occasion, when Dusty Springfield was due to perform, the singer, who was suffering from a bad cold, refused to go on, causing ripples of panic through the production team. After some persuasion she eventually agreed to perform. In an interview with the *NME* in that year, she had expressed concerns that her preparations for her Talk of the Town show were behind schedule, which had perhaps added to her anxiety. A temporary demonstration of vulnerability did nothing to dilute Dusty Springfield's reputation as one of the greatest, most soulful voices of all time, but working at The Talk of the Town, Rosalyn Wilder saw both the good, and the more temperamental sides, of a great many stars.

Others who worked at Talk of the Town have their own memories. Roberta Mitchell was an employee in the late 1970s and early 1980s,

Grand finale of the 1979 floor show, *Bubbly*, a glittering homage to champagne.

in the final years before it closed, initially as secretary to the sales manager Bill Salter, looking after VIP clients and helping to produce and deliver The Talk of the Town promotional newsletters, which were distributed to the foyers of all the major hotels in London's West End. She remembers Eamonn Andrews surprising Anita Harris in the foyer as a prelude to *This is Your Life*, and the acts who were particularly friendly to The Talk of the Town staff; among them, the singer Grace Kennedy and The Drifters. Tony Monopoly, a former Carmelite monk who briefly but spectacularly hit the big time after winning Opportunity Knocks, was another favourite. She later had the opportunity of working backstage as a dresser, "a completely new and exciting experience", if a somewhat stressful one. She would be assigned to five or six dancers and showgirls and was responsible for ensuring they were in and out of their costumes in double-quick time. Timing had to be spot on and the costumes, which were such an integral part of the spectacle on stage, often needed positioning or arranging just so before the girl stepped onto the stage. Handing over the loops on a principal dancer's train for the male dancers to carry was often one of the most tense moments with huge potential for disaster.

For the dancers themselves, it was a glamorous but tough job, starting with the humiliating audition process, where hopefuls had to parade in very little on the stage and were often dismissed with barely a glance. For the ones who made the grade, there were rules to abide by. Diana Schooledge and Carolyn Irving were among the dancers who considered themselves fortunate to have succeeded at auditions for several Talk of the Town shows and between them spent many happy years there with Diana going on to become ballet mistress. More than fifty years later they can reel off the house rules for dancers. All girls had to be in the theatre by the "half" (the thirty-five minute call before the beginning of the performance); there would be no tolerance of latecomers. They were not allowed access to front of house unless they had expressly asked permission to watch the star. Nor could any girls sit among the customers; if they wished to sit somewhere, they had to go upstairs and find an empty table, and if there were no empty tables, then they would have to go backstage. There was to be no drinking front of house, and absolutely no eating or drinking in costume. There were to be no complaints about costumes, and all hair, clothing, wigs, shoes and tights were to be worn exactly as directed with no variation allowed. While girls did their own make-up, if the choreographer or 'Mr. Nesbitt' disapproved, they would be required to change it. There was, inevitably, the stricture that weight should be kept under control. They were, they will tell you with a smile, required to remain what Mr. Nesbitt called his "long-stemmed roses". If any dancer was thought to have gained weight, they would have to stand on scales and were ordered to diet to promptly lose any excess. With so much invested in each revue, performers were required to sign contracts for the run of the show. Extra payments were given for understudy work (known as Swing), solo work, and to the ballet mistress. As showgirls were meant to measure at least six feet in heels and headdresses, they had to be five foot nine in their stockinged feet; dancers had to be at least five foot seven tall. The rules extended to the male dancers too, who needed to measure a minimum of five foot eleven. As girls were committed to a show for most of a year, they would supplement their income with other jobs ranging from promotional work at motor shows or selling perfume to more lucrative television work; some girls who worked at The Talk of the Town in later years were among the famous Hill's Angels on the Benny Hill Show. Lindsey Williams performed at The Talk of the Town in 1971, as principal dancer in *Tonight's the Night*, which took as its theme the 1930s. As principal,

View from the stage – the illuminated Talk of the Town awaits the first arrivals of the night.

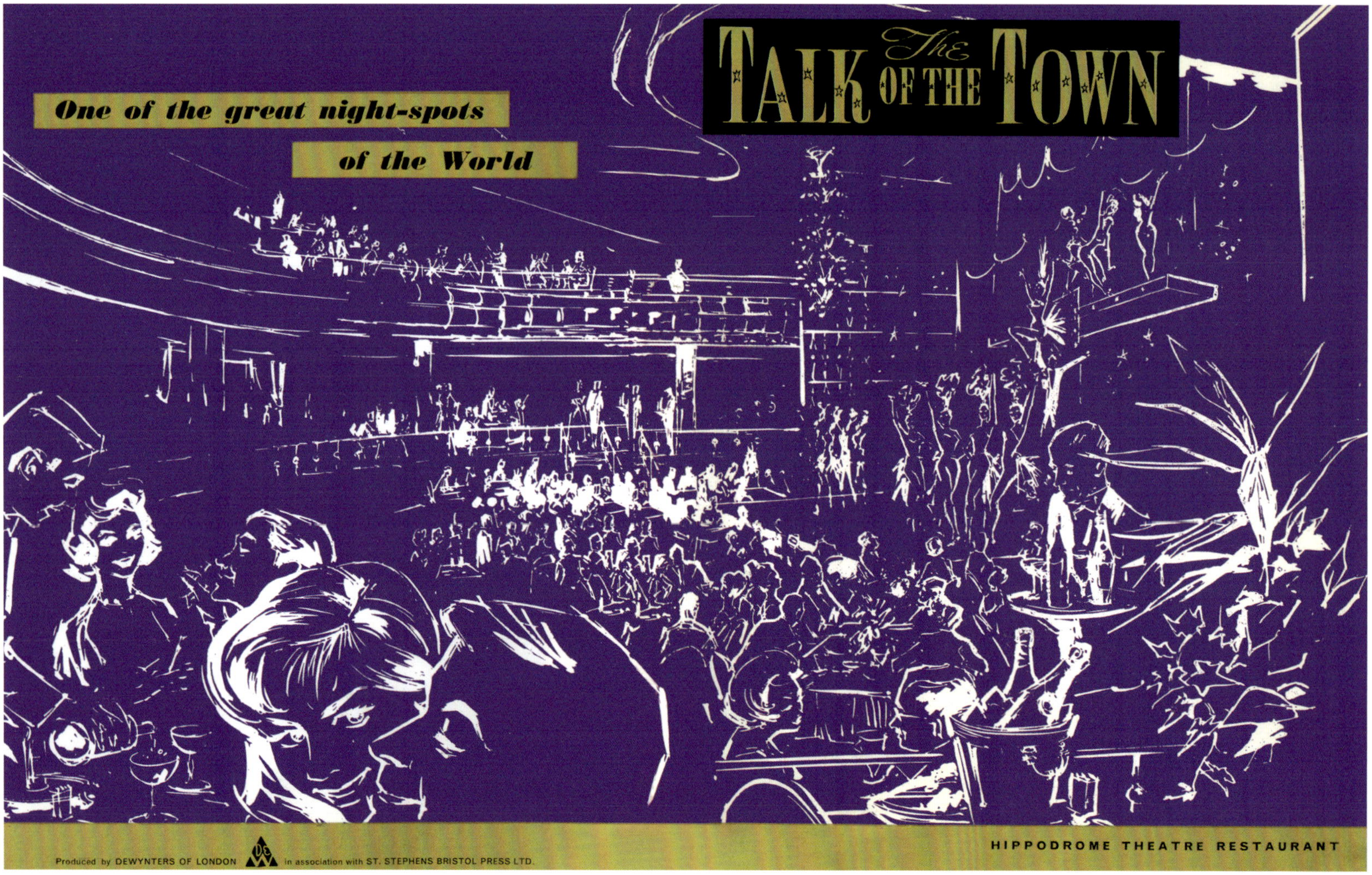

Cover for The Talk of the Town's brochure, during the run of *Dangerous Curves*, 1966.

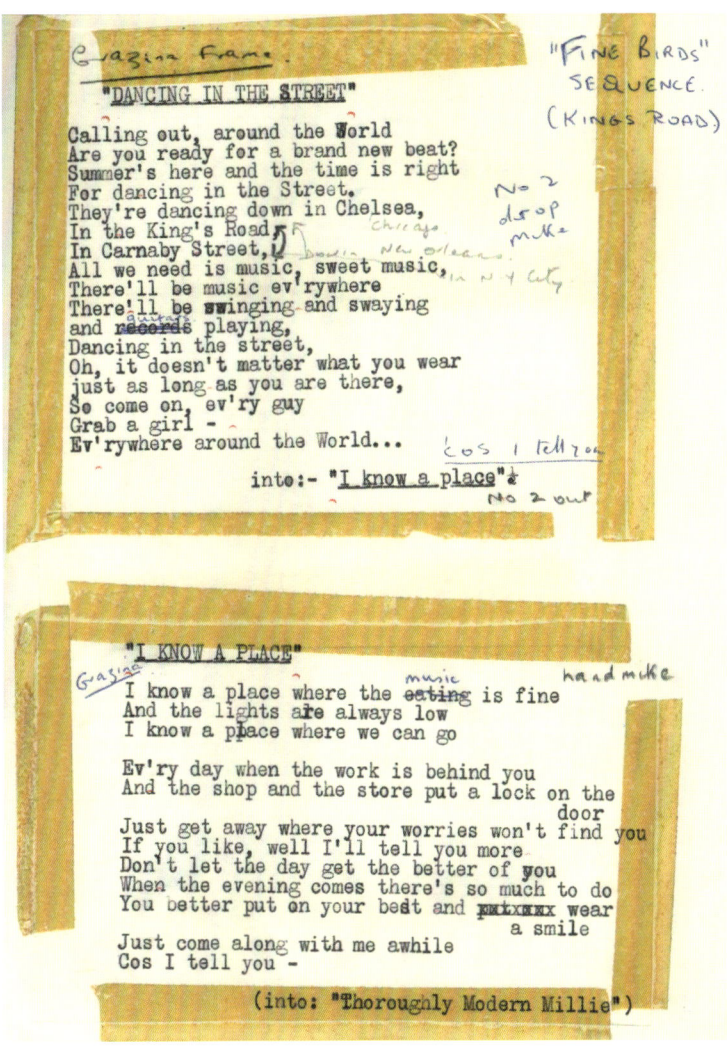

Script with notes and annotations belonging to Rosalyn Wilder for the 1968 revue *Fine Feathers*, during which Judy Garland appeared as the star attraction. Among the songs featured were crowd-pleasing, toe-tapping contemporary hits including 'Dancing in the Street' and 'The In Crowd'. Both were performed by Grazina Frame who was another alumnus of the Hippodrome, having appeared in *The Famous Five* matinee show in 1956. She had gone on to appear in numerous West End shows with great success.

Robert Nesbitt deep in discussion with Cliff Richard and the Shadows prior to their appearance at The Talk of the Town in January 1966.

she shared a dressing room with three singers rather than the other dancers, where they would prepare before the 9pm show. She had been appearing in *Promises, Promises*, the Burt Bacharach musical at the Prince of Wales Theatre, based on Neil Simon's *The Apartment*, and received the same pay at The Talk of the Town – £30 a week. She remembers standing in heels at the top of the staircase below the stage, which would then be raised up, and clearly recalls the iron bars still fixed to the perimeter of the area under the stage, a legacy of when various animals were tethered there in the 1900s.

Grazina Frame, who had performed at the Hippodrome in *The Famous Five* in 1956, returned to the venue to perform in its floor shows including, in 1968, as leading lady in *Fine Feathers*. Grazina's stage school training and confidence meant she was an entertainment all-rounder – a dancer, an actress and with a voice that she admits "could belt out" songs. She had already starred in *Let Yourself Go* at the Palladium while still a teenager and Robert Nesbitt, aware of her abilities, took her under his wing. He and his wife Iris took her to Le Caprice and taught her to eat lobster. "He understood glamour," she says, "and he moulded me to his vision of glamour." Grazina's talent and effervescent personality would take her to a highly successful career in a number of hit West End shows including the lead in Lionel Bart's *Blitz!* in 1962.

Those who performed at The Talk of the Town look back on those years with immense fondness and an enduring camaraderie that comes from that shared experience. It was undoubtedly hard work, but also full of fun and glamour and in some cases, The Talk was where they met their future partners. Diana and Carolyn both recall the frenetic pace of life and speak of doing the show at The Talk of the Town before sometimes dashing off later to take part in another performance at the Savoy or some other late-night venue. There was the learning of new routines, the long and relentless rehearsal hours, costume fittings and rubbing shoulders with some of the era's biggest stars. It is perhaps no surprise that many ex-Talk of the Town dancers regularly meet and remain friends to this day. They are an elite club; an intrinsic element of an entertainment phenomenon that was at its zenith during London's swinging decade.

With three kitchens, up to eight hundred customers an evening, two orchestras, an army of serving staff, a cabaret extravaganza followed by an internationally famous main act, The Talk of the Town had to operate like a well-oiled machine. Even the revue show, with its elaborate moving stages and lifts, gave the impression of effortless spectacle. The raised apron stage consisted of two inner halves which could be lowered to make way for the massive scenic lift, usually brought into play for the grand finale of the floor show, with a Rolls-Royce, a fountain or something similarly ostentatious rising up and surrounded by a bevy of spangled showgirls. At the same time as the lift rose, a scenic bridge would be lowered from the ceiling, similarly embellished, and would come to rest at the exact point the lift was rising from below (once, the bridge lowered the Tree of Life down to the stage, complete with a reclining Lynda Baron dressed as Eve).

Rosalyn Wilder is familiar with these scenes and explained what happened at the end of the show: "At end the scenic lift went down, the two halves joined and when they had reached the top level the whole thing was lowered once again to form the dance floor and the show band was lowered under the stage, while the dance band rose from below on the opposite side and slid across the centre and dancing began! All totally seamless."

AT NINE-THIRTY

BERNARD DELFONT

PRESENTS

AT ELEVEN O'CLOCK

ROBERT NESBITT'S

REVUE

WILD WEST END

Choreographed by BILLY PETCH

Costumed by ST. JOHN ROPER

Decor by TOD KINGMAN

Orchestrations by BURT RHODES

assistant to the choreographer: ROBERT CHANDLER

special material written and composed by BILLY PETCH

DANCING TO THE MUSIC OF

THE PHIL PHILLIPS GROUP

* * *

FRANK DENIZ and his LATIN RHYTHMS

* * *

THE BURT RHODES SHOW BAND

Heading for the Golden West

ON THE ATCHISON-TOPEKA-SANTA FÉ

THE CHARACTERS

The Sheriff:

MICHAEL ROWLATT

The Rough Ridin' Gal:

JUDY COLLINS

The Girl with a heart of Gold:

JACQUELINE JONES

The Bad Man:

ROD McLENNAN

CATTLEMEN, GAMBLERS, SALOON GIRLS, COWBOYS and INDIANS

WHERE THE ACTION IS

DEADWOOD CITY

'Hoedown' Sheriff's Song – 'Hoop d'Dingle' 'The Wild One' 'Heart of Gold'

THE GOLDEN NUGGET SALOON

'Come along with Me' 'The Swingin'est Bad Man'

THE COUNTY JAIL

'Jailhouse Rock'

'BACK AT THE RANCH

'Bless your Beautiful Hide' 'Navajo Trail' Square Dance – 'Might as well be Spring'

THE OLD HORSE OP'RY HOUSE

'Ev'rybody loves a Western' 'Go West Young Man'

INDIAN COUNTRY

'Cherokee'

'WESTERN A GO-GO'

Finale – THE COMPANY

TOM JONES

THE TALK OF THE TOWN is proud to present, for the first time in Cabaret — Britain's Sensational Singing Star, King of the Hit Parade

Musical Director: JOHNNY HARRIS

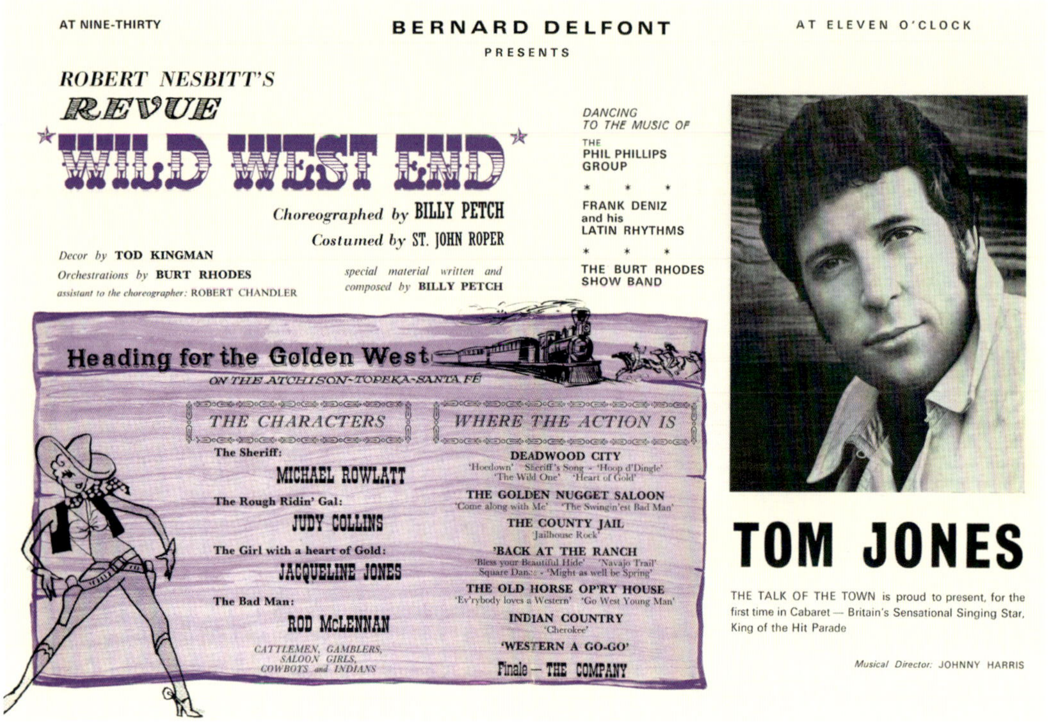

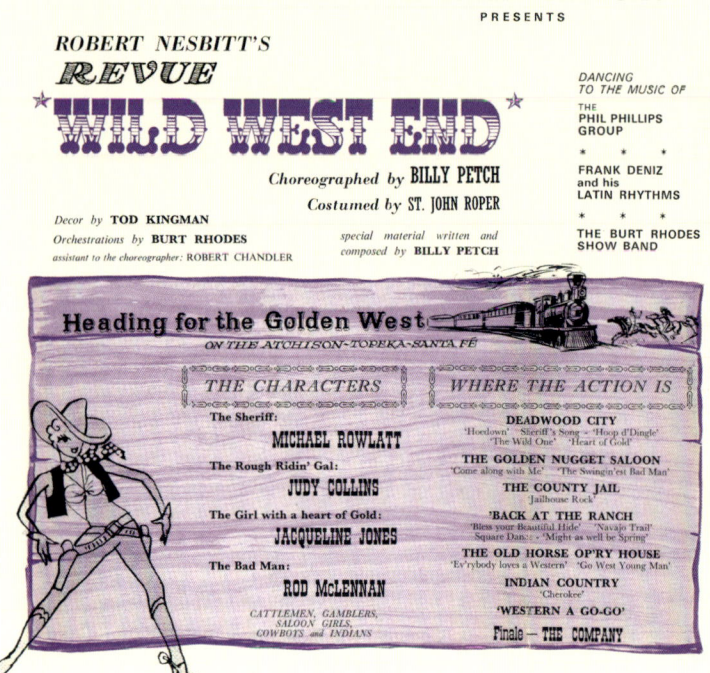

Programme for the 1967 revue, *Wild West End*, with the star slot filled by Tom Jones.

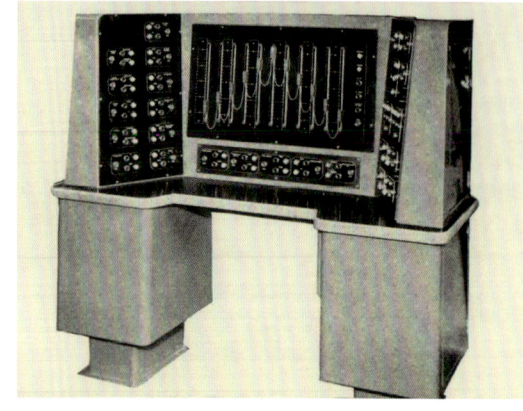

The stage console, ultra-modern for its time, controlled all the lifts and stage equipment; a separate console controlled the lighting.

From Robert St. John Roper's stunning costumes to Tod Kingman's mastery of set design, Robert Nesbitt's backstage team were pivotal in the success of the venue. His early involvement with Stanley Earnshaw and Frank Bentham of Rank Strand made them pioneers of modern stage lighting design. Billy Petch's choreography, the musicians, wigs, the best girl and boy dancers and principals, stage and lighting crews – all handpicked – meant everyone knew they were part of an "A" team that created the dazzling reality of a Robert Nesbitt production and guaranteed The Talk of the Town lived up to its name.

Plumes and sequins in abundance for the grand finale of *Tonight's the Night*, Robert Nesbitt's 1971 revue.

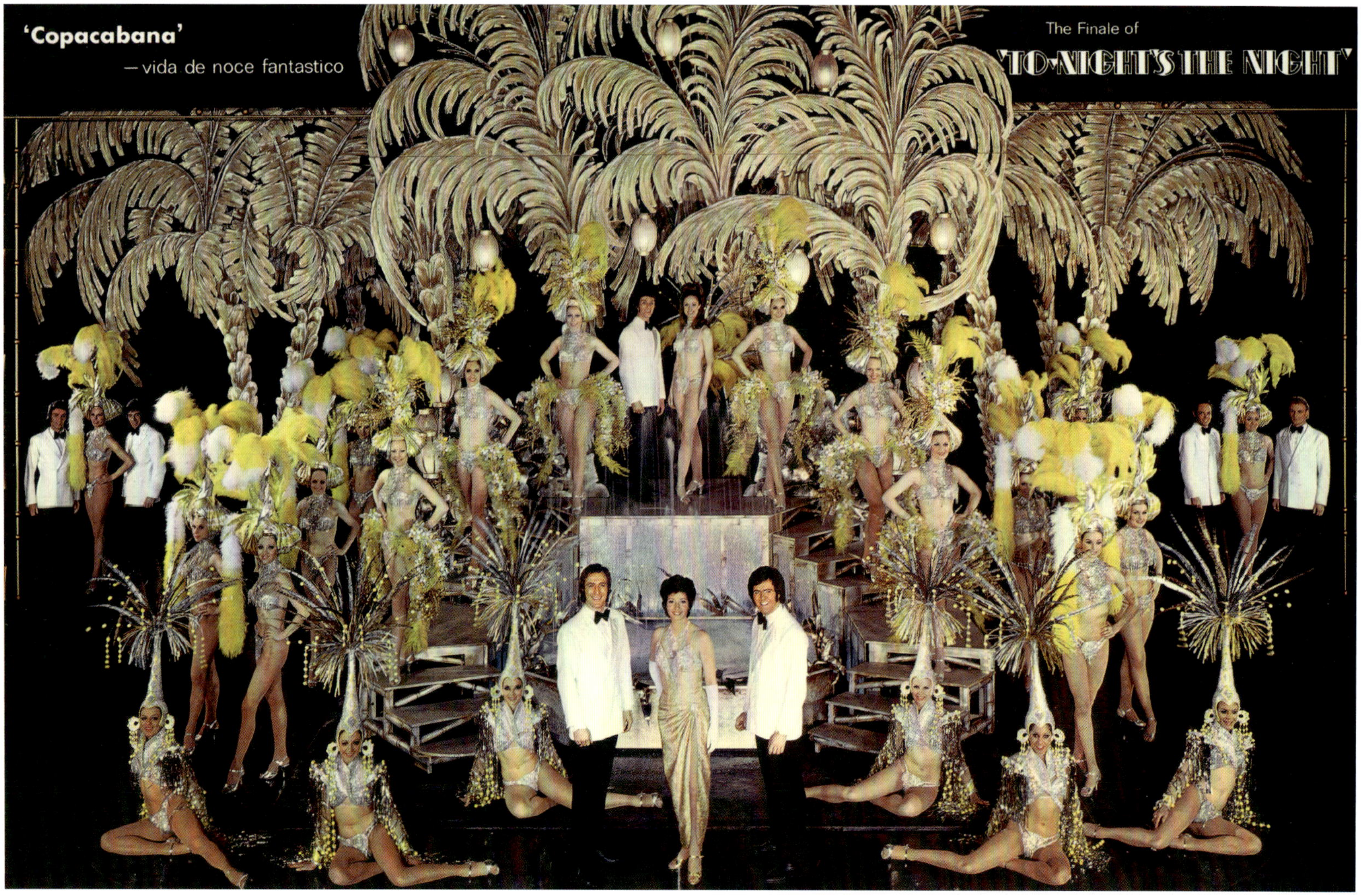

In 1965, Robert Nesbitt's show was given the enticing title *Fatal Fascination*. Its main star was Lynda Baron, whose long career in acting and entertainment has continued. She is probably best known for her role as Nurse Gladys Emmanuel in the TV comedy series *Open All Hours*.

Talk of the Town dancers in costume, from left: Carolyn Irving, Sorralyn Croston and Joyce Court. Dancers had to be a minimum of five foot seven while showgirls measured five foot nine. With the addition of makeup, sequins, heels, head-dresses or hats, they brought a breath-taking brand of style to The Talk of the Town stage.

It was an ingenious but complicated system and could sometimes succumb to technical hitches.

"It was a challenge," recalls Rosalyn. "The people who installed it were Hall's Stage Equipment – really the only people capable of dealing with machinery on that scale – you have no idea how heavy or dangerous it was. We practically had an open line to Hall's – we were their biggest customer – there was a mass of other machinery besides and the entire evening depended on every single piece working! Never hurt anyone, never trapped anyone but definitely a LOT of very hairy moments and running the show was a split-second operation where you kept 110% attention on EVERYTHING for every single moment!"

Disruption of a different kind came with extra-curricular trade shows and television recordings, most squeezed in between the close of The Talk of the Town at night and its re-opening to customers the following evening. There were limitations over what could be done due to the comparatively small scenic dock doors, inconveniently located down an alley, and the stage lift which was usually fitted with the semi-permanent stage show sets. However, it was a lucrative sideline so efforts were made, and extra hours were worked to accommodate a variety of companies ranging from Ford and Chrysler (who bought out the venue for two whole days and nights) to Avon cosmetics and Gloria Vanderbilt jeans. Despite access issues, and after much mayhem, on one occasion a huge tractor was wheeled into place in the centre of the venue. Television shows caused similar levels of upheaval, with crews moving in on a Saturday night at close of business and filming right through until early Sunday evening. It was a punishing schedule, where The Talk of the Town was effectively dismantled and then reassembled in less than twenty-four hours. Rosalyn Wilder particularly remembers the frequent disagreements over the changing of the floor from black to white and then back to black each time. From 1966, the BBC filmed *International Cabaret* at The Talk of the Town, directed by Stewart Morris, one of the top producers of light entertainment, who signed up Kenneth Williams to present a mix of well-known stars such as Vera Lynn and Johnny Mathis as well as novelty acts – acrobats and jugglers – from around Europe. There were also a series of specials simply called *Talk of the Town* directed by Michael Hurll, another well-known name, with Alyn Ainsworth as musical director. The performers in each episode tended to reflect The Talk's usual roster of stars: Sammy Davis Jr., Bruce Forsyth, Cliff Richard and Charles Aznavour. In 1972, Thames Television, in association with Lew Grade's ATV, broadcast *Tony Bennett – Live at The Talk of the Town*, thirteen half-hour episodes with Bennett, joined by the Canadian-born composer and conductor Robert Farnon and a forty-piece orchestra, introducing a number of acts such as Cleo Laine and Matt Munro. Bennett was keen to concentrate on the music and ignore the awkward chit-chat that blighted many other celebrity-led music shows. It was a laudable approach but Bennett was also vocal about the state of the music business, finding the rise of rock music perplexing; he therefore chose a selection of guests who would appeal to the tastes of an older, more conservative audience.

A new challenge faced The Talk of the Town's management in the autumn of 1975 when around 100 staff, mainly kitchen workers and waiters, went on strike in support of a closed shop as part of the Transport and General Workers' Union. In a decade punctuated by industrial action, Charles Forte resisted any attempts at union encroachment into his catering empire and for a month, employers and employees were at deadlock. With the kitchen unable to produce

Showgirl costume design by Robert St. John Roper, 1973.

Far right: Cocktail menu from the 1970s; the prices reflect the fact that The Talk of the Town was for special occasions.

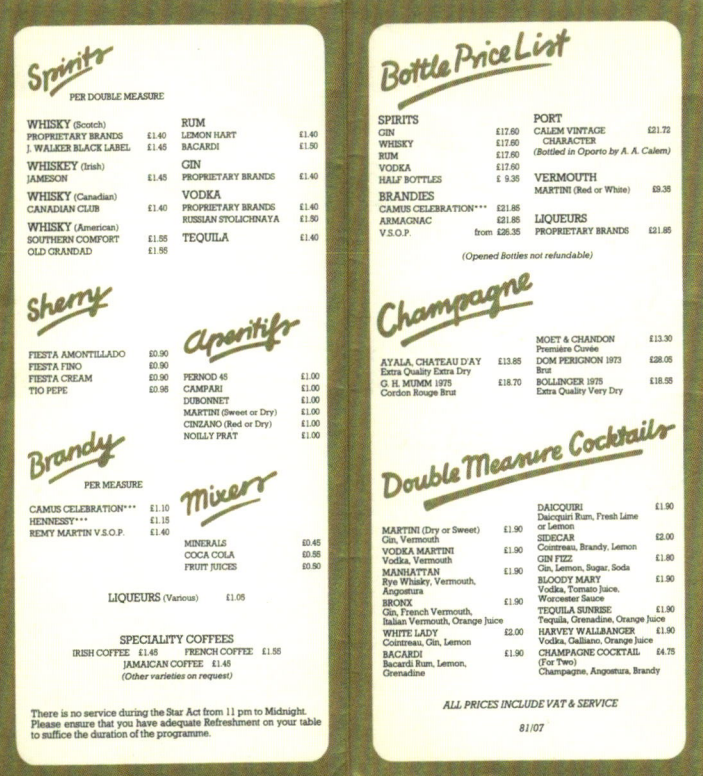

its usual high standard of fare, airline-style ready meals were instead provided from another branch of Forte's business, with occasional cold buffets as an alternative. Customers, who were given a discount to compensate for this inconvenience, seemed unperturbed by the situation and rather enjoyed the novelty of airline meals so continued to fill the venue, where Roy Castle and, later, Salena Jones were playing. Meanwhile, members of the management team stepped in to help out. Rosalyn Wilder worked the cloakroom one evening, afterwards pooling her tips with Sir Leslie Joseph, a board member of Theatre Restaurants, the company that controlled The Talk of the Town. Some of those passing the picket line may have noticed Vanessa Redgrave standing in solidarity with the strikers. *The Observer*, reporting on the strike after a month, revealed there was a real threat that The Talk of the Town would be closed if the Musicians' Union also came out in support of the strike. But members of the orchestra crossed the picket line, and eventually the crisis passed.

A week or so later, a big splash about The Talk of the Town appeared in *The Stage*. With the headline, "A VERY SPECIAL SHOWCASE: The Talk of the Town Gives that Special Cachet to today's Top Entertainers" it went on to describe the success of the venture, and to emphasise that big plans were afoot for the future. Billy Marsh of London Management, who booked acts for Bernard Delfont, "surveys the world scene for future star attractions", while Robert Nesbitt's revues "become more potent as an escapist entertainment with each successive production". Considering the timing of the article, just a month after the strike, it suggests a public relations exercise in damage limitation. The last thing The Talk of the Town's management wanted was for the talent to get cold feet about signing contracts. Ironically, on the same page, a stop press article informed readers that EMI were going to buy The Talk of the Town. There were certainly discussions in this direction (Bernard Delfont would later become chief executive of EMI) but by July the following year, newspapers were reporting that the deal was off.

While it is tempting to pinpoint this moment as the beginning of The Talk of the Town's decline, it in fact still had another six and half years to run. Arguably its best years were behind it, though it continued to operate as it had always done and it was only towards the final few months that it was seen to be seriously struggling. Roberta Mitchell remembers the auditorium becoming more sparsely populated and a review of Matt Munro's *Talk of the Town* show by *The Daily Telegraph* on 3rd February 1982 described it as "an increasingly flaccid hour". The end, when it came, was swift and unexpectedly brutal. In December 1981, the lease expired on the building, and Bernard Delfont was hit with a rent increase of £200,000 per annum from £15,000. A new general manager, Colin Hayes, was brought in and told the staff at first that the building was closing temporarily for refurbishment. But then, in June 1982, *The Times* ran the headline, "Talk of the Town to be closed". Delfont defended his actions to the press, telling the paper, "I have always tried to give value for money for the ordinary man in the street who wants a night out. And I think £23 to £24 a night is too much." Having looked at alternative ways to keep the venue going he was adamant he did not want to bring in nude entertainment ("I do not want to bring Soho into Leicester Square"), but claimed the increased rent and rates, VAT and demands by the Musicians' Union made the business unsustainable. "Rising costs had already damaged ticket prices: from a two guinea entrance in the early sixties we were now up to twenty-four pounds," he explained in his memoirs. "The latest jump in overheads would put us into the fifty pounds bracket, far too much for a family of middling

Talk of the Town poster for *Dream Machine* with Cliff Richard filling the star spot, 1973.

> **Rising costs had already damaged ticket prices: from a two guinea entrance in the early sixties we were now up to twenty-four pounds**
>
> Bernard Delfont partly explaining the demise of The Talk of the Town

Talk of the Town promotional leaflet from 1980, featuring Pearl Bailey. These were distributed in the foyers of major West End hotels, with the intention of attracting tourists in London, and changed with the introduction of each new act.

From left: Talent agent Billy Marsh, Joe Longthorne, Burt Rhodes and Robert Nesbitt bid farewell to The Talk of the Town in June 1982.

income who wanted a good night's entertainment without feeling as if they had to take out a second mortgage." The other problem was finding big enough stars who were willing to do a stint of a week or more at The Talk of the Town. Why put in the hours, when in one or two nights at Wembley Arena or a similar-sized venue, they could play to a larger number of people?

For the three hundred people employed at The Talk of the Town, the news that it was being closed for good came as a shock. Most of them were immediately out of a job, including Roberta Mitchell who feels, "It was not handled well." She went to work for Carlo Sparteli, owner of the club Xenon. Rosalyn Wilder had departed The Talk of the Town two years earlier, to work as booking manager at the Barbican Centre. Bernard Delfont, by now Lord Delfont, was philosophical about the eventual demise of his grand project. "I had to face the fact that The Talk of the Town had had its innings, at least as a theatre restaurant; a very respectable twenty-four years. In show business there are few centuries."

London's *Standard* newspaper announces the closure of The Talk of the Town after twenty-four years.

Talk of the Town 1958-1982

Robert Nesbitt – The Prince of Darkness

Robert Nesbitt was one of the West End's most glamorous and well-respected figures; suave, debonair, articulate, smooth-mannered, the consummate professional, and yet one with a permanent sense of occasion. Francis Neville, a lighting engineer who had worked at the Talk of the Town, reminisced in *Cue* magazine in 1982 about how 'Mr. Nesbitt' carried out all the functions associated with being a producer, "in a rather grand manner from a table where he appeared to live in some style". Rather than tea and biscuits, elevenses in the Nesbitt office frequently meant the popping of a champagne cork, remembers Rosalyn Wilder, who worked with Nesbitt at the Talk of the Town for two decades. Champagne was a recurring theme, an accessory that cemented Nesbitt's reputation as a connoisseur of the finer things in life. When interviewed by Roy Plomley for 'Desert Island Discs' in 1973, his chosen luxury was a bottle of vintage 1966 Moët et Chandon. It seems particularly apt therefore, that when Angus McBean took Robert Nesbitt's photograph for *The Tatler* in 1950 he chose to portray him in immaculate evening wear against an enormous bottle of champagne, a coupe of bubbly held elegantly in his hand.

This glamorous veneer never interfered with his work ethic, or his ability to form a cohesive creative and technical plan for his many revues, most of which began with "a clean piece of white paper". Rosalyn Wilder describes him as "a magical man to work for, elegant beyond belief with an amazing imagination". This imaginative flair was instinctive and never seemed to leave him. He would percolate ideas and form an entire show in his head before going through it with others, scene by scene. Joan Davis, Nesbitt's dance director during the Hippodrome days, said of him, "He inspires us all with his accuracy of vision. Through his eyes we can see a complete picture of what will eventually happen on stage." When directing or auditioning he remained diplomatic, bending others to his will by sheer good manners. Rather than bellowing commands, Nesbitt would phrase requests so they appeared to be collaborative rather than autocratic: "Don't you think this would work better?" or "Can we try it this way?" *Everywoman* magazine, covering The Talk of the Town in 1959, corroborated this, reporting, "Many stars have paid tribute to Nesbitt's soothing manner at rehearsals. He gets what he wants – but does not rant and rave." In a 1945 profile in *Illustrated* magazine, Alan Reeve summed up Nesbitt's unruffled character: "I don't believe any other producer gives birth to a spectacle with less flurry."

Nesbitt was educated at Heathmount School in Hampstead (where Evelyn Waugh and Cecil Beaton were fellow pupils), then Repton and Oxford, before going into advertising and journalism. While doing so he moonlighted as a lyricist and writer for the vibrant cabaret scene of late 1920s London and produced his first show, *Ballyhoo*, at the Comedy Theatre in 1932. He moved to work for Andre Charlot, one of the great impresarios and masters of revue, and later began to produce pantomimes for Tom Arnold. As a schoolboy, Nesbitt had often visited the Hippodrome for the matinees produced by Albert de Courville during the Great War. He adored seeing Shirley Kellogg lead the chorus girls down the gangplank and in his boyish daydreams imagined watching the show while enjoying his favourite meal of sardines on toast. In some of his recorded reminiscences, Nesbitt wondered if these juvenile memories had planted the seeds of an idea for a theatre restaurant like Talk of the Town, where an entertainment spectacle combined with fine dining.

Robert Nesbitt, the maestro of glamorous revue, seen planning his next revue and in discussion over a stage set with director of dance Joan Davis.

> "When they come to write the history of twentieth century entertainment in this country they'll be hard pressed to find anyone else who has dedicated so many years and so much cash to the single-minded task of turning all that glitters into box-office gold"
> Sheridan Morley

Light Fantastic

A key aspect of Nesbitt's creative vision was his pioneering use of technically advanced stage lighting. He worked with Stanley Earnshaw and Fred Bentham of Strand Electric, the only company to provide lighting for London's theatres and with a long-standing relationship with the Hippodrome of old. By using dimmers and colour changes, Strand Lighting were able to realise Nesbitt's creative ideas, and the dazzling effects earned Nesbitt the moniker 'The Prince of Darkness'. Stage histories rarely give much credit to the technicians behind the scenes, but the combination of Nesbitt's imagination with Bentham's technical know-how revolutionised the way a stage set could look. "Nesbitt is a master of the art of lighting," wrote David Clayton in *Illustrated* magazine. "He uses electricity as cleverly as Picasso uses a palette. The difference is you can understand the end-product."

Robert Nesbitt (1906–1995) photographed by Angus McBean for *The Tatler*, 21 June 1950. McBean perfectly captures Nesbitt's smooth, unflustered persona, elegance and sense of occasion by picturing him in a dinner jacket against a large magnum of champagne, coupe of bubbly in hand.

Talk of the Town programme, December 1968–January 1969.

Judy Garland at The Talk of the Town

December 1968 in a photograph by Bryn Campbell for *The Observer*. Her sequinned trouser suit had originally been designed by William Travilla for her role in the 1967 film *The Valley of the Dolls*. She was fired from the movie but got to keep the suit.

Renee Zellweger as Judy Garland in a still from the 2019 film *Judy* directed by British director Rupert Goold. Zellweger immersed herself in the role, watching interviews and performances by Garland and spending time with Rosalyn Wilder (who was played by Jessie Buckley in the film) to learn as much as possible about her time at The Talk of the Town. She won several awards for what was a deft and sensitive portrayal of the beleaguered star, including an Academy Award for Best Actress.

Far right: Rosalyn Wilder worked at The Talk of the Town over two decades in the role that was described as 'production assistant' but in fact encompassed a wide range of responsibilities including liaison with performers. During Judy Garland's appearance at The Talk of the Town in 1968–9, Rosalyn found herself providing help and support to the beleaguered star.

On 30th December 1968, Judy Garland began a five-week residency in the cabaret slot at The Talk of the Town. The first night was a triumph. She seduced the audience from the start by opening with 'I Belong to London' and by the end, Bernard Delfont recalled the audience reaction rivalled a football crowd at a cup final in its very vocal appreciation. Reviewing the show a few days later, *The Stage* wrote, "There are few artists who create an emotionalism – almost amounting to hysteria – minutes before they actually step foot onstage. Of these, probably the greatest is Judy."

But behind the sequins, pizazz, sly wisecracks and declarations of love between performer and audience, Garland was struggling. Hugely in debt, painfully thin and relying on a cocktail of drugs to bring her up and then help her sleep, her reputation had become increasingly frayed. A string of failed marriages only exacerbated the fragility of a woman who had been exploited by the Hollywood studio system since childhood, causing a lifelong battle with her weight and self-esteem. Her latest paramour, Mickey Deans, a discotheque manager a decade younger than Garland, was widely thought of as a chancer, and a completely unsuitable for a woman who needed stability. She was considered a liability, her erratic timekeeping and lapses of commitment making her unemployable in the States. But on a good night, she could hold an audience spellbound. The 30th December was one of those nights.

It was not to last. Judy Garland's appearances at The Talk of the Town became increasingly unpredictable. She had already arrived without any band parts causing Burt Rhodes to have to completely rewrite the score at short notice. She once turned up at 1:50am for a performance – over two hours late. "You never knew if she'd turn up on time. If she would perform the whole repertoire, or more than the repertoire," remembers Michael Hirst, who was The Talk of the Town's general manager. Her behaviour could be eccentric, such as the time she borrowed, without permission, The Talk of the Town's guard dog, a German Shepherd called Rex, keeping him at her suite at the Ritz for several nights. On more than one occasion, when Garland failed to appear on time, her legendary rapport with the audience curdled. Many guests, irritable by that point, threw rolls or cigarette butts and heckled as she walked onto the stage. For a performer who desperately craved audience approval, it only added to her anxiety. And for those involved in keeping the show running, it was a nerve-shredding experience.

Rosalyn Wilder, practical, firm, and outwardly unruffled after a decade dealing with the caprices of The Talk of the Town's various performers, found herself supporting Garland during her time there. She recalls how, in an age well before mobile phones, there was no knowing Garland's whereabouts once she had left the Ritz and before she arrived at The Talk of the Town. "We just had to wait and pray," she remembers. One night, Garland came to her at the last minute and confessed that she did not think she could go on, and certainly not without taking her pills. Some careful negotiation followed with the conclusion that Rosalyn promised to stand in the wings with a glass of water and the pills as a safety net. "After a certain amount of persuasion, she went out, the orchestra struck up and there was Judy Garland. You saw the performer who was deep down in the soul of her. And she did her act. And when she came off, she looked suitably impressed with herself. She'd achieved it."

> **Judy Garland was one of the greatest entertainers, ever. Nothing that ever happened, can ever take away from that**
> Rosalyn Wilder

On reflection, Rosalyn believes Garland was too vulnerable and ill to have performed there. Bernard Delfont recounted in his memoirs how after three weeks, it was becoming clear that Garland's health was jeopardising the show and he only agreed she could perform if declared fit enough to do so by a doctor. Garland's doctor, John Treherne, confirmed that with a weekend of rest, she would be well enough to perform. She got through the final fortnight with a combination of Ritalin to fire her up before a performance, and Senecol to help her sleep afterwards. Sometimes she took both together. It was a lethal combination, resulting in a loss of appetite, continuing weight loss and stomach pains.

Nobody knew it at the time, but The Talk of the Town show would be Judy Garland's final bow. On 22nd June 1969, her husband Mickey found her dead in the bathroom of the Chelsea mews house they were staying at, having taken an accidental overdose of barbituates. She was forty-seven.

Rosalyn Wilder, who stood witness to Garland's last days on stage, believes the tragedy of those final months should not taint the star's legacy as one of the world's most iconic and life-enhancing figures of stage and screen.

Peter Stringfellow and staff pose for a photograph underneath the Hippodrome's extravagant and somewhat temperamental state-of-the-art light system in 1983 when it was opened as 'the greatest disco in the world.' The club remained a landmark in London's nightlife scene throughout the decade and typified the excess and flamboyance of the 1980s.

The greatest disco in the world 1983-2009

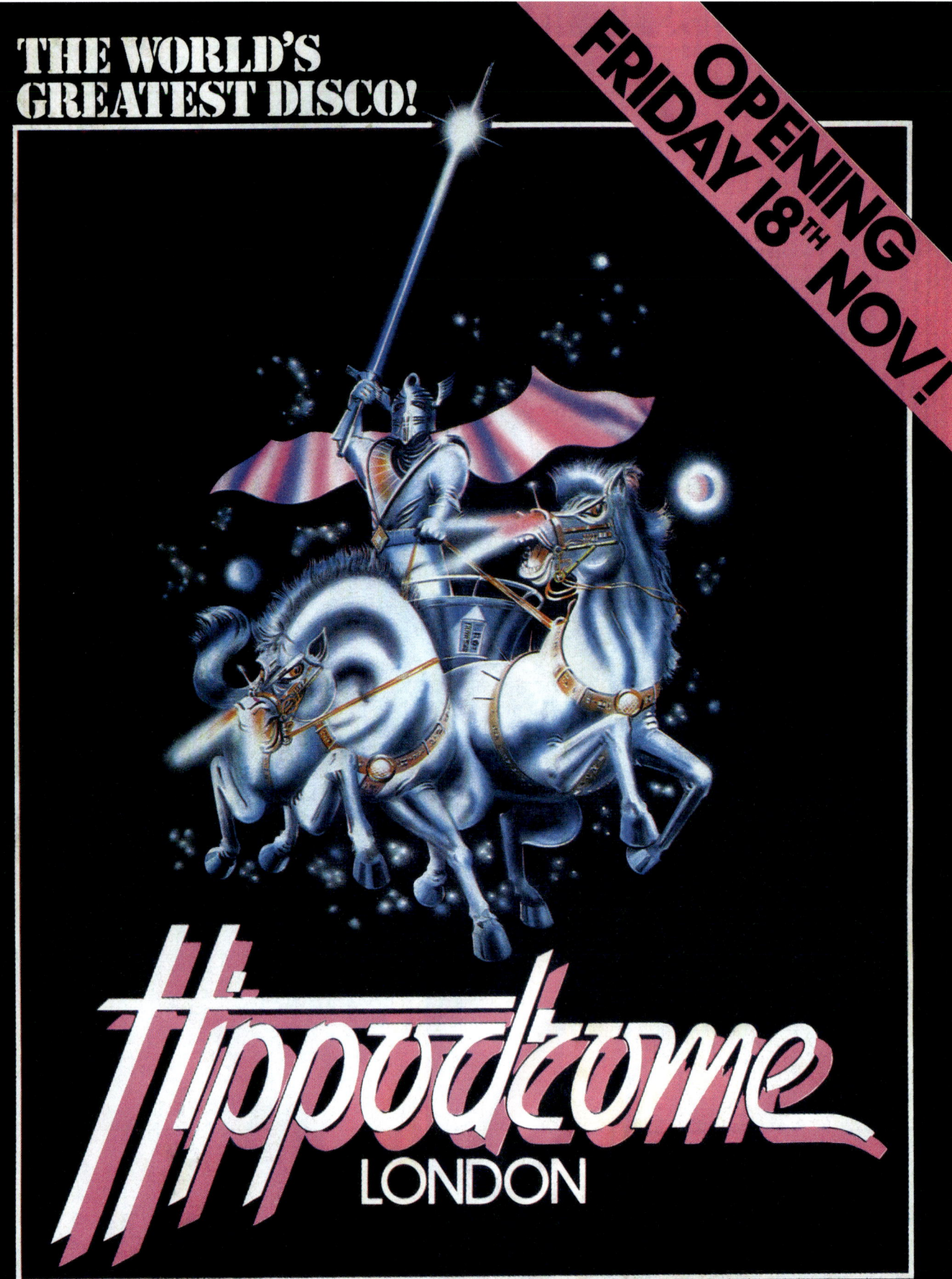

Peter Stringfellow poses outside the Hippodrome in 1983, shortly after acquiring the venue, which he planned to transform into "the greatest disco in the world".

Boy George with his mother at the London Hippodrome's party following the charity gala performance of London Festival Ballet's *Night Creatures* in March 1987. The singer, a controversial figure at the time, was reported to have chatted to the Princess of Wales during the evening.

Left: A full-page advertisement in the *Record Mirror* for the soon-to-open "World's Greatest Disco", brimming with typical Stringfellow audacity.

In 1980, when Buddy Greco was playing at The Talk of the Town, Peter Stringfellow paid a visit one evening. The son of a Sheffield steel worker, he was known as the 'King of Clubs' and had recently, with much fanfare, opened Stringfellow's, a gentlemen's club a short walk away in Covent Garden.

As someone who was rapidly gaining a reputation as London's most prominent showman, Stringfellow's opinion of The Talk of the Town was less than complimentary – "the place looked tired and lacked atmosphere". And yet the visit had sparked an interest. Two years later, with the building by that time closed and standing empty, he admitted, "The Talk of the Town screamed at me every time I saw the building".

Stringfellow was shown around by the caretaker Phil, who would regale him with stories of the building's glorious past, and in particular of Sir Edward Moss, with whom Stringfellow immediately felt an affinity.

"I don't believe in reincarnation, but it is strange how my life echoed that of Edward Moss. Our personalities, our aspirations – even our attempts at innovation – were uncannily similar. Once I knew its history, I wanted the place."

He went ahead and signed the lease without consulting anyone else in his management team. Despite the building being "damp, smelly and full of bits of 1950s kitsch", the Hippodrome had cast its spell over another impresario.

In many ways, however, Edward Moss and Peter Stringfellow were diametrically opposed personalities. Stringfellow divided opinion. He was amiable but also brash, flamboyant and a renowned womaniser; Moss courted publicity out of necessity for his business but was otherwise the epitome of quiet respectability. Where Stringfellow opened strip clubs and controversially populated his other clubs with scantily clad women, Edward Moss had strived to offer a cleaned-up version of the music hall for family audiences. But there were also parallels; the vision, the pioneering instinct, the determination to innovate, to be the best at what they did, and that 'gut feeling' which many successful entrepreneurs often claim to have. The *Guardian* described Stringfellow's tastes as "profitably bizarre" and the same could be said of Moss, when it came to booking acts for the Hippodrome. Both men had also started in the provinces, Moss in Edinburgh, Stringfellow in Sheffield, then Leeds and Manchester, both building their businesses up from nothing before conquering London's West End. If Sir Edward Moss had lived through the 1980s rather than the 1880s, would he, instead of a theatre, have decided to open a huge nightclub on the corner of Cranbourn Street and Charing Cross Road? That is precisely what Peter Stringfellow decided to do. As his general manager Julian Russell confirms, in buying The Talk of the Town, Stringfellow's ambition was to create the greatest disco and nightclub in the country.

Moss, Stringfellow and the other Hippodrome alumni would all have agreed on something else: that no expense should be spared

The greatest disco in the world 1983-2009

Clubbers dance under the famous state-of-the-art lighting system of the London Hippodrome on 24th November 1989.

The hip and happening faces of 1980s London were gathered together for the opening night of the transformed London Hippodrome. Journalist, presenter and style maven Magenta Devine was there with boyfriend Tony James of the band Sigue Sigue Sputnik, as was Malcolm Maclaren. In addition, anyone with a provocative or flamboyant sense of style was positively encouraged.

Whitney Houston, a relative unknown, makes her UK debut on the stage of the London Hippodrome in 1983.

> **I don't believe in reincarnation, but it is strange how my life echoed that of Edward Moss. Our personalities, our aspirations – even our attempts at innovation – were uncannily similar. Once I knew its history, I wanted the place**
>
> Peter Stringfellow

in transforming The Talk of the Town into a 1980s mega-club. The interior was painted black, and Stringfellow ordered in specially commissioned plastic champagne flutes at a cost of £30,000, which turned out to scratch easily and to jump around in the dishwashers. He also insisted on black and silver leather seats, but when the seats arrived, nobody wanted to sit on them because the silver rubbed off on clothing. Costs escalated rapidly. The focus was on fitting the club with the best lighting and sound system available, investing in a huge thirty by twenty foot video screen costing $65,000 and a system of multi-coloured, water-cooled lasers. Designers John Franks and Paul Roberts were drafted in to oversee the overhaul, and Mark Fisher and Jonathan Park were in charge of the light and sound, tasked with training the flashing lights and music to pulse together in beat-perfect harmony. At one point, just a few weeks before its scheduled opening, there were three hundred workmen and technicians employed in a bid to achieve Stringfellow's ambitions. An unlikely friendship formed during this period between Stringfellow and the incumbent Robert Nesbitt, who, despite being heartbroken at the demise of The Talk of the Town, liaised with the new owner over the removal of machinery and installation of the new state-of-the-art equipment. Nesbitt found Stringfellow amiable, and was naturally interested in the technical side of the refurbishment. The pair formed quite a bond, and Nesbitt, together with his wife Iris, would occasionally dine at Stringfellow's restaurant on Upper St. Martin's Lane.

Meanwhile, Peter Stringfellow had experienced an epiphany over the name of his new club. Having initially decided that the name 'Space' summed up the futuristic venue he was planning (Talk II had been another option), one day he woke up from a dream where he had been standing in front of The Talk of the Town only to see its sign fall away to reveal the words of the Hippodrome carved above the entrance. It sounds improbable but nevertheless, Stringfellow decided to give the grand old building back its original name. Not only that, the iconic horse-drawn Greco-Roman chariot, still standing proudly on top of the dome on the roof, was to become the club's distinctive brand logo. In time it would even be incorporated into the light show.

While the name and logo were settled, despite the money and manpower being thrown at the new Hippodrome, the fit-out was beset with problems. It was taking time to get the lasers to work, and the computerised console controlling the lights was still a work in progress too. The spiralling debts and constant setbacks led Stringfellow to declare he knew he would never die of a heart attack, "because if I was going to have one, I'd have had one then".
A corporate event for a city firm a few days before the grand opening gave the team a chance to test everything, but when the rising stage carrying Sarah Vaughan at the piano jammed at her head height, this served to highlight just how far behind the preparations were. Nevertheless, Peter Stringfellow, ever the optimist and showman, and never short of a superlative or ten, brazenly set out his stall for the press.

"We have the best sound system, the most sophisticated air-conditioning, the most fabulous laser show in the world, and an incredible computerised lighting system," he told *The Times*, which disdainfully described him as "a 43 year-old who dresses like a teenager".

To Stringfellow's dismay, on the opening night, 17th November 1983, the famous lights that he had claimed were the best in the world failed to work properly, lowering from the ceiling but then staying there for

Seduced by the idea of aristocratic connections, Stringfellow booked Lady Theresa Manners, daughter of the Duke of Rutland, to perform at the Hippodrome with her band, The Business Connection. Theresa's grandmother, Margaret, Duchess of Argyll, who had achieved notoriety in the 1960s with a scandalous divorce case, came along to see her granddaughter perform, but found the noise so unpleasant she demanded some ear plugs. Ear plugs were not in plentiful supply at the Hippodrome and in desperation, Stringfellow, in typical slapstick fashion, offered her a makeshift pair, hastily adapted from tampons acquired from a dispenser in the ladies' toilets. So relieved was the Duchess to have the raucous sounds around her muffled, she appeared not to notice the strings hanging unceremoniously from each ear.

Frequently used as a venue for after-show parties and publicity launches, in 1984 the Hippodrome saw members of The Beatles descend to celebrate Paul McCartney's new album, Give My Regards to Broad Street.

The Beverley Sisters camping it up for an adoring audience in February 1985. "We haven't played this theatre for eighteen years," said Teddy, one of the younger twin sisters, "and though coming here now with all these laser beams is a bit like walking into an air raid (and we remember those) the crowd loved us. A lovely boy with very nice skin told me he had all our albums – he knew all the words to all our songs."

Champagne lifestyles catered for at the Hippodrome courtesy of a scantily clad waitress in 1989.

the rest of the evening rather than rising back up again. Having drunk rather too many glasses of the champagne being liberally poured out for the 1500 guests, Stringfellow took to the stage to give a rambling explanation for the technical hitch. It was completely unnecessary. The crowd, similarly well lubricated by the free champagne, simply applauded and carried on dancing. Ironically, the next day's review in *The Evening Standard* gave particular praise to the "magnificent £1 million lights" which "dazzled us all". There were plenty who were quick to criticise Stringfellow's profligate spending. *The Sunday Telegraph* reported on rivals who claimed he was offering nothing new or unique, and charging a small fortune for what was basically "a 1980s-style dance hall". It was pointed out that laser beams and video screens had first been done at New York's Studio 54 seven years earlier, and the Camden Palace's refit had cost a mere £300,000 compared to Stringfellow's extravagant £3 million investment. He had taken on a high-risk venture, and the vultures were circling in the hope that he would fall victim to his own ambition. Stringfellow had a lot to prove.

Slowly but surely, the Hippodrome began to fill up night after night. The engineers continued to tinker with the lighting system after the club closed, and within a few weeks, all components of the Hippodrome's spectacular technical theatrics were fully functional. The stage lift, such an integral part of The Talk of the Town's cabaret shows, continued to do good service. In 1985, as part of a publicity tour, Little Richard arose from below playing a white grand piano, a shining beacon in the gloom of the Hippodrome's cavernous space.

The Hippodrome, in its new incarnation, encapsulated much of the bold excess of 1980s Britain. Price of entry was between £5 and £7.50, more expensive than nearly any other well-known nightclub in the West End, and the cost of drinks, once inside, was correspondingly wallet-shrinking. There was a stringent door policy, in which the bouncers had carte blanche to admit or refuse entry to customers based on their appearance. These were all factors that served to contrive an aura of exclusivity, catnip to tourists and out-of-towners, who had either read about the Hippodrome, or seen it – or Stringfellow – on the television. In a survey of nightlife in the 1980s *The Times* interviewed a couple from Dartford who were at the Hippodrome for the night, and, while they admitted shock at the admission price, they felt reassured knowing the club "didn't let in any riff-raff". The lights were "flash", they enjoyed sinking into the deep sofas and asked, "Have you seen the lavatories? Hair spray, cologne, the lot! What experience. Out of this world!" In reality, the truly fashionable crowd went elsewhere – to the nearby Wag Club or the Limelight; many in the New Romantic tribe favoured the Camden Palace run by Steve Strange. The Hippodrome, in an effort to grab some hip cachet for itself, would frequently admit for free anyone with an eccentric or outrageous sense of style. "We attracted people from across the social spectrum," wrote Peter Stringfellow in his memoirs, "from punks on the dole to affluent hoorays."

The journalist James Delingpole, who visited the club on behalf of *The Illustrated London News* in July 1988, was not convinced, noticing, "the queue, the watchful bouncers, the £10 entry fee were all part of the cultivated image of exclusivity". Once inside he noted, "It has an atmosphere of cheap titillation," going on to describe the club's lights as "a huge death machine, which swoops down, lights flashing, spewing out smoke on to the bored groovers beneath". He tried to ask for a glass of tap water but was given short shrift and told he had to buy something first, and when he claimed one of the black chairs

Charles Spencer, Lord Althorp (now Earl Spencer), brother to Diana, Princess of Wales, was a frequent visitor to the Hippodrome and friend to Peter Stringfellow. He is seen here arriving with friend for a gig by The Business Connection in December 1985.

Sarah Ferguson, prior to her marriage to Prince Andrew, was one of the guests at the Hippodrome on 26th June 1985 to also see aristocratic rock band The Business Connection. The band's name was appropriate, considering the well-connected audience. Also present was David Linley, son of Princess Margaret, together with his then-girlfriend, Susannah Constantine, Lady Helen Windsor and rock royalty in the form of Mick Jagger.

Hair gel and clouds of aftershave filling the entrance foyer of the Hippodrome as a "typical Essex crowd" queue to enter on a weekend night in 1988.

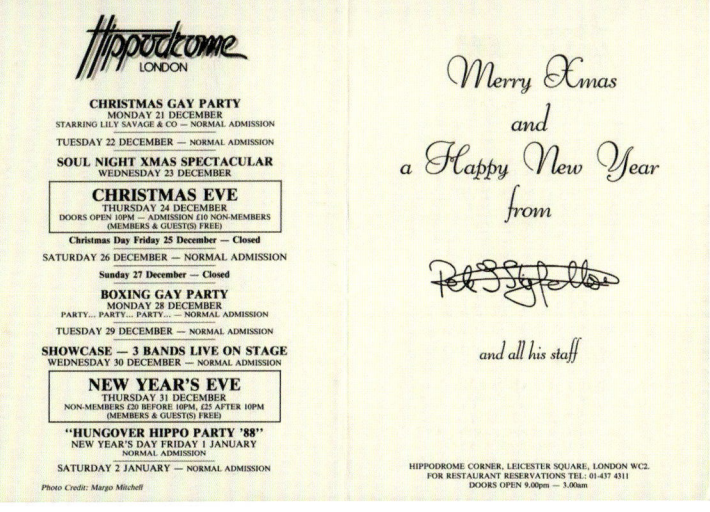

Promotional Christmas card featuring Stringfellow and his cast of fun-makers at the Hippodrome, including his girlfriend Frizzby Fox (top right behind him). Note that part of the Christmas programme includes the appearance of Lily Savage at the 'Christmas Gay Party'.

overlooking the dance floor was moved on as the area was reserved for champagne drinkers only. The one beacon of civility, he felt, was the men's lavatories, where "the attendant had carefully arranged a shrine to male beauty. On a table before the mirror were laid out nine varieties of aftershave, five types of brush, and assorted gels, sprays, mousses and unguents. A nearby dish was covered in £1 coins – never anything less – and it seemed obligatory to reward the attendant for his trouble."

Aged nineteen, Adrian Pel worked at the Hippodrome in 1986 as one of these attendants, but in the infrequently visited VIP men's toilets on the top floor, dispensing the spray and fragrances that had so impressed Peter and Tracey from Dartford. As a keen clubber himself, Adrian would visit the club when not working, but usually only on a Thursday night when admission was free, and then as a stop-off on the way to somewhere else. He remembers eighties pop stars such as Boy George and Marilyn frequenting the club (not to mention Peter Stringfellow giving him a £20 tip after a visit to the gents; generous, but if anyone was aware the attendants relied on tips, Stringfellow was) but agrees that the majority of customers were not particularly sophisticated. Yet the Hippodrome had a kind of flamboyant notoriety. It was as ostentatious and unapologetic as its owner, and while its exclusive character may have been a sham, there was still a sense of occasion about the place. Customers came to dance, drink, flirt and to briefly indulge in the extravagant hedonism it promoted.

Peter Stringfellow ensured there was more to his club than just lights and music, booking celebrity appearances and novelty acts to entertain his customers – frequently, it seems, invoking the spirit of his predecessor Edward Moss with circus stunts, and casting himself as ringmaster. On one occasion, Stringfellow got his then girlfriend, the DJ Frizzby Fox, to be assistant to a knife thrower, and on another he volunteered to sit on the shoulders of a tightrope walker, instantly regretting the decision when he realised the slightest mistake would probably mean death. A wild animal evening went dangerously wrong when a lioness broke free, dragging her trainer horizontally across the club's floor, though the animal was quickly secured with the help of nets; Adrian Pel remembers the drag queen Divine once making an entrance astride a baby elephant. There were other ideas bordering on the bizarre, and often crossing the boundaries of good taste (among various ill-judged ideas was a 'Bad Taste' night which recreated a car crash). A Miss Glamour Wear 1989 competition, judged by a panel that included Christopher Biggins, Su Pollard and Lemmie from Motorhead, in which the participants paraded in underwear in front of clubbers, seems very much a relic of another era.

And yet among the mayhem and the occasional vulgarity, the Hippodrome under Stringfellow seemed equally as capable of rising to the occasion. The UK premiere of Michael Jackson's 'Thriller' was on the Hippodrome's vast video screen. It was also the setting for the battle in 1987 between chess masters Gary Kasparov and Nigel Short, and, incongruously, it hosted an event for young Liberals, where the diminutive David Steel was introduced to the Amazonian Cleo Roccos for a predictably compromising photo opportunity. Among the frequent guests at the club was Charles Spencer, the brother of the Princess of Wales. Stringfellow formed a friendship with Charlie, who would join him, Frizzby, Stringfellow's daughter Karen and the Hippodrome's MC Bradley White at the Sun Luck Chinese restaurant where they could drink after hours. Stringfellow was introduced to Diana at Charlie's 21st birthday at Althorp and eventually invited her to the Hippodrome to a special gala performance of the

The Hippodrome's state-of-the-art lighting system, 1980s. Futuristic and complex, the lights had some operational hiccups in the early days.

The trusty stage mechanics of the old Talk of the Town were still providing service for events at the Hippodrome, including an appearance by Little Richard at a book launch in 1985, where he emerged from beneath the stage seated at a white grand piano.

Right: Flyer for an after-show party at the Hippodrome on the night the Artist formerly known as Prince was performing at Wembley Arena as part of his New Power Soul tour in 1998. He played a full concert at the Hippodrome the following night before moving on to Brixton Academy on 28th August.

Far right: By the 1990s, the Hippodrome had tapped into the rave scene. This flyer advertises one of its 'Orange' all-nighters held on 27th December 1992.

The Most Famous Discotheque In The World

The Hippodrome

is proud to announce

The Artist
formally known as
Prince
is appearing and hosting his

"AFTER SHOW PARTY"

on
Wednesday 26th August 1998

10PM - 3AM　　　　　　　　　　　STRICTLY OVER 18's
CASUAL DRESS　　　　　　　　　　　　　　　R.O.A.R

TICKET'S AVAILABLE AT THE DOOR, ON A FIRST COME FIRST SERVE BASIS. DOORS OPEN AT 10PM

THIS IS THE PARTY OF THE YEAR!!!

The Hippodrome, Hippodrome Corner, Leicester Square, London
Tel: 0171 437 4311

Inside the Hippdrome in the late 1980s. Peter Stringfellow sold the business in 1989 but the venue continued as a club throughout the 1990s.

London Festival Ballet to celebrate their hundredth anniversary. The Hippodrome went into overdrive preparing for the royal visit. Stringfellow's Star Bar was refurbished with antique furniture to the tune of £35,000, and the chef David Miles even created a special dish, a Papillon steak, of a beef fillet in the shape of a butterfly with a mushroom and Boursin sauce, in her honour. She arrived looking chic in a tuxedo and cheekily told Stringfellow to tuck his Issey Miyake shirt in. Nervously drinking rather more than he should have done, Stringfellow found himself indulging in some mild flirtation with his royal guest but when he asked how he could address her informally, she very firmly told him that, "Princess will do nicely thank you." Sadly, when she was invited to inspect the new-look Star Bar, she politely declined, saying she did not have enough time.

One of Peter Stringfellow's most successful innovations was the introduction every Monday of a gay night, the first time a high-profile, mainstream mega-club had run a specific event for a gay audience. Apart from Heaven, run by Richard Branson, major gay venues in central London were practically unknown during this period, but Stringfellow felt instinctively that attracting the gay market would be the key to his success. It was a bawdy, sexually charged atmosphere, spiced with acts ranging from porn stars to camp legends like the Beverley Sisters, who played there in February 1985, delivering a schmaltzy set to an adoring audience. The Beverley Sisters had slipped into the Hippodrome one night to see their daughters perform as a band called the Little Foxes, and Stringfellow, ever the opportunist, asked them to come out of semi-retirement to perform there themselves. It was a categorical triumph. "After the show they were mobbed for autographs and carried shoulder high from the theatre, three middle-aged women from Barnet," reported *The Observer*. The American drag artist and pop star Divine was a guaranteed draw, regularly filling the Hippodrome to capacity. Stringfellow paid Divine generously, and in return Divine obliged with an exuberant show, once rising up onto the stage draped in the American flag for a special Independence Day celebration, before removing the stars and stripes boxer shorts belonging to the dancers. Stringfellow's hunch had been right. Mondays at the Hippodrome quickly became a notable fixture of London's gay scene.

The rest of the week catered to different crowds. There was a rock-themed night on Tuesdays, Battle of the Bands on Wednesday, Frizzby Fox on Thursdays, when entry was free, and then what Julian Russell described as a more "normal Essex crowd" on Fridays and Saturdays, arriving in a cloud of hairspray, with plenty of cash to spend at the champagne bar. Like The Talk of the Town before it, the Hippodrome would often be hired out at weekends. One Sunday, an impressive line-up consisting of Cliff Richard, The Shadows, Jimmy Ruffin and Long John Baldry were recording at the Hippodrome, but the venue was lacking the atmosphere generated by a live crowd. Julian Russell remembers having to pay passers-by to come in and form an audience, as nobody they approached believed who was inside on a Sunday afternoon.

In 1989, wishing to expand his empire further in America, and needing cash as settlement for a second divorce, Peter Stringfellow sold the Hippodrome to Michael Ward of European Leisure for £7 million. It had been a riotous six years, and the Hippodrome had allowed him to give free rein to his imagination, but Stringfellow was also a businessman, and the Hippodrome had made him a tidy profit. European Leisure invested in successful businesses rather than building them from scratch, and in that respect, the Hippodrome,

La Clique opened at the Hippodrome in 2008 and in many ways echoed the vision of Edward Moss more than a century earlier with its curious melange of novel and awe-inspiring acts.

> **Pre-World War II Germany had the Weimar cabaret. Post-crash England has La Clique**
>
> The Evening Standard

Captain Frodo, one of the performers in *La Clique*'s subversive circus act show in 2008 to 2009, absorbed in passing his entire body through a tennis racquet head.

David O'Mers of *La Clique* setting pulses racing with his aerial bath routine.

on a prime London spot and with a healthy turnover, was a good investment.

And so the Hippodrome continued, without its chipper ringmaster now, but in roughly the same format. As the eighties turned into the nineties, the introduction of rave nights signified a slight adjustment to fall into line with musical tastes, but the Hippodrome's usual eclecticism remained, and in between or combined with club nights were fashion shows, hairdressing competitions, celebrity appearances, lookalike contests – one in August 1995 had Mark Anthony voted as Britain's number one Prince lookalike by the Hippodrome 'ravers'. Prince, the actual one, had played an after-show concert at the Hippodrome until 5:30 in the morning around the same time.

The millennium marked the Hippodrome's centenary, but also an uncertain future. Its owners were now Luminar Leisure, who in 2003 decided not to renew the lease on the building. There had been growing concern, particularly from supporters of theatrical heritage, about the potential fate of the Hippodrome. In 2002, a planning application to turn the building into shops and residential flats was met with a thunderous opposition. Many hoped it could be restored as a fully functioning theatre once again and there were suggestions that the RSC could use it as a temporary home, or that Andrew Lloyd Webber should step in to buy it. Then in 2004, it was reported that a group of investors had plans to make the Hippodrome an entertainment venue once more, with live music on Friday nights and Moulin-Rouge-style acts on Saturdays. It seemed a promising concept but the Hippodrome's malaise continued. Without any proper purpose, it became a prime spot for private events and corporate functions, particularly theatre and film premiere after-show parties. Then in 2008, a show arrived that appeared tailor made especially for the Hippodrome.

La Clique, which had first captivated audiences at the Edinburgh Fringe Festival, was a witty hybrid of sophisticated circus and burlesque, seamlessly blending sauce, sex and silliness to bring a show that chimed in time with recession-hit Britain.

"Pre-World War II Germany had the Weimar cabaret. Post-crash England has La Clique," quipped *The Evening Standard*, who declared it the perfect form of escapism, "with the economy gurgling down the toilet". It was an opinion that had been echoed through the decades by theatre critics visiting the Hippodrome. When times were tough, theatre, and particularly the imaginative spectacles the Hippodrome did so well, could offer a welcome diversion. *La Clique* was the variety programme of the Hippodrome's Edwardian heyday reimagined for the twenty-first century, an artful and erotic subversion of those glory days. Among the internationally harvested acts were Yulia Pakhtina spinning multiple hula hoops, and David O'Mers, who performed a bath-time aerial routine. Captain Frodo, a Norwegian contortionist, somehow squeezed himself through two stringless tennis racquets, while Ursula Martinez's infamous 'hanky panky' routine saw her produce handkerchiefs from increasingly unmentionable places. *La Clique* was cool, clever, slickly produced and the press was unanimous in its praise. It played at the Hippodrome from October 2008 to June 2009, the first time in twenty years the venue had hosted a long-running live show. It might have remained there longer, but just as it opened, a licence was granted to United Leisure Gaming to convert the Hippodrome into a casino, and by the summer of 2009, preparations were underway for the 109-year-old building to undergo yet another regeneration.

Princess Mary, Countess of Harewood pictured outside the London Hippodrome in July 1931 with her two sons (left), George and Gerald, and a number of curious members of the public after attending a charity matinee performed by the young pupils of Madame Vacani's dancing school. Seen centre, in charge of proceedings, is 'Mac' (aka Mr. MacGrath), the Hippodrome's long-serving front-of-house manager. The little girl at the front is Margaret Elphinstone, niece of the Duchess of York (and cousin of the present Queen), who was one of the performers.

> "Roger Moore chatted to Princess Anne while among the guests on the Queen's table was Neil Armstrong, the first man on the moon. It is difficult to think of two more iconic dinner companions"

By Royal Command

The Hippodrome has enjoyed the royal seal of approval throughout its history, from the Shah of Persia arriving to enjoy the aquatic thrills of *The Bandits* in 1902 to George V chuckling at comedian Milton Hayes at the Royal Command Performance in 1921. Queen Alexandra had made friends with one of Richard Sawade's tiger cubs in 1905, and royal family members from Princess Mary to the Duke of Edinburgh regularly lent regal cachet to the Hippodrome and Talk of the Town's many charity functions through the years. During the Second World War, King George VI and Queen Elizabeth came to see *Black Velvet*, and in 1945, brought Princesses Elizabeth and Margaret to *Meet the Navy*. Even in the 1980s, when the Hippodrome was reborn as a discotheque under Peter Stringfellow, it received a much-publicised visit by Princess Diana in March 1987. Dressed in a chic tuxedo suit, she arrived to support a charity performance of London Festival Ballet's new jazz ballet, *Night Creatures*. The Princess, who the papers reported "liked pop music", was ushered into the building by Stringfellow, and spent some time that night talking to singer Boy George, who was a controversial figure at the time having admitted publicly to a drugs problem. There were also occasions when members of the royal family attended informally. The future King Edward VIII and his brothers came to enjoy the revues and comedy musicals of the 1920s, while Princess Margaret visited The Talk of the Town on at least one occasion.

But on 18th November 1970, The Talk of the Town hosted an event that was to eclipse all others in terms of royal prestige. The Royal Gala in aid of the World Wildlife Fund not only boasted a star-studded line-up, which included Engelbert Humperdinck, Petula Clark, Tom Jones, Rudolph Nureyev and Bob Hope, but counted no fewer than eighteen members of British and European royalty among the audience, including Queen Elizabeth II and the Duke of Edinburgh, Prince Charles, Princess Anne, Queen Juliana and Prince Bernhard of the Netherlands, and King Constantine and Queen Anne-Marie of Greece. The comparative informality of The Talk of the Town's layout led to an unusually relaxed atmosphere, with royalty and celebrities mixing on each table, and everyone dining on melon in port wine, chicken stuffed with pâté and truffle, followed by ice-cream cake in the shape of a panda (the WWF's logo). On one table, Cary Grant sat with Queen Juliana of the Netherlands and Prince Philip; Prince Charles was positioned opposite Bob Hope on another. Roger Moore chatted to Princess Anne while among the guests on the Queen's table was Neil Armstrong, the first man on the moon. It is difficult to think of two more iconic dinner companions. "It's the West End's most Fantastic Night Out Ever – as 18 Royals Go Out on the Town" screamed the *Daily Mirror*'s headlines, which was particularly enamoured with the idea of the Queen going 'clubbing'. Bob Hope, always with a topical quip up his sleeve, took to the stage, surveyed the scene before him and remarked it was like looking at a chess board. The only hiccup was when Rex Harrison, who was acting as compere, mistakenly introduced Petula Clark instead of Rudolf Nureyev, causing Robert Nesbitt to stand up and say, "No, no dear boy, you've got the order wrong." Harrison apologised, bowed, retreated back into the wings, and came back on to sympathetic applause and laughter. With seats costing anything from £25 to £500, the evening raised a total of £100,000 for the World Wildlife Fund. It was one of The Talk of the Town's most glittering occasions.

In 1976, royalty was out in force once more for *Once Upon a Century*, a gala dinner and entertainment celebrating the centenary of St. John Ambulance. On this occasion, Robert Nesbitt adapted numbers from the current cabaret, *Sweet Temptation*, staged a version of 'What a Swell Party This Is' from the film *High Society* (which seemed particularly appropriate given the company), and booked Andy Williams in the star spot. Nesbitt counted the two royal galas as among his most satisfying achievements, "for when else have 18 royal personages been present in a theatre restaurant," he wrote in his unpublished memoirs, "and indeed when has H.M. The Queen ever been seen seated at a table watching a West End floor show?"

Stars and royalty meet and mingle at the 1970 World Wildlife Fund Gala. Bob Hope and Tom Jones are presented to The Queen, while twenty-year-old Princess Anne chats with Roger Moore. At the time, Moore was famous for playing Simon Templar in the TV series *The Saint*, and was still three years away from taking on his most famous role as James Bond.

The Queen, the Duke of Edinburgh, Prince Charles and Princess Anne arrive at The Talk of the Town for the World Wildlife Fund Gala, 18th November 1970. They were joined by fourteen members of European royalty for an event which was one of the most dazzling evenings witnessed by the venue in its seventy-year history. The Talk of the Town's team liaised with Buckingham Palace in planning a minute-by-minute schedule to ensure any royal event ran with military precision.

17th March 1987: the Princess of Wales steps onto the red carpet at the Hippodrome in a tuxedo and pink bow tie ensemble that earned column inches in the press. She jokingly asked Peter Stringfellow why he hadn't tucked his own shirt in.

More than one hundred and twenty years since it first opened its doors, the Hippodrome remains a familiar landmark on the corner of Charing Cross Road and Cranbourn Street. While its interior has gone through many transformations through the decades, its founder Sir Edward Moss and the building's architect, Frank Matcham, would still recognise the flamboyant façade of red sandstone, brick and terracotta, which has changed little since its Edwardian heyday.

The Hippodrome Casino 2009-present

The shell of the Hippodrome's auditorium, with layers of its history revealed at the start of renovations in 2009. The work would take three years and £40 million to complete.

As work gathers pace, the brand-new Hippodrome Casino prepares to emerge from its chrysalis.

Detail of the new plasterwork, a sensitive reinterpretation carried out by Locker and Riley, inspired by Frank Matcham's ornate interior which had been lost during the remodelling of the building into The Talk of the Town in the 1950s.

In 2012, the firm received an award in the heritage category at the FPDC Plaisterers' Awards, for exemplary craftsmanship shown in the Hippodrome renovation.

A large, landmark building in a prime location in one of the world's greatest cities cannot help but attract the attention of anyone with an entrepreneurial eye for a business opportunity. But the London Hippodrome offers far more than a set of boxes for investors to tick. It resonates with a rich and romantic history; casts a spell over each new generation; ensnares, seduces and stirs the ambitions of entertainers and impresarios; and, as each new owner or tenant steps into the shoes of the last, they become the custodian of not just a building, but a priceless piece of the past.

When Robert Nesbitt, the creative force behind the entertainment at The Talk of the Town, joined forces with Bernard Delfont and Charles Forte in the 1950s, his memories of going to see the glamorous Hippodrome revues of the Great War era were never far from his mind. Peter Stringfellow had an epiphany after visiting The Talk of the Town in 1980, sparking his grand ambition to create what he called the greatest disco in the world.

Like Nesbitt and Stringfellow before him, Jimmy Thomas felt a special connection to the Hippodrome, kindled by a visit to The Talk of the Town in 1966 when the Andrews Sisters were performing. He and his friends, none of whom had much money at the time, bought a show-only ticket, afterwards choosing the more economical option of a bacon sandwich and cup of tea at the Fiori restaurant over the road. He had enjoyed the show but was more intrigued by the building, taking note of the false ceiling and hints of old plasterwork falling away. When one of his friends asked him what he planned to do about it he announced, "I'm going to buy it one day and restore it! I'll bring it back to its former glory and turn it into one of the biggest entertainment centres in the country."

It was an audacious declaration, but more than half a century on, Jimmy Thomas has made good on his promise, and today the Hippodrome is once again at the heart of London's West End, thriving as the country's largest casino, but with the addition of a cabaret theatre, eight bars including a rooftop terrace and an award-winning restaurant. In 1900 it opened as a theatre of varieties, and arguably, the Hippodrome's twenty-first century incarnation continues to offer variety to visitors who can choose to try their luck at the gaming tables, eat at the Heliot Steak House, enjoy a cocktail, play poker or take in a show. Jimmy Thomas, now in his late eighties, is the president of the company and can often be spotted there, chatting to guests. Simon Thomas, his son, CEO and Chairman of the Hippodrome Casino, describes him as, "a wise, experienced operator who still loves being involved in the business". For both father and son, the satisfaction of seeing the Hippodrome revived and revitalised is all the sweeter considering the rocky road they travelled to achieve their vision. "If I'd known then what I know now, I'd probably have

Birds-eye view of the casino's main gaming room, formerly the old Hippodrome's arena and auditorium. The huge dandelion clock lights which illuminate the central atrium were inspired by a report in *The Daily News* from December 1899, describing the reaction of the first visitors to the building prior to opening: "They walked around the new building astonished, puzzled and delighted, like Alice in Wonderland. Every now and then they had almost to pinch themselves to make sure they were awake." Then, as now, the Hippodrome was a place of fantasy and escapism.

Jimmy Thomas and Bruce Forsyth share a joke as they pose with commemorative plaques outside the Hippodrome Casino on 7th August 2013. Sir Bruce's plaque records his own eight performances at The Talk of the Town, while Mr. Thomas holds one commemorating Sammy Davis Jr. appearing at the venue in August 1969.

"I soon realised if I was to do the job properly I had to bring back much of the original vision of Frank Matcham, all the while making it the best casino the country had ever seen." Simon Thomas, Chairman and co-founder of the Hippodrome Casino, pictured with his grand design.

> **I'm going to buy it one day and restore it! I'll bring it back to its former glory and turn it into one of the biggest entertainment centres in the country**
>
> **Jimmy Thomas**

Boris Johnson tries his luck at roulette at the opening of the Hippodrome Casino on 13th July 2012. Then Mayor of London, he was encouraged to put his chips on number ten but the future Prime Minister declined. Mr. Johnson described the renovation as, "simply stunning" and highlighted the advantages of a business that would attract tourists and see "money pouring into London".

walked away!" remarks Simon wryly, admitting to numerous sleepless nights during the course of the Hippodrome's renovation. Yet, in quoting Hannibal, his mantra is, "I will find a way, or I will make a way," demonstrating the tenacity and determination with which he approached the project and which were necessary to make it a success.

The Thomas family's expertise was originally in bingo halls. In the early 1960s Jimmy launched Thomas Automatics, which built and supplied amusement and leisure equipment, and over the next twenty-five years he grew the business to include the Showboat amusement centres and Beacon bingo halls, selling most of the business to the Rank Organisation in 1987.

After working for the City firm Singer & Friedlander, Simon joined the new family company, Thomas Estates Ltd, working on the amusement and bingo portfolio retained from the Rank deal. His move coincided with the deregulation of bingo in the 1990s which allowed bingo halls to advertise for the first time in thirty years. It was a boon to the Thomases' business, resulting in a 2,700-seater purpose-built flagship bingo hall in Cricklewood. Complete with three bars, two restaurants, two cabaret stages, a wedding licence and a cinema licence, it was the largest bingo venue in Europe. The experience of creating it helped inform the Hippodrome development.

In the early 2000s, Simon was president of BACTA, one of the industry's trade associations, and was keeping a watchful eye on the proposals for a new Gambling Act. The Labour Government's proposals were looking good for casinos, giving them the freedoms that bingo was given in the 1990s and that he had learnt to use effectively. For the first time casinos were going to be able to advertise and promote themselves, as well as offer live entertainment and alcohol on the gaming floor. Importantly, customers would be able to walk in off the street without joining as a member 24 hours before. These changes would, he realised, transform the sector and open it up to a larger audience. British casinos would finally be able to offer both gambling and entertainment on a par with European operators or Las Vegas; good food, drinks and theatre or cabaret shows could sit comfortably alongside the gaming tables. Customers could drink as they played and there was no longer the 24-hour 'cooling off' period, formerly required for new members. Instead, people could just walk in and sit down at the table. It also allowed for the reframing of the casino experience into something that was no longer taboo or intimidating; a place that bridged the gap between the high-end, high-stakes Mayfair clubs and those that were considered far from salubrious.

The smoking ban was announced at a similar time as the new Act. Simon's analysis was that the impact of this, and the new regulatory changes, was going to be worse than the market expected. So taking advantage of the strong credit market and demand for leisure stocks, he sold Thomas Estates in 2006 and started the Hippodrome project.

Simon knew the increased freedom and flexibility would allow them to bring a sophisticated and exciting concept to a mass audience; inviting both locals and tourists into a space that was glamorous and distinctive, but also welcoming and inclusive. The London Hippodrome, which had spent most of the past decade without a dedicated purpose, but with tens of thousands of people passing by its door every hour, appeared to be the ideal setting and negotiations commenced with the landlord, Gascoyne Holdings.

Prince arriving at the Hippodrome Casino on 5th June 2014, where he played an intimate late-night gig in the Matcham Theatre. During the two hour set, the audience were treated to a virtuoso performance of his many hits including 'When Doves Cry', '1999' and 'Purple Rain'. It would be the last concert the multi-talented musician would give in the UK before his untimely death in 2016.

In a show that blended song, dance and reminiscences from her fifty-year career, Bonnie Langford was joined on stage on 31st March 2016 by ballroom king Anton du Beke, for a rendition of 'Let's Face the Music and Dance'.

A veteran of musicals and television, including the hit show *Glee*, Matthew Morrison appeared at the Hippodrome on 16th May 2017, treating the audience to a mix of standards and favourites, backed by a jazz band.

There had already been conversations with both Lord Lloyd Webber and Cameron Mackintosh about the viability of converting the Hippodrome back to a theatre, an option favoured by Gascoyne Holdings and various heritage groups. But they could not see a way of making it a commercial success. Other members of the theatrical community hoped it might, with its famously superior sight lines engineered by Matcham, become a new London performance venue for the Royal Shakespeare Company. Turning it into a retail space with the addition of a roof-level restaurant overlooking the West End was also considered. But the Thomas proposal, which sought to preserve and restore the building *and* would see more immediate income generation, job creation and stimulus to the local economy, was beginning to seem like a good fit. The building's days as a nightclub were over especially as Westminster council had taken away its alcohol licence, being keen to move away from anything that would negatively impact on the area's image. In 2005, Jimmy and Simon Thomas signed the lease and set to work.

Like many grand designs, the project soon became a labour of love. "It was a mess," recalls Simon Thomas. "In its various incarnations down the years its tenants had systematically ripped the heart and soul out of the building and I soon realised if I was to do the job properly I had to bring back much of the original vision, drama and splendour of Frank Matcham, all the while making it the best casino the country had ever seen."

Nor were the incomers welcomed immediately with open arms. "Quite rightly there were many historical trusts, heritage organisations, theatrical luminaries, police and local councillors, who all treated us with suspicion. There were letters in the press suggesting the building should not be repurposed in this way. Of course, everyone had the Hippodrome's best interests at heart. They made us jump through many hoops and I would have done exactly the same."

The architects Cadmium Design, headed by Paula Reason, were engaged to work on the rebuild and renovation. As experts in designing entertainment venues, it became clear to both architect and client as plans progressed that they needed to increase the floor space of the building if they were to build the casino they envisaged. Jimmy likens the building to an Easter egg: "It's huge but there's a lot of space that is simply fresh air. Of course, that's wonderful on the eye and has significant dramatic impact, but it's still surprisingly short on useable space." On the hunt for more square footage, Simon approached Gascoyne Holdings about potentially acquiring Cranbourn Mansions, a block of Edwardian gentlemen's apartments that abutted the theatre and shared a light-well. Many of the rooms had served as Hippodrome offices over the years. While work continued on the transformation of the main theatre, this extra property, a warren of rooms overlooking Leicester Square, complete with the original fireplaces and sash windows, was woven into the project. Further space was provided by the Crystal Rooms, a former amusement arcade which had run along the Cranbourn Street aspect of the building.

Cadmium's brief was to create an environment that could combine the practical requirements of the casino with a spectacular interior, encompassing all this within a sensitive restoration which would do much to return the Hippodrome to its former grandeur. The false ceiling which had been installed during The Talk of the Town refit was removed, and £700,000 was spent on replacing much of the ornate plasterwork and mouldings by experts at Locker and

In a nod to the building's theatrical heritage, the Matcham Theatre has hosted a series of successful cabaret shows featuring stars from the stage and screen in its relaxed, intimate space. Michael Ball, who first found fame in the West End playing Marius in *Les Misérables* back in 1985 and has gone on to become one of Britain's favourite television and radio personalities, took to the stage at the Hippodrome Casino on 21st July 2016 in a sell-out concert.

The upper floor of the three-tier outdoor roof terrace, constructed in 2020 during the temporary closure of the Hippodrome due to the pandemic. The open-air space, with room for up to 150, gives guests a good view of the building's famous cupola topped with its charioteer.

Singer, songwriter, actor and Broadway star Tituss Burgess, 22nd September 2016.

The Heliot Steak House, decorated with more awards for 'best steak restaurant' than any other in London, was named after the lion tamer Claire Heliot, who once fed her charges with raw meat in the arena below.

Riley, who, in cooperation with English Heritage and the Theatres Trust, recreated the ten-metre-wide proscenium arch and balcony fronts. A team from the Museum of London came to check there was nothing of archaeological interest before work could progress, and everyone prayed that a rumoured subterranean water source, which purportedly had once run right under the Hippodrome, was no longer extant.

Even the most seasoned speculator might shy away from the challenges of not only renovating the historic building, but moulding it into an efficient, profit-making business. But Simon Thomas had a fundamental belief the concept could work. "The skills I used to create the largest bingo hall in the country – a mass-market monolith – were transferable. I'd previously done much of what I was trying to achieve. Together with a highly skilled architect team, I was now building a multi-product business where all the elements were related, but for the first time with a casino at its core. We were the first; pioneers in fact, enabled by the enlightened changes to the Gambling Act and were interpreting the new rules to the max. It was a once-in-a-generation opportunity to reshape an industry steeped in tradition and demonstrate its true potential. Fortunately, I now had two buildings that, once combined, were big enough to accommodate the vision and ambition."

While there was no lack of confidence or belief in the venture, for a venue that had seen so much on-stage drama over the years, it was perhaps no surprise that during the course of the renovation there were one or two nail-biting moments worthy of an Edwardian melodrama. To keep on top of cashflow, the Thomases mortgaged their houses but when a promised loan from Barclays Bank was withdrawn at the last minute, it was a serious blow – thankfully, a temporary one. At the time of this setback, Simon Thomas was watching the news one night when his interest was piqued by an interview with Bob Diamond, Chief Executive of Barclays Bank, in which he spoke about how the bank was fully committed to supporting the recovery of British businesses through renovation, regeneration and job creation. Simon wrote Mr. Diamond an email that night explaining his situation and how they were trying to do everything Barclays espoused, and Barclays were doing the opposite of supporting them. He received a reply the following day. Barclays Bank would, after all, support the project.

Five years and £40 million after originally signing the lease, the Hippodrome Casino was opened on Friday 13th July 2012 by Boris Johnson, at that time Mayor of London, and Councillor Robert Davis, former deputy leader of Westminster Council. Mr. Johnson gamely took a turn at the roulette table and said of the West End's latest opening: "This huge project has not only restored and retained the glorious fabric of this historic building, but it has also created 450 new jobs for the capital at a very important time. It is a simply stunning venue with every conceivable attraction in a James Bond-style environment where people can get as plastered as this very ceiling!" He added it was vital for the city to continue to provide developments that would attract tourists, "lavishing foreign currencies and pouring money into London". Interviewed by BBC News on launch day, Simon Thomas summarised the significance of this new era for the Hippodrome, explaining it could "redefine the way in which visitors to the West End celebrate an evening out".

Unlike a West End show, which prepares for its opening night with months of rehearsals, the assembled staff at the Hippodrome Casino

In November 2014, two heavyweights of the sporting world, Rafael Nadal and Ronaldo, took part in a poker game at PokerStars Live at the Hippodrome. The Grand Slam champion prevailed, winning $50,000 for the Rafa Nadal Foundation. Meanwhile, one of the world's greatest football stars took a penalty of a different kind: doing the dishes in the Hippodrome's kitchens.

Below: *Magic Mike Live*, a theatrical spin-off from the 2012 film devised by one of its original stars, Channing Tatum, began in Las Vegas and came to London in 2018 where it took up residence in the Matcham Theatre, renamed the Magic Mike Live Theatre having undergone a £3 million remodelling to support and enhance a theatrical event unlike anything else in the West End. Described by *The Independent* as "like *Strictly* on Viagra", the cast of top international dancers treat audiences to ninety minutes of seductive spectacle, jaw-dropping choreography and, according to *Time Out*, "more abs than Brazil's Olympic diving team" in a steamy show that is firmly intended for the 21st-century female gaze.

> **Building a cabaret space was a key part of our ambitions in retaining a core theatrical element for the Hippodrome, the location for so many incredible performances down the years**
>
> Simon Thomas

Channing Tatum and the cast of *Magic Mike* pose for a picture in Piccadilly Circus where their arrival in London was emblazoned across the famous illuminated hoardings.

instead prepared themselves for a baptism of fire. Nobody could quite predict how many people would come through the door, especially as the opening coincided with the staging of the Olympic Games in London. Twelve thousand customers a week had been the original year one projection, yet by week four, they hit their year two projection of eighteen thousand visitors a week, and by the end of 2012, the business was operating 50% over financial projections. Open twenty-four hours, seven days a week, the Hippodrome Casino was soon running smoothly, the only hiccup occurring on Christmas Eve 2012 when realisation dawned that, after five and a half months of being open round the clock, nobody actually knew how to lock up the building!

On the day the Hippodrome Casino opened, Simon Thomas had told reporters, "Work has only just begun." His father Jimmy reiterated this in an interview with *Gambling Insider* – "I know we'll spend a lot more – we're not satisfied yet" – and in the intervening decade, the venue has continued to adapt and innovate. Simon is renowned for metaphorically 'moving the furniture' to make the building better suited to the business and his customers. "There has not been one day since opening when I haven't thought: what if…?" he admits. The Hippodrome's intimate Matcham Room cabaret theatre has played host to a string of talented singers, musicians and performers from Michael Ball, Bonnie Langford or Anita Harris to the Boom & Bang Circus, billed as a "cavalcade of late-night exotic acts", similar in style to *La Clique*. Boom & Bang even paid tribute to the acts of the Hippodrome's Edwardian heyday with one routine mimicking Little Tich, the star of the theatre's first water spectacle, 'Giddy Ostend'.

Today, in addition to the three casino floors – the Grand Casino, Lola's and The Gods – the PokerStars poker rooms on the third floor, its restaurant and eight bars, the Hippodrome now hosts *Magic Mike Live* in its redesigned 326-seat theatre, which occupies the space within the confines of the former stage and proscenium arch. The self-contained theatre was an essential addition to the casino according to Simon: "Building a cabaret space was a key part of our ambitions in retaining a core theatrical element for the Hippodrome, the location for so many incredible performances down the years." It has been an investment that has paid off. *Magic Mike Live* remains one of London's hottest tickets. And as part of a complete night out, audience members can also choose to sip a pre-show cocktail in The Boozy Tea-room, designed by Rachel O'Toole, Production Designer of *Magic Mike Live*. Or they might take the lift up to the three-tier rooftop terrace for drinks and a view of the Hippodrome's famous cupola and charioteer as the sun sets over the West End of London.

Simon Thomas recalls how the show was brought to the Hippodrome: "An extraordinary meeting took place on a quiet Sunday morning on our cabaret stage where I had an appointment with one of Hollywood's A-listers, Channing Tatum. Channing had launched a spectacular music and dance adaptation of his hit film *Magic Mike* in Vegas and was looking to London for its European debut. A member of the Hippodrome team was sent to Vegas and had given it a resounding thumbs-up so the next stage was to meet the man himself.

"Channing was looking at several other venues but after meeting us we just clicked; I signed the deal in California. The cabaret theatre was transformed into a £3m, 326-seat light and music experience with state-of-the-art technology. Channing launched the show on ITV's *Britain's Got Talent* which saw *Magic Mike Live* quickly become one of the fastest selling shows in the history of the West End. We were even able to arrange for the iconic lights in Piccadilly Circus to

" The London Hippodrome has had a chameleon life, changing to suit the fluctuating tastes of the times. It remains a familiar and well-loved fixture of London's landscape, cherished for its memories yet always moving with the times. Above all, it continues, immutably, the legacy of Sir Edward Moss, who, back in 1900, delivered on a promise to his customers – to provide something we all want on a night out – an entertainment of unexampled brilliance "

The Hippodrome by Peter Blake – mural created for the Hippodrome Casino, 2012.

During renovations, Simon Thomas commissioned the godfather of British pop art to create an original artwork for the soon-to-open Hippodrome Casino. "We wanted to put some real pieces of British art into the building," he explained, "because the building is almost a piece of art in its own right. It's such an iconic London environment, we couldn't think of anyone better than Sir Peter Blake to create a piece of original Hippodrome art."

Inspired by the building's past performers, Sir Peter Blake collated posters, graphics and portraits of personalities, ranging from Claire Heliot the lion tamer to Tom Jones, in his trademark montage style. The result is a fitting and flamboyant celebration of the Hippodrome's eclectic heritage.

be changed for 45 seconds in order to welcome Channing and the boys to London – a first for the capital."

Magic Mike has been a huge success and is the culmination of a decade in which the Hippodrome has played host to some of the world's most high-profile stars. Simon Thomas is the first to admit it has been a thrilling rollercoaster ride.

"I get all the best jobs. I can shake the hand of the Chinese Ambassador in the morning atop a red London bus during London's legendary Chinese New Year celebrations; welcome 800 NFL fans for a vital clash; talk to a group of Michael Ball fans queuing four hours in advance of his performance so they're assured a front row seat; meet Ant & Dec in the bar; congratulate a player lucky enough to win £20K on a slot machine; even perform a song and dance routine alongside my father to celebrate another year's anniversary.

"There have been so many highlights it's difficult to single out just one. I've stood beside soccer legend Ronaldo as he washed up in the Heliot Steak House kitchen. This was his forfeit for losing a very high-profile poker match played on our main stage against tennis ace Rafa Nadal. Football's 'il fenomeno' and the fourteen-time Grand Slam winner met for a charity game organised by our partners PokerStars with $50K eventually going to the Rafa Nadal Foundation."

Undoubtedly one of the most memorable moments occurred just two years after the Hippodrome Casino opened in May 2014, when pop superstar Prince chose to perform at the Hippodrome's theatre in what would tragically be his last ever UK performance. Prince had performed at an intimate after-show gig at the Hippodrome in 1998 and had put in a special request to return. Everyone cleared their schedules, gave his crew *carte blanche* access to the cabaret theatre and laid a new red carpet. He arrived with minimal fanfare and by all accounts gave a superlative performance.

Entertainment has been at the very heart of the London Hippodrome since Edward Moss opened his theatre at the beginning of a brand-new century in a fanfare of publicity. Just a year after opening, *The Sketch* magazine declared it, "one of the handsomest, brightest and most comfortable theatres in the world; the Hippodrome eminently merits the popularity it enjoys; and the entertainment continues to be judiciously diversified". Through one hundred and twenty years of change it has inspired a succession of innovators to take an original approach to the entertainment business. As the latest in a long line of Hippodrome owners, Simon Thomas shares the same passion for the place as his predecessors. He believes the Hippodrome Casino brings a unique brand of glamour and fun to London's West End, setting a gold standard for the industry. It is a source of pride to him and his father that American casinos now come to visit the Hippodrome to see how things are done at the UK's largest casino. The venue's slogan is, 'Life can be extraordinary'. That mantra feels all the more genuine when played out against the backdrop of this building which brims with magical atmosphere, exuberant energy, and a vivid, fascinating past.

The London Hippodrome has had a chameleon life, changing to suit the fluctuating tastes of the times. It remains a familiar and well-loved fixture of London's landscape, cherished for its memories yet always moving with the times. Above all, it continues, immutably, the legacy of Sir Edward Moss, who, back in 1900, delivered on a promise to his customers – to provide something we all want on a night out – "an entertainment of unexampled brilliance".

Acknowledgements

This book has been possible with the help and generosity of a number of people and institutions.

First of all, Ian Haworth of the Hippodrome Casino recognised that the building's rich and varied history deserved to be recorded and came up with the original concept for this book. He has provided encouragement and support from day one and it is down to him, and his passion for the project, that the Hippodrome's past is documented for posterity.

Rosalyn Wilder's memories of her years at the centre of things at The Talk of the Town have been an invaluable resource in documenting that period of the Hippodrome's history. Rosalyn has given her time, shared her network of contacts, opened up her archive, helped to secure images from various contributors and been an honest, accurate and constructive consultant. This book is undoubtedly better for her involvement.

Andrew Humphries and Louise Sword from Memory Lane Media, as publisher and designer respectively, have been a pleasure to work with. Louise's creativity and enthusiasm for the subject has resulted in a dazzling book that truly reflects the Hippodrome in all its glitz and glory. In managing the project, Andrew has been patient, diplomatic, unruffled and has kept the book - and us - on an even keel through occasionally stormy seas.

Various people have kindly shared their own experiences of working at or attending the Hippodrome, including Grazina Frame, Diana Morrice, Lindsay Williams, Michael Hirst, David Drummond, Julian Russell, Roberta Mitchell, Marion Clapson and Adrian Pel. And thanks also to all those who helped to make this book such a visual feast by supplying or lending images including Geoffrey Bowden and David Reed at The British Music Hall Society, The Museum of Music History, Tonie & Valmai Holt, Diana Morrice, Rosalyn Wilder, Bryn Campbell, Ray Stevenson, Michael Diamond, Randy Bryan Bigham and Michael Pick. Special mentions to Tony Shrimplin from the Museum of Soho, Alison Griffiths, who has done a sterling job as proof-reader and Tom Gillmor for admirable Photoshop skills that have given new life to old ephemera. I also want to acknowledge the help of Rob Baker, Terry Parker, Gary Chapman of the Jazz Age Club, Simon Ornstein at Click Studios, Radlett, Herts., Classic Framing, Radlett, Herts., Sarah Hedger and other colleagues at Mary Evans Picture Library.

Finally, my thanks to Simon Thomas, whose deep regard and respect for the heritage of the building he took over more than a decade ago, is applauded by historians everywhere.

Lucinda Gosling

As this book so wonderfully illustrates, the Hippodrome has been central to the lives of tens of thousands down the years, and entertained millions along the way.

My stewardship of this iconic venue is a privilege, but only came about through the hard work, vision and inspiration of many people.

The danger of thanking individuals of course is that I am going to miss someone off the list, so I humbly apologise if that's the case. But I would like to personally thank the following for their contribution, in no order of precedence:

Frank Matcham, Jimmy Thomas, Boris Johnson MP, Lord Grade of Yarmouth, Dame Shirley Bassey, Rosalyn Wilder, Peter Stringfellow, Nickie Aiken MP, Robert Davis, Bob Diamond, Audrey Lewis, Philippa Roe, Craig Bayliss, Leslie MacLeod-Miller, Gerald Gouriet QC, James Rankin, Paula Reason, Brian Turner, Matthew King, Josh Edwins, Jeremy Delf, Peter McNally, Oliver Caroe, Bob Diamond, Lord Salisbury, Lord Cranborne, Adam Wiles, Beck Construction, Channing Tatum, Vincent Marini, Rachel O'Toole, Briggs & Forrester, Cllr Tim Mitchell, Cllr Louise Hyams, Cllr Mark Shearer, Ros Morgan, Robin Hibbert, CT Tang OBE, Christine Yau MBE, Joe Davey, David Doyle, Locker & Riley, Ian Watson, Tom Roberts, Andy Hixson and my darling wife Fiona Thomas.

I also want to thank the people who now work at the Hippodrome as members of the core staff team of 700 and our suppliers and partners. The building is, without doubt, magnificent but it's the people who work here, care for its infrastructure and provide the very best service in the West End, that truly bring it to life. Always with a smile.

Life Can Be Extraordinary.

Simon Thomas

Selected Bibliography and Sources

Andrews, Julie. *Home, A Memoir of My Early Years* (Orion Publishing, 2009)
Baker, Rob. *High Buildings, Low Morals* (Amberley, 2017)
Boulton, David. *Jazz in Britain* (W. H. Allen, 1958)
Cartland, Barbara. *We Danced All Night* (Foyle's Quality Book Club, 1970)
Chaplin, Charles. *My Autobiography* (Simon & Schuster, 1964)
De Courville, Albert. *I Tell You* (Chapman & Hall, 1928)
Delfont, Bernard. *Presents... East End, West End* (Macmillan, 1990)
Gosling, Lucinda. *Great War Britain, The First World War at Home* (The History Press, 2014)
Kirkwood, Pat. *The Time of my Life* (Robert Hale, 1999)
MacQueen-Pope, Walter James. *The Footlights Flickered* (H. Jenkins, 1959)
Murphy, Janet. (ed.) *The Girl from Gneeveguilla – Memoirs of Peggy O'Neill* (Google Books, 2017)
Nesbitt, Robert. (with Robert Walne) *Light up the Town* (1989, unpublished)
Noble, Peter. *Ivor Novello, Man of the Theatre* (Falcon Press, 1951)
Oliver, Vic. *Mr. Showbusiness* (Harrap, 1954)
Robey, George. *Looking Back on Life* (Constable & Co., 1933)
Stringfellow, Peter. *King of Clubs* (Little, Brown, 1996)
Walker, Brian Mercer. (ed.) *Frank Matcham, Theatre Architect* (Blackstaff Press, 1980)
Willson Disher, M. *Winkles and Champagne* (Batsford, 1938)

Digital, audio and archive resources:
Theatre and Performance Collection, V&A Museum
Michael Diamond Theatre Collection
Rosalyn Wilder Collection
Hippodrome Casino archives
British Newspaper Archive – various contemporary press, including *The Era* and *The Stage*
Mary Evans Picture Library – *The Sketch, The Tatler, The Illustrated Sporting & Dramatic News, The Graphic, The Illustrated London News, The Bystander* (searchable via BNA)
'Judy Garland – The Final Rainbow' – Radio 4, broadcast 5th October 2019

Picture credits

Alamy, p.115, p.131 btm, p.134 top right, p.137 top, p.164, p.167 btm left, btm right, p.174, p.178 top; **Darren Bell**, p.175–7; **Deborah Benton**, p.108–9; **Randy Bryan Bigham**, p.125 top left; **Bridgeman Images**, p.24–5 (© Art Institute of Chicago/Friends of American Art Collection, Goodman Fund/Bridgeman Images), p.52 btm left (© Bonhams, London, UK), p.94 (R. Mander & J. Mitcheson Theatre Collection); **British Music Hall Society**, p.50 (colourised by Tom Gillmor), p.59 top, p.117 btm, p.118; **Bryn Campbell**, p.150 main pic; **Christian Couzens**, p.170–1; **Grazina Frame**, p.120 left, p.132 top; **Lucinda Gosling**, p.137 btm, p.154, p.162 btm right, p.163 btm right; **Getty Images**, p.19 top, p.64–5, p.68 top, p.82 btm, p.90 btm right, p.93, p.96–7, p.129 top, p.130, p.136 btm right, p.155 top, p.165 btm; **Harry Ransom Centre, University of Texas**, p.33 top; **Hippodrome Casino**, p.10–11, p.12 btm left, p.13 top, p.35 top, p.69, p.70 top right, p.78, p.80 left, p.81, p.82 top right & left, p.84 top right, p.87 top, btm, p.90 top left, btm left, p.92, p.99 top, p.101, p.102 btm, p.103 btm right, p.106, p.107, p.110 top left, p.111 btm, p.112, p.113, p.114, p.116 right, p.119 btm, p.120 right, p.121, p.122, p.145, p.147 top left, p.168–9, p.172 top, p.173 top (photograph by Steve Gregson), btm, p.180–1 (artwork by Sir Peter Blake); **Tonie & Valmai Holt**, p.58 left, top right; **Trevor Leighton**, p.178 btm; **Library of Congress**, p.47 top; **Look & Learn**, p.18 top left; **Mary Evans Picture Library**, p.15 btm, p.16 btm, p.48 left; **Mary Evans Picture Library/AF Archive**, p.117 top; **Mary Evans Picture Library/Grenville Collins**, p.23 btm; **Mary Evans Picture Library/Harry Price Library of Magical Literature**, p.40 top left; **Mary Evans Picture Library/Historic England**, p.9; **Mary Evans Picture Library/Illustrated London News**, p.12 top left, p.13 btm, p.14 top, p.15 top, p.16 top left, top right, p.17 btm, p.20 top left & right, p.21 top & btm, p.22 btm left, p.23 top, p.26–7, p.28–9, p.30–31, p.32, p.33 btm, p.34, p.35 top, p.36–7, p.38–9, p.41, p.42–3, p.44–5, p.46, p.47 btm, p.48 right, p.49, p.51, p.52 top left, btm left, p.53, p.54 btm, p.55, p.57 btm, p.58 btm, p.59 btm, p.60 btm, p.63 top left, btm, right, p.66 right, p.68 btm, p.71, p.72, p.73, p.74, p.75, p.76 top left, p.77, p.79, p.80 right, p.83, p.84 top left & btm, p.85, p.86 left, p.89, p.90 top right, p.95 btm x 3, p.99 btm, p.100, p.103 btm left, p.104, p.110 btm left, p.116 left, p.123 top left, p.124 btm right, p.125 btm left, centre, p.148, p.149 (photograph by Angus McBean for *The Tatler*); **Mary Evans Picture Library/Jazz Age Club**, p.61 btm, p.67, p.70 btm, p.95 top x 3; **Mary Evans Picture Library/John Frost Newspapers**, p.63 top right, p.98, p.128; **Mary Evans Picture Library/Land of Lost Content**, p.86 top right; **Mary Evans Picture Library/March of the Women Collection**, p.52 top right; **Mary Evans Picture Library/Michael Diamond**, p.14 btm, p.18 right, p.22 right, p.40 top left, p.54 top left, top right, p.56, p.57 top, p.63 btm left, p.70; **Mary Evans Picture Library/Michael Pick/Madame Yevonde**, p.125 top right; **Mary Evans Picture Library/Courtesy Everett Collection © Roadside Attraction**, p.151 top left; **Mary Evans Picture Library/Terry Parker**, p.61 top, p.66 left; **Chris McAndrew/UK Parliament**, p.7; **Diana Morrice**, p.147 right; **Museum of Music History**; p.62; **National Fairground Archive, University of Sheffield**, p.12 right; **Adrian Pel**, p.161; **Shutterstock**, p.102 top left, top right, p.110 left, p.111 top, p.132 btm right, p.152–3, p.155 btm, p.156 top, p.157, p.158, p.159, p.160, p.162 top, btm left, p.163 top, p.165 top, p.166, p.172 btm; **Ray Stevenson**, p.156 btm x 3; **V&A**, p.17 top, p.105; **Rosalyn Wilder Collection**, p.8, p.126–7, p.131 top, p.132 left, p.133 top, p.134 top left, p.135 btm, p.136 top left, p.136 btm left, p.140, p.141, p.143 top, p.146, p.150 top, p.151 top right; **Rosalyn Wilder Collection/Illustrations by Russ Eglin**, p.129 btm, p.134 btm left & btm right; **Rosalyn Wilder Collection/Designs by Norman Hartnell**, p.103 top, p.125 btm right x 2; **Rosalyn Wilder Collection/Illustration by Robert St. John Roper**, p.144; **Rosalyn Wilder Collection/Photography by Houston Rogers & Jeremy Grayson**, p.133 btm, p.138–9, p.142 btm, p.143 top, p.147 btm left.

Every effort has been made to trace the source or copyright owners of all images.
Text from Julie Andrews, 'Home' reproduced by kind permission of Orion Publishing Group.

THE LONDON HIPPODROME